D0499942

The Internet Revolution
A Global Perspective

Information technology has become a constant presence in contemporary life, infiltrating community, business and state affairs. This book discusses the current uses and problems of IT in both developing and advanced countries, focusing on the ways in which IT changes society, without neglecting the problematic aspects of the Internet revolution such as computer crime and the lack of professionals with computer literacy, particularly from a developing country's perspective. It examines such issues as the characteristics of network economies, connectivity pricing, Internet access, regulation, changes in supply chains, IT gaps between supply and demand, productivity increases, and the digital divide. Emanuele Giovannetti, Mitsuhiro Kagami, and Masatsugu Tsuji have gathered together a group of international experts in economics and trade who discuss the impact of this revolution globally, looking at countries or regions including the UK, the EU, Central and Eastern Europe, the USA, Japan, India, Malaysia, Singapore, Thailand, China, and South Africa.

EMANUELE GIOVANNETTI is Research Associate at the Department of Applied Economics, University of Cambridge and New Scholar of the CEPR. He is also Tenure Research Fellow in Economics at the University of Rome "La Sapienza." He obtained his PhD from Trinity College, Cambridge, and has written on the economics of innovation and the Internet for various journals, including *Information Economics and Policy*, the *International Economic Review*, the *Journal of Industrial Economics*, and *Economic Notes*.

MITSUHIRO KAGAMI is Executive Vice President of the Institute of Developing Economies in the Japan External Trade Organization. He obtained his PhD from Hiroshima University. His previous publications include *The Voice of East Asia: Development Implications for Latin America* (1995); *Learning, Liberalization and Economic Adjustment* (with J. Humphrey and M. Piore, 1998), and *Privatization, Deregulation and Economic Efficiency: A Comparative Analysis of Asia, Europe and the Americas* (with M. Tsuji, 2000).

MASATSUGU TSUJI is Professor of Economics at the Osaka School of International Public Policy, Osaka University. He obtained his PhD from Stanford University, and has written on the economics of telecommunications and IT-related issues for various journals including *Technology and Health Care* and *Mathematics and Computers in Simulation*. His previous publications include *Privatization, Deregulation and Economic Efficiency: A Comparative Analysis of Asia, Europe and the Americas* (with M. Kagami, 2000) and *Private Initiatives in Infrastructure: Priorities, Incentives and Performance* (with S. Berg and M. Pollitt, 2002).

University of Cambridge
Department of Applied Economics

Occasional Papers 66

The Internet Revolution
A Global Perspective

Recent books in this series

The Internet Revolution
A Global Perspective

EDITED BY

EMANUELE GIOVANNETTI
University of Cambridge and University of Rome "La Sapienza"

MITSUHIRO KAGAMI
Institute of Developing Economies, Japan External Trade Organization

AND

MASATSUGU TSUJI
Osaka University, Japan

CAMBRIDGE
UNIVERSITY PRESS

PUBLISHED BY THE PRESS SYNDICATE OF THE UNIVERSITY OF CAMBRIDGE
The Pitt Building, Trumpington Street, Cambridge CB2 1RP, United Kingdom

CAMBRIDGE UNIVERSITY PRESS
The Edinburgh Building, Cambridge, CB2 2RU, UK
40 West 20th Street, New York, NY 10011-4211, USA
477 Williamstown Road, Port Melbourne, VIC 3207, Australia
Ruiz de Alarcón 13, 28014 Madrid, Spain
Dock House, The Waterfront, Cape Town 8001, South Africa

http://www.cambridge.org

© Department of Applied Economics, University of Cambridge, 2003

This book is in copyright. Subject to statutory exception
and to the provisions of relevant collective licensing agreements,
no reproduction of any part may take place without
the written permission of Cambridge University Press.

First published 2003

Printed in the United Kingdom at the University Press, Cambridge

Typeface Times 10/12 pt   *System* LATEX 2_ε [TB]

A catalogue record for this book is available from the British Library

ISBN 0 521 82372 2 hardback

Contents

Figures

Tables

List of contributors

SOON-YONG CHOI *Center for Research in Electronic Commerce, University of Texas at Austin*

EMANUELE GIOVANNETTI *Department of Applied Economics, University of Cambridge, and University of Rome "La Sapienza"*

KUMAR IYER *Faculty of Economics and Politics, University of Cambridge*

MITSUHIRO KAGAMI *Institute of Developing Economies (IDE), Japan External Trade Organization (JETRO)*

PAUL KATTUMAN *Department of Applied Economics, University of Cambridge*

TANGA MCDANIEL *Department of Applied Economics, University of Cambridge*

HIROMI OHKI *Japan External Trade Organization (JETRO)*

MASATSUGU TSUJI *Osaka School of International Public Policy, Osaka University*

YASUSHI UEKI *Institute of Developing Economies (IDE), Japan External Trade Organization (JETRO)*

ANDREW B. WHINSTON *Department of Management Sciences and Information Systems (MSIS), Center for Research in Electronic Commerce, University of Texas at Austin*

NORIHIKO YAMADA *Institute of Developing Economies (IDE), Japan External Trade Organization (JETRO)*

Preface

This book is the product of a research project entitled "A New Trend in the International Division of Labour: the Influence and Issue of Information Technology for Developing Countries," which was coordinated and financially supported by the Institute of Developing Economies (IDE), Japan External Trade Organization (JETRO). Globalization and the information technology (IT) revolution are two distinctive phenomena occurring simultaneously in the world today. Globalization, together with liberalization and deregulation, has been swiftly spreading to developing economies as well as advanced countries. This book focuses on the IT revolution, analyzing current developments and problems in developing countries such as India, Malaysia, Singapore, Thailand, South Africa, and Eastern Europe, as well as advanced economies such as Japan, the EU, and the USA.

We held an international workshop in Tokyo on December 2000 and these chapters reflect the preparatory work and the ensuing discussion of the workshop.

Special thanks go to Professor Masatsugu Tsuji who effectively started the entire project. Any opinions expressed in this volume are those of the authors and not of the organizations they are affiliated to. Emanuele Giovannetti and Tanga McDaniel acknowledge support from the Economic and Social Research Council grant R000238563. Special thanks to Beth Morgan for her indispensable help in editing the entire book.

Introduction

Emanuele Giovannetti, Mitsuhiro Kagami, and Masatsugu Tsuji

Information technology (IT) has dramatically changed both business practice and people's lifestyles, especially since the late 1990s. The impact and influence of this new technology is powerful and far-reaching, and has had a marked effect on almost every aspect of society. At the core of the IT revolution is the Internet, originally developed and opened to the public domain in the late 1960s by Dr. Robert W. Taylor and his group at the US Defense Department. Aided by the reduced cost and increased availability of computers and computer-related products, as well as technological advances in telecommunications, online networks spread rapidly throughout the world over the late 1990s.

Globalization, backed by a market-oriented philosophy of liberalization and deregulation of economic activities, is another factor in stimulating the use of the Internet as the global strategies of multinational corporations have changed. Outsourcing and "fabless" enterprises have become mainstream and their objective functions have expanded to include consumer satisfaction at each stage of the supply chain. Contract manufacturers emerged and have been thriving, whilst established manufacturing companies have been transformed into service industries dedicated to design, R&D, and marketing under brand names. Their regional centers have been established close to the world's three main markets – Western Europe, East Asia, and North America – but they procure parts and components worldwide using electronic data interchange (EDI). The Internet has been extensively used for business activities, and instantaneous information exchanges have become a daily phenomenon. Old hierarchical parts-purchasing systems have broken down and many workers' skills are rapidly becoming obsolete due to the appearance of CAD/CAM systems and sophisticated machine tools.

Ordinary individuals' lifestyles have also been dramatically affected by access to the Internet and its most popular applications, the World Wide Web and e-mail. People can download worldwide entertainment contents, such as music and movies, within minutes in their own living rooms. E-mail makes speedy communications with family and friends living anywhere in the world cheap and

1

easy, and e-business has allowed individuals easy access to worldwide products such as books, cars, and airline tickets.

Deregulation and privatization of state-owned enterprises are closely correlated to the progress of the IT revolution. Where electricity and telecommunications are state monopolies, the progress of the revolution is slow and expensive, as can be seen in some developing countries. Online networks need efficient, low-cost access to the local loop networks that are usually monopolized by existing, or formerly, public enterprises. Thus, the degree, speed and mode of the process of privatization and deregulation of these incumbent enterprises is of great importance.

In this book, we concentrate on the impact of the IT revolution on:

1   the changes affecting production and trade in terms of information, communications, and technology-related products;
2   network infrastructures;
3   new forms of business activities through electronic online services such as e-commerce (business-to-business [BtoB] and business-to-consumer [BtoC]);
4   pricing and charges for online access, services, and e-commerce;
5   society, in terms of both the digital divide within and between countries, and the changes induced in business practices and organization (for example online procurement and supply chain management).

This book presents a timely review of the present state of the IT revolution in a wide range of economies, major advanced ones (Japan, Europe, and the USA) as well as several developing and transitional ones (India, Malaysia, Singapore, Thailand, South Africa, and Eastern Europe), plus a scrutiny of its impact on the emerging problems of "digital divide" and computer crimes.

In chapter 1, Tsuji analyzes present progress and problems in the Japanese IT revolution and its relation to the Japanese production and social systems. He spells out Japan's need for urgent deregulation in the telecommunications industry and the labor market, since the low penetration rate of the Internet and e-commerce is largely due to high charges for telecommunications services. Tsuji also finds the strongest obstacle to the diffusion of the information society to be the Japanese way of thinking: to adhere to tradition and to react with friction when mastering or confronting a new system. Finally, the author advocates the necessity for not only organizations but also the Japanese people themselves to undertake a cultural transformation in order to be able to capture the relevant economies of network made available by the IT revolution.

In chapter 2, Kagami analyzes the dichotomy between the current high-tech monopolies in computer programs, business models and telecommunications standards, and the open-source philosophy of the initial Internet. After an introduction to Japan's legal infrastructure, and government plans to promote the IT revolution, Kagami provides a fascinating description of two unique Japanese ideas: the TRON operating system, based on an open-source philosophy like Linux (and able to widen the use of Chinese characters and of other Asian languages) and i-mode cellular phones as an alternative to PC-based Internet access.

In chapter 3, Tsuji describes the local call market and modalities for Internet access in Japan and maintains that, whilst the Internet penetration rate in Japan lags behind that of other advanced economies, there is strong potential for the diffusion of high-speed broadband and wireless Internet in Japan. However, to fulfil this potential the right public policies are needed, for example radio-wave spectrum auctions, as is a transition toward an m-economy where mobile and wireless will be dominant means of access to the Internet.

In chapter 4, Ohki studies world IT trade and production and thoroughly analyzes the structure of the international division of labor in IT-related production in East Asia. In particular, he provides a description of the migration of Taiwanese firms to Southern China, especially to the Chu-Chiang River Delta, in response to changes in cost and outsourcing patterns. He also describes the evolution of multilayered cobweb relations along the supply chain and their transnational trends.

Chapter 5, by Ueki, sheds light on the evolution of supply chain management in the electronic industry in East Asia. He draws an updated Asian electronic map of comparative advantages, where Singapore plays an important role as regional hub and where China is catching up in the production of new electronic commodities such as DVD players and mobile handsets.

Chapter 6, by Yamada, portrays the IT situation in three ASEAN countries: Singapore, Malaysia, and Thailand. He describes the IT policies started twenty years ago which made Singapore one of the world's most advanced IT countries (including the early introduction of computers into secondary schools) and describes the Malaysian Multimedia Super Corridor Plan launched in 1996. Yamada's chapter also focuses on the drawbacks of the Southeast Asian experiences, such as oversupply of government-led infrastructure and services in Singapore, the regional gap between rural and urban areas, and the increasing gap between rich and poor in Internet penetration rates, due to policies which have often neglected these issues.

In chapter 7, Giovannetti reviews the regulatory debate which has been informing the ongoing liberalization process in the European Union. Compared to the USA, Western Europe has indeed arrived late in liberalizing the telecommunications sector, and this shows in their different Internet penetration levels. All of the 380 million people of the European Union now live in a fully liberalized telecommunications market. Nevertheless, in all EU member states the incumbents continue to hold a firm bottleneck control on competition in the local loop. As a consequence, whilst competition in long-distance and international telephony is developing at a rapid pace, the incumbent operators still dominate the local markets where prices are crucial for Internet penetration. Giovannetti describes how the European Commission tackled this problem by launching, in December 1999, the *e*Europe initiative with the objective of speeding up the process of bringing Europe online. The chapter also discusses some of the theoretical and practical problems associated with pricing the access of network components required by the unbundling process, and the human capital shortages facing Europe in the coming years.

In chapter 8, McDaniel discusses many of the IT issues confronting Central and Eastern European countries (CEECs). The conditions among these countries differ for a number of reasons; location, the magnitude of foreign direct investment, labor force skills, electricity infrastructure, and private sector participation also influence national access to and use of information. In this chapter, McDaniel argues that for the CEECs, the information age has corresponded to an age of transition from centrally planned to market economies, and their adoption of IT is associated with transition reforms. Communication infrastructure varies in CEECs and can be outdated or insufficient. The need for significant upgrading expenditures along with the benefits of being connected to neighboring networks can provide additional incentives for economic reforms. Moreover, McDaniel describes how the dangers of lagging behind in e-commerce for the CEECs can be seen in business-to-business (BtoB) transactions where there are a number of obstacles for entrepreneurs in Central and Eastern Europe. Among these are several psychological barriers due to national experiences with corruption. Others are more tangible and include the lack of transaction security as expressed by the low number of secure sites. This is seen as an indication of a country's potential to take advantage of online commercial activity.

In chapter 9, Kattuman and Iyer describe the beneficial window of opportunity open for India by the IT revolution. The Indian software and services industry is estimated to have grown at nearly 50 percent annually over the last five years. Over the next five years, software and services might come to account for 25 percent of total Indian exports, up from the current 5 percent. Indian firms hold 18.5 percent of the global market in customized software and attracted close to 40 percent of Fortune 500 companies as clients in 2000. Kattuman and Iyer give a fascinating account of this enclave of international competitiveness: since the 1950s, the publicly financed higher education system has increased the output of science and engineering graduates at an impressive rate. But the growing stock of human capital did not find rewards within the country as long as planning and regulations undermined the basis for the growth of private enterprise. The economic liberalization process started slowly in the 1970s with the software sector, and gathered pace in the late 1980s. This coincided with the explosive growth of the international IT market. The combined effect drew both entrepreneurship and human capital into the sector. The cost advantage and size of the pool matched the occupational requirements of the software industry for programmers and analysts. In the meantime, the flow of Indian students emigrating since the 1950s had grown into a sizable stream, and by the late 1980s a good number of non-resident Indians (NRIs) had worked their way up the executive structures of multinationals. As the industry took off, these NRI executives helped in matching buyers of software services from the West with sellers from India. The developments in the Indian software industry show a vivid leapfrogging example.

In chapter 10, Giovannetti describes the South African experience of privatization, its slow liberalization of the telecommunications sector and its impact on Internet penetration and the digital divide. The chapter focuses on the trade-offs given by the need to foster competition whilst, at the same time, extending universal service. In this chapter, Giovannetti also describes the implementation of policies aimed at extending Internet penetration via shared access. A typical example is given by the establishment of Multipurpose Community Telecenters that are public multifunctional loci of shared access where demand for connectivity can be pooled, and supply becomes commercially feasible and self sustaining after an assisted start-up period. These are typical and relevant examples of the technological possibilities created by the IT revolution and show how access can be increased in a segmented and geographically dispersed society.

In chapter 11, Choi and Whinston focus their attention on the current situation and problems of the IT revolution in the USA, with special emphasis on its productivity effects. The authors show how the growing importance of the IT sector in the US economy is demonstrated by the rapid growth in labor productivity since 1995. Its share of the overall economy, employment, and contribution to economic growth has been phenomenal. But besides these measurable indicators, the true impact of IT is felt in the way firms are organized and operate in the new world of e-business. A distinguishing feature of an IT-intensive firm is its highly flexible organization and implementation of IT or e-business drivers that enable the horizontal division of labor which promotes distributed enterprises.

In chapter 12, Choi and Whinston describe the effects of the IT revolution on firms and on the global economy. The authors discuss several studies and empirical evidence indicating the rapid development in networked e-business firms which maximize the benefits of IT and the Internet. They find that the strongest performance and success by IT industries and users have been shown since the introduction of the Internet.

Chapter 13, also by Choi and Whinston, investigates whether or how the Internet affects the way in which firms are organized and operated in the world economy. Unlike the vertical division of labor witnessed in the manufacturing-driven twentieth century, the Internet and IT enable a horizontal division of labor that addresses the need to be flexible in the newly emerging value web. Firms dependent on IT are virtual firms, often producing digital products and services which can be transported via the Internet. On the global implications of the IT revolution, Choi and Whinston point out how, for developing economies, the shift towards the service sector and the reliance on IT and the Internet poses a serious threat in development policies. On the one hand, highly skilled workers can be retained, lowering the risk of brain drain through the promotion of IT infrastructure and software and other digital product and service projects; on the other hand, the required level of education and training is far higher than for manufacturing jobs. Choi and Whinston conclude this chapter by analyzing how the gap between developing countries and the underdeveloped world seems to be growing as we move into a full-fledged service economy of the digital age.

Thus, this book provides a bird's-eye view of the IT revolution in numerous, and representative, countries of the world, together with an attempt to point out its merits and demerits whilst closely analyzing the economic and social trade-offs faced by the policies that are aimed at facilitating IT diffusion.

1 Transformation of the Japanese system towards a network economy

Masatsugu Tsuji

Introduction

The Japanese economy is facing its longest period of stagnation since the 'bubble' burst in 1990, and is experiencing its poorest performance in terms of growth and unemployment in the post-war period. This period is referred to as the 'lost ten years' as the Japanese economy failed to adjust itself to shifting economic trends. As a result, it lags considerably behind the general trend towards the information society.

This is clearly evident in data on the Internet and e-commerce. It is estimated that the number of Japanese Internet users was about 27 million at the end of 1999, compared to the USA's 163 million, and the EU's 70 million. As for the Internet penetration ratio, the USA is about 40 percent, ranked 5th in the world, and the UK 24 percent. For Japan, on the other hand, it is 21.4 percent and ranked 13th, the lowest of the OECD economies.[1] According to the survey carried out by the Electric Commerce Promotion Council of Japan (ECOM), the size of e-commerce, business to business (BtoB) as well as business to consumer (BtoC) is as summarised in Tables 1.1, 1.2a, and 1.2b. Although Japanese e-commerce has achieved remarkable growth, it still lags behind the USA, and the gap seems to be growing.

The long stagnation in the 1990s occurred as the Japanese economy entered a stage of stable, but low growth, with an aging population and in a period of globalization. The Japanese economic system was formed during the rapid growth of the 1960s, and is based on the assumption of continuous economic growth. Once the Japanese economy matured and entered a stable growth era, it resulted in the collapse of the assumptions on which the system was based. The old basis, which had been a source of strength, no longer provided any positive effect. As will be discussed later, the success of the Japanese economy in the 1970s and 1980s was due to the "Japanese system," which was based on economies of scale or economies of scope. Since the 1990s, the efficiency of the system has come from "economies of network," which the Japanese system

Table 1.1 *The size of Japanese e-commerce, 1999–2005 (US$ billion)*

	1999	2000	2001	2002	2003	2004	2005
BtoB	–	220	360	510	670	870	1,110
BtoC	3	8	17	34	56	94	133

Source: ECOM.

Table 1.2a *Comparison of e-commerce in Japan and the USA: EC ratio of BtoB, 1999–2005 (percent)*

	1998	1999	2000	2001	2002	2003	2004	2005
Japan	1.5	–	3.8	6.1	8.5	11.0	14.0	17.5
USA	2.5	–	4.9	7.1	9.7	13.1	17.9	23.1

EC ratio denotes the share of e-commerce to the total charges.
Source: ECOM.

Table 1.2b *Comparison of e-commerce in Japan and the USA: EC ratio of BtoC, 1999–2005 (percent)*

	1999	2000	2001	2002	2003	2004	2005
Japan	0.1	0.25	0.56	1.1	1.9	3.1	4.5
USA	0.6	1.37	2.16	3.16	4.25	5.51	6.99

Source: ECOM.

is not structured to exhibit, and this has led to the low penetration rate of the Internet and e-commerce.

In what follows, we will focus on Japanese economic systems in the areas of employment and production, which are fundamental to Japanese international competitiveness. We then discuss the source and importance of economies of network in the age of the information society. We make a comparison with the US economy, which has an entirely different economic system, and show how the US economy has changed to take advantage of economies of network. Finally, possible reforms of the Japanese system will be suggested.

Economies of network[2]

Definition

A network is defined by nodes and arcs: in economic terms, the former are agents and the latter are channels connecting the agents. Firms, consumers, governments, organisations, and groups of nations such as the EU and APEC are examples of nodes, and telecommunications cables, roads, railroads, airlines, and electricity cables are arcs.

Economic agents connect to a network to receive a service from it: by using a telephone we can talk to someone in a distant place. The merit of subscribing to this service is measured in terms of utility. In addition to direct utility, agents receive extra utility through the network; the more agents that participate in the network, the more utility they gain. This is the definition of economies of network, or network externality. Externality has the standard economic meaning where one person's utility is affected by the action of others.[3] In the business world, economies of network are widely recognised, and competition for subscriptions in the broadcasting, newspaper, and telecommunications industries are typical examples.

A network gives rise to negative as well as positive externalities in the form of congestion. This commonly occurs in a network with limited capacity such as telecommunications and public utilities. Beyond a certain level of participation, negative externality outstrips positive externality.

Basis of economies of network

Economies of network have the following three characteristics:

1. Outsourcing of managerial resources: agents can receive all kinds of information via the network that they themselves do not own. If it is costly to obtain those resources by themselves, they can purchase information from other agents, and thus specialize their own activities. This is a primitive example of efficiency through division of labor.
2. Quick response to changes in the environment: they can receive information on ongoing changes in real time and thus react immediately.
3. Economies of speed: real-time information speeds up decision-making and aids forward and strategic planning.

Economies of network stem from developments in telecommunications technology, especially digitalization and multimedia. Digitalization enables all information to be processed by computer. By combining digitalization and optic fibers, a huge volume of information can be transmitted all over the world in seconds.

Economies of scale and economies of scope

In this section, other concepts of efficiency will be examined. First, let us consider economies of scale that are related to economies of mass production, that is, where an increase in inputs leads to a greater increase in output. In other words, with the increase of production, the average cost is decreased. Economies of scale arise from: (a) the existence of a fixed cost; (b) indivisibility of production plants; and (c) the nature of physics. Typical industries of this nature are heavy industries such as steel, chemical, and petroleum. These commonly have large-scale production plants.

Secondly, economies of scope: the cost of production of several products within one factory is less than if they are produced separately. The source of this economy is the existence of a common factor of production. Financial institutions typically exhibit economies of scope. Banking and securities are separate activities, but they are quite similar in nature, so if one branch can handle both businesses, it would be less costly than doing them separately. Numerically controlled (NC) machine tools, which are a combination of mechanics and electronics, also share factors of production, as does the assembling and processing industry that includes automobiles, household electrical appliances, and precision machinery.

Japanese employment system

The Japanese system consists of several subsystems (see Figure 1.1): (a) the employment system, which relates to households and firms; (b) industrial groups which connect firms with other firms; (c) the relation between firms and the government sector; and (d) the political relationship of the government sector with the households where there are voters. The first two of these are discussed in this and the following section.

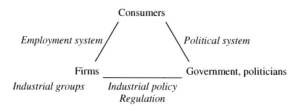

Figure 1.1 The Japanese system

Table 1.3 *Comparison of the employment systems of Japan and the Western economies*

Japanese economy	Western economies
Lifetime employment	Lay-offs
Seniority	Ability
Bonus system	Only for executives
Retirement payment	None
Company union system	Trade union system

Characteristics of the Japanese employment system

The most important system in an economy is the employment system, since it is the basis of not only economic, but also social, life. Table 1.3 compares the employment systems of Japan and the West.[4]

In the seniority system, wage levels and promotions within the firm are based on the number of years employed there. Moving firms results in loss of seniority and a lower wage level. Lifetime employment and seniority systems are meaningful when both are in effect.

Economic foundation of the Japanese employment system

The Japanese employment system is based on a long-term implicit contract relationship rather than the market mechanism of the Western economies. Without signing a formal contract, workers and firm implicitly agree that labor will be supplied and the firm will employ them until retirement. Promotions and wage levels are determined inside the firm, and it is very rare for the firm to recruit middle management, for instance, from outside the firm. Thus, firms serve as a resource allocation mechanism and create an internal labor market. A long-term implicit contract relationship does not use the market mechanism. On the other hand, in a Western firm, vacancies are usually filled by hiring from outside the firm. The allocation of human resources is based on a competitive market.

Thus the economies show a marked contrast. Which is the more efficient? We can compare them from the viewpoint of transactions and information costs in the market. In order for firms to carry out smooth transactions, they have to bear costs, among which is the cost of information. After hiring a worker, it is too late to learn then that they are not very capable. Thus time and energy is spent in examining applicants prior to hiring. On the other hand, when the firm promotes its own employees, it is well informed about their background. This merit of the Japanese employment system thus saves the cost of transaction and information.[5]

In addition, since workers remain in one company over a long period of time, it is worthwhile investing in the human resources that become the basis of productivity growth. This would be a risky investment for a Western firm, as high productivity workers can seek higher wages elsewhere. So firms only invest in non-transferable skills.

The most important mechanisms for maintaining the morale of the workers are incentives and monitoring. In a Japanese firm, the bonus system provides an incentive for workers to contribute to the profit of the firm, as the higher the profit the larger the bonus. Transactions in the market have to be monitored all the time. In a market economy, if there is no concrete monitoring system, moral hazard and adverse selection result from asymmetric information, and overcoming these problems is costly. A long-term relationship between the firm and its workers can save all these costs.

Japanese industrial group

Firms do not exist in isolation, but are interconnected with one another and form groups. Japanese firms form groups in a unique way, and it is these industrial groups that make Japanese management more competitive than those of other economies.

Horizontal group: Zaibatsu *Group*

There are six major industrial groups in this category, namely Sumitomo, Sanwa, Mitsui, Mitsubishi, Fuji, and Ikkan. The historical background of these groups can be traced back to *Zaibatsu* before World War II. When the economy was democratised under the allied forces, the holding companies of *Zaibatsu* were abolished. Soon after the end of the occupation, however, *Zaibatsu* groups reassembled around banks rather than holding companies, and each group was named after its bank. This system is referred to as the "main bank system," and those banks are called the "main bank."

The term horizontal implies that firms from all kinds of industries are members of the group. They make close connections with each other by having interlocking directors and mutual stock holding. The reasons for this formation can be summarized as follows:

1   long-term contract relationship: as mentioned in the previous section, this saves transaction and information costs. CEOs of the major firms in these groups meet regularly to exchange information and discuss new joint projects, etc.
2   risk sharing: by combining with firms of different industries they can diversify the risk of management and takeover;

3   growth sharing: one can never be certain which industry will become
     a major one in the future.

Since the group has firms in all industries, they can shift funds and human
resources to a budding industry from the smokestack sector, and the group as a
whole can adjust to new environments and enjoy continuous growth.

Vertical group: hierarchical production structure

Firms in vertical groups are interconnected by a flow of materials, parts, and
final products. Typical examples are found in the assembling and processing
industry. The key characteristic of these industries is that their products consist
of many components. Efficiency of production heavily depends on how these
parts suppliers are organized. The solution for Japanese firms is the hierarchical
production system. Parts suppliers are called subcontractors or *Keiretsu*. For
example, firms related to Toyota can be broadly classified as follows:[6]

1   Primary parts manufacturers: The firms in this category supply parts
     directly to Toyota. They supply complete items such as air condition-
     ers, clutches, brakes, and shock absorbers. These firms are quite big,
     and some are independent of Toyota. Toyota owns part of their stocks
     and sends directors to their Boards. Toyota currently has 168 primary
     parts suppliers.
2   Secondary parts suppliers: Manufacturers of this type supply sec-
     ondary parts such as cylinders, brake linings, and thermostats. These
     firms are generally medium to small. Secondary parts suppliers have a
     strong tie with primary parts suppliers. There are 5,437 parts suppliers
     in this category.
3   Tertiary parts suppliers: Firms in this category are small and depend
     on family labor. As subcontractors of secondary parts suppliers, their
     main business is of a processing nature such as casting and forging.
     These are labor intensive and their productivity is low. The number
     in this category is the largest and totals more than 40,000.

Since certain firms supply parts to firms belonging to the different categories,
with the omission of double counting, its is said that Toyota has nearly 36,000
parts suppliers. Toyota, however, purchases parts directly from less than 200
firms. Next, let us compare Toyota with GM. The production structure of GM
is non-hierarchical, and it has only 12,000 parts suppliers. This implies that its
ratio of domestic production is much higher than Toyota's. A comparison of
the two systems is summarized in Table 1.4.

How does Toyota organize its huge hierarchical structure? It can be summarized as follows:

Table 1.4 *Comparison of Toyota's and GM's systems*

Toyota	GM
Low domestic production: 20–25%	High: 40–50%
200 trade partners	Much larger
Dominates parts suppliers	Equal partner
Long-term commitment on quality and price	Market-based relationship
Parts suppliers investment in specific equipment	General equipment

1 *Kanban* method or just-in-time system synchronizes production. This is a system of delivering the right parts to the right places at the right time. This saves the cost of inventories. Because of this, most factories are located close to Toyota production factories.

2 Joint activities such as R&D, quality management (QM), and total quality management (TQM). The last two are known as *Kaizen*. Primary parts suppliers include eleven firms called the 'Toyota Group' whose businesses are related to the automobile industry. Their relationship with Toyota is so close that they engage in joint activities such as R&D and improve the quality of parts through QM and TQM. These are the basis for the high quality of Toyota products.

Toyota also has cooperative organizations of parts suppliers such as *Kyohokai* and *Kyoeikai*. Their ties with Toyota are also strong.

Economic basis of the hierarchical production system

Toyota's relationship with its parts suppliers can be explained by a long-term implicit contract. Once Toyota opens trade with a certain supplier, it is accepted that it will continue that trade over a long period. This saves transaction and information costs, and suppliers can invest in equipment specifically for the production of Toyota parts. In addition to this, the efficiency of the hierarchical production structure can be explained by the "principal–agent model," where Toyota is the principal and parts suppliers are agents. The agent has more skill than the principal in manufacturing components so it is more efficient to subcontract that part of the production process to it. Subcontracting is commonly adopted in industries such as construction, since it improves the efficiency of a large organization.[7]

In order for this type of hierarchical production system to function effectively, two factors are required, namely monitoring and an incentive scheme. Toyota can easily monitor quality and continuously supervizes the suppliers. This is of prime importance as the quality of the parts determines the quality of Toyota automobiles. The incentive for nearly 36,000 subcontractors to support the hierarchical production system is "growth-sharing." When Toyota grows, the parts suppliers also grow,[8] and most Toyota Group firms are now world-scale enterprises. Toyota is said to be very strict in price negotiations; prices are based on cost calculations, and suppliers' profit margins are based on some historical value, since a severe cut in price would spoil the incentive to work with Toyota.

Economies of network and the Japanese system

In this section, we attempt to analyse the Japanese system from the perspective of networks and information. We also show that the system which fully exhibits economies of scale and economies of scope might not be the best system for economies of network. In contrast to Japanese firms, US firms have been utilizing IT, and tend to take advantage of the information society.

Traditional information interchange inside Japanese firms

Information is largely paper based and passes down through the hierarchy, though importance is also placed on face-to-face communication. In this transmission process, an important aspect that is peculiar to Japanese firms is "groupism," or *Nemawashi* (rooting), which helps to achieve a harmonious relationship between labor and management. Through this system of sharing information, labor can feel that it is participating in decision-making and so has an incentive to contribute to the firm. Japanese workers belong to a specific section of management and they work together as a team. This would not be possible without the lifetime employment and seniority systems.

It should be noted, however, that there is the risk of bureaucratic management and sectionalism when information is kept within a particular group. In this context, the Japanese system is a closed network. As mentioned earlier, the Japanese system makes less use of the market mechanism and tends to be less transparent. Asymmetric information between insiders and outsiders is much greater than in economies with a market mechanism.

Transformation of the US economy and economies of network

Between 1991 and 2000, the US economy enjoyed an economic boom and was said to have entered a new stage of development, a 'New Economy.' This resulted from the IT revolution which exploited economies of network. In what follows, three cases have been selected to examine these phenomena.

Concurrent engineering

During the 1980s, the Japanese automobile industry showed its supremacy over that in the USA. All technological innovations introduced in the US automobile industry in the fifteen years since the late 1970s came from Japan, namely, just-in-time production and QM (*Kaizen*). In 1993, however, Chrysler shocked the Japanese automobile industry by announcing "Neon" to the market. It had a 2,000cc engine but was priced at only US$10,000. This was half the price of a comparable Japanese car. The secret to this low price was concurrent engineering, that is, sharing information between different sections of the firm such as production, R&D, and design. In the development of Neon, Chrysler cut R&D time and costs dramatically, to thirty-one months and US$1 billion respectively. The average period for Japanese assemblers was forty-two months, and sixty-two months for the USA. R&D for GM's Saturn took seven years and US$3.5 billion, and the Ford Escort required four years and US$2 billion.

With concurrent engineering, different sections engaged in R&D are interconnected through a network of computers, and each can monitor or trace the current stage of development of the others. The usual method of development is linear, that is, results are passed from section to section in sequence.[9] If one section finds an error or something that could be improved, the work is returned to the previous section. Concurrent engineering, on the other hand, is multidimensional, and all sections can be engaged in development simultaneously.

Contract manufacturing

Another factor leading to the recovery of the US automobile industry was sourcing parts from all over the world by establishing supply chain networks. Since they do not have fixed subcontractors, they can choose parts suppliers of better quality and cheaper prices, and can freely extend the network of parts suppliers. The same strategy is also taken by US PC makers, who can sell PCs at far lower prices than their Japanese counterparts.

The key element of US manufacturers' global supply chain networks is contract manufacturing, which handles production needs of manufacturers on contract and organizes their own parts suppliers networks. By aiming to achieve maximum customer satisfaction in each market, the US manufacturers decided to use external (foreign) companies to produce their products (outsourcing) and concentrate company efforts on design, R&D, distribution, and marketing operations. Thanks to advanced IT, particularly the Internet, information can be communicated instantaneously and processed immediately. Speed, resolute decisions, and dramatic reforms have supported the prosperity that US manufacturers enjoy today.[10]

Venture business

Venture businesses, which were also important in the recovery of the US manufacturing sector, are small businesses oriented exclusively to high-tech or R&D activities. They are also young businesses. Large numbers of venture businesses can be found in industries related to computers, computer software, biotechnology, telecommunications, and new materials. Deregulation of business activity during the Reagan administration of the early 1980s was one factor in promoting venture business. Other factors were the nature of the labor market, the technology transfer and funding.

A large number of entrepreneurs are needed to start a new business. Since a venture business is technology based, its entrepreneurs are likely to be engineering specialists, but they need others to take care of management. The highly flexible labor market can supply these specialists.

Venture businesses require new technology. Universities have technology transfer centres that supply this new technology to the commercial sector. Examples can be found in the relationship between Stanford University and Silicon Valley, or MIT and Route 128.[11] Universities are at the core of research parks, and play a coordinating role by interconnecting university laboratories and entrepreneurs.

The US financial market has already been deregulated and there are many different channels for funding venture businesses. These are angles, venture capitals, NASDAQ, and public funds. Thus, in the USA, there is an abundance of funds for investing in venture businesses that seek high returns by accepting high risk.

Toward the Japanese system in the twenty-first century

Thus far, we have analysed the economic basis of the Japanese system and found that it does not suit the curent economic transformation. Here, we will discuss possible reforms that will enable the Japanese economy to benefit from economies of network.

Transforming the Japanese economy and the Japanese system

The Japanese economy is characterised by a low growth rate, an aging population, and globalization. The Japanese system is not constructed to cope with these factors – on the contrary, they will destroy the basis of the Japanese system.

The lifetime employment and seniority systems are based on the continuous growth of the economy, that is, firms increasing in size with increasing employment opportunities. Under the seniority system, wages increase as workers become older. This is possible since the younger generation receives relatively low wages that subsidize the older generation's relatively high wages; it is an intergenerational subsidy system. However, in an aging economy, as the younger cohorts shrink, total employment costs increase. Due to this, more firms have shifted from a seniority system to one in which wages are based on working ability. In addition, senior workers are either forced to move to affiliated firms, or are simply fired.

Globalization is another challenge. Japanese firms have been shifting their activities overseas by means of direct investment. They have to decide where to build a factory, where to sell a product, where to engage in R&D activity, etc. Globalization makes it necessary for Japanese labor to compete with the low-waged labor of less developing countries (LDCs). This will have a serious effect on the Japanese employment system. Japanese automobile assemblers have been increasing overseas production but in the host countries they are levied on local content, that is, some components have to be purchased from local firms. As a result, it has become harder to maintain *Keiretsu* in Japan. The hollowing-out of the economy is now becoming a reality.

Possible reform of the Japanese system

As shown in the previous section, the US economy recovered from nearly twenty years of stagnation following the oil crises in the mid-1970s, by information innovation and venture business. A key factor was their ability to take advantage of economics of network. We have also shown that the Japanese economy cannot rely on the same strategies since appropriate conditions for their success have not yet been established. The traditional scheme of information sharing in firms is still firmly rooted and the Japanese system is too conservative for ambitious entrepreneurs to emerge from the employment system to start up venture businesses. Students still aspire to a job in a traditional, large firm. Banks do not wish to invest in risky venture businesses, and they ask for real estate as collateral – ideas or know-how is not sufficient. Local, as well as central, governments provide public funds to venture businesses, but the procedure for application is too bureaucratic, and the funds are not in great demand. Typical examples of successful venture businesses are Sony and Honda. Most new or venture businesses emerge from industrial groups, as analyzed previously. They take the form of affiliated companies with funds and manpower supplied by their parent companies. Thus, US-style venture business is very rare in Japan.

Under these circumstances, what reform is possible? As shown previously, economies of network can be fully exhibited in a flexible and diversified economy, since networks interconnect economic agents in many different ways. One essential reform is deregulation. Free and competitive activities by the private sector are the only source of affluent and diversified networks. The government cannot create such flexibility. In the underlying context of an information society, deregulation is urgent in the telecommunications industry and in the labor market. The low penetration rate of the Internet and e-commerce is due to high charges for telecommunications services. Deregulation in the labor market would make it both more flexible and more mobile.

Socio-economic systems change slowly. The strongest obstacle to an information society is our way of thinking, that is, inertia in the old system. We tend to prefer to adhere to tradition, since it is rather comfortable to do so. Friction is encountered when mastering or confronting a new system. This is the true reason why Japanese firms are reluctant to make use of e-mail and intranet systems. It is necessary not only for organizations, but us, ourselves, to undergo change in order to capture economies of network.

Notes

1. Ministry of Posts and Telecommunications 2000.
2. This section is based on Tsuji and Nishiwaki 1996, Chapter 2.
3. This similarity is pointed out by Katz and Shapiro 1985.
4. A concise exposition of the Japanese employment system is found in Ito 1992, Chapter 8.
5. For a more detailed discussion, refer to Aoki 1988, and Aoki and Dore 1994.
6. The reality is much more complicated. More detailed classification of parts suppliers and their relation with Toyota is presented in Tsuji 1991.
7. For more detailed discussions on the economic explanation of the hierarchical production structure, see Asanuma 1992, and Tsuji 1991.
8. The growth of the firms in the Toyota Group in terms of the amount of capital and the number of employees is also analysed by Tsuji 1991.
9. R&D teams of Toyota and its group companies meet regularly on a face-to-face basis when they develop new automobiles. The long-term relationship makes this possible.
10. The top ten contract manufacturers in the world are Solectron, SCI Systems, Celestica, Jabil Circuit, Avex Electronics, Manufacturers' Services Ltd., Dovatron International, Flextronics, NatSteel Electronics, and Venture Manufacturing Ltd. The first seven are US firms, while the last three are located in Singapore. For more details on the relationship between US manufacturers and contract manufacturers, see Kagami and Kuchiki 2000.
11. The Ministry of Education deregulated the activities of universities. Universities have started to commercialize their technology following the US example.

References

Aoki, M. 1988, *Information, Incentives and Bargaining in the Japanese Economy*, New York: Cambridge University Press.

Aoki, M. and Dore, R. (eds.) 1994, *The Japanese Firm: The Sources of Competitive Strength*, New York: Oxford University Press.

Asanuma, B. 1992, Risk absorption in Japanese subcontracting: a microeconometric study of the automobile industry, *Journal of the Japanese and International Economy*, 6(1), 1–29.

Ito, T. 1992, *The Japanese Economy*, Cambridge, MA: MIT Press.

Kagami, M. and Kuchiki, A. 2000, Silicon Valley in the South: new management networks emerging in Guadalajara, paper presented at the international workshop on "A Study on Industrial Networks in Asia," Institute of Developing Economies, JETRO, January 2000.

Katz, M. L. and Shapiro, C. 1985, Network externality, competition, and compatibility, *American Economic Review*, 75, 424–440.

Ministry of Posts and Telecommunications 2000, *Telecommunications White Paper 2000* (in Japanese), Gyousei, Tokyo.

Tsuji, M. 1991, Structural shift in the Japanese economy and regional adjustment: Tokai Region and automobile industry, *Proceedings of the First Pacific Rim Conference on the Resource Management*, National Chiao Tung University, Taiwan, 563–593.

Tsuji, M. and Nishiwaki, T. 1996, *Nettowa-ku Mirai (Future of Network)*, Nihonhyoron-sha (in Japanese).

2 The IT revolution and its meaning for society

Mitsuhiro Kagami

Introduction

The Industrial Revolution began in the last half of the eighteenth century in the UK when the steam engine and other mechanical innovations dramatically increased industrial output and drastically altered society. The second wave of industrialization came with mass production methods, represented by the automotive industry, at the beginning of the twentieth century. Then the third industrial revolution occurred during the 1980s, driven by technological breakthroughs in the computer industry.

The emergence of powerful desktop computers has affected both industrial production and people's lifestyles. The appearance of the Internet, in particular, has had a profound impact on society. There were around 4.5 million Internet users worldwide at the beginning of the 1990s rising to 260 million in 1999 (see Table 2.1). A network system such as the Internet can cross national boundaries and time zones. This creates fundamental complications for current territorially based systems of regulation, law, and administration, as well as for economic and social institutions.

This chapter describes the characteristics of the third industrial wave, its pros and cons, and some measures to counter the resulting problems. The advantage of global cooperation in the information age is viewed, and recent IT developments in Japan are introduced with special attention to made-in-Japan OS systems (TRON) and wireless Web (i-Mode).

Basic characteristics of the information age

The third industrial revolution comes from a combination of computer and telecommunications technologies, especially the development of the Internet, which has brought about global linkages between individuals, regardless of distance and time. This in turn has produced fundamental changes within society.

Table 2.1 *Telecommunications indicators, 1999*

	Main telephone lines (thousands)	Cellular phone subscribers (thousands)	Internet users (thousands)	Internet users per 10,000 inhabitants	Estimated PCs (thousands)
Japan	70,530	56,846	18,300	1,447	36,300
Germany	48,300	23,470	15,900	1,935	24,400
France	34,100	21,434	5,660	961	13,000
UK	33,750	27,185	12,500	2,128	18,000
USA	188,331	86,047	110,000	3,982	141,000
China	108,716	43,296	8,900	70	15,500
India	26,511	1,884	2,000	20	3,300
Korea	20,518	23,443	6,823	1,468	8,500
Malaysia	4,431	2,990	1,500	687	1,500
Singapore	1,877	1,631	950	2,946	1,700
Thailand	5,216	2,339	800	132	1,382
Argentina	7,357	4,434	900	246	1,800
Brazil	24,985	15,033	3,500	208	6,100
Chile	3,109	2,261	625	416	1,000
Colombia	6,665	3,134	600	144	1,400
Mexico	10,927	7,732	2,500	257	4,300
Venezuela	2,586	3,400	400	169	1,000
World	910,624	489,483	260,095	440	387,071

Source: ITU 2000.

In the computer industry, the centralized batch system was replaced by PCs and their networks. The mass production system, which forced people to work on production lines, was divided and replaced by the module production system, or even the cell production method (a group of workers in charge of all production processes, i.e., the 'mini' production system). In short, there was more decentralization and individual participation in production as well as in consumption.

However, there have also been negative effects from the computer age. New products or software with extremely high-tech knowledge can dominate the market. These 'locked-in' phenomena can typically be seen in the computer software industry. Thus, monopoly or oligopoly develops. Moreover, hegemonic competition in obtaining 'de facto standards' among multinational corporations (MNCs) becomes fierce, and is sometimes backed by advanced countries' governments, for example, digital TV transmission, satellite telecommunications, and code/decode systems.

Decentralization and demand considerations

With a PC, an individual can communicate through the Internet network and participate in worldwide electronic commerce (e-commerce), so traditional concepts on location and time have to change. People can easily communicate with people at the opposite side of the globe, crossing national borders through cyberspace. Instantaneous transmission has also changed our concept of time, fully utilizing the 24-hour day. For example, information-related industries can be set up in developing countries, skipping the normal stages of technology development (Kagami 1998). This leapfrogging effect can be observed in service industries, especially in the computer-related software sector. In India and Taiwan it has been realized by directly connecting local offices to Silicon Valley via satellite to develop software programming on a 24-hour basis, thereby utilizing time, cost and location differences.

Decentralization is another important aspect of the network society. On the production side, individual workers can participate in production decisions, so information flows horizontally as well as vertically. Workers are no longer the slaves of machines. Production lines can be divided into several blocs or modules to decentralize production processes with flexible specialization (what Piore and Sabel [1984] called the second industrial divide). In Japan, several manufacturing companies have adopted the cell production method which abolishes the mass production system. This also corresponds to changes in demand.

As demand diversifies, production has to respond to many varieties and differences in taste. Consumers can participate in, or order, desired products over the computer networks linking them directly to producers. This connection surpasses time and location. The greater the network coverage, the greater the end-user satisfaction (so-called 'network effects' or 'network externalities'). Personal network communication works efficiently when emergency or natural disasters occur. People can transmit their real situation and express their real needs to the outside world more quickly and effectively than mass communication professionals such as CNN and the BBC. Recent instances of this were observed in the Bosnian war, the Kobe earthquake, and the Timor riots. People's voices were heard firsthand.

As decentralization and individual participation are the basic principles of democracy, not only in the political sphere but also in the social domain, democratization proceeds.

High-tech hegemony

In the network market, good products (hardware and software) have a tendency to be locked into their markets. Once supremacy of such goods is established, they can occupy the market and enjoy absorbent monopoly rents. A recent dispute between Microsoft and the US Department of Justice over Microsoft's package deal of Windows 98 with its Internet Explorer (browser) program is a typical example of monopoly power. Extremely high-tech products are apt to be produced by MNCs because they necessitate accumulated knowledge gained through huge R&D inputs and expensive sunk costs. Antitrust laws are therefore necessary, particularly on a worldwide basis.

Another major feature of the new situation is the hegemonic struggle for global rules and standards amongst advanced countries, including MNCs and governments. For example, it is said that the UK government succeeded in having UK standards in environmental management accepted as the global standard (ISO14000 series). In the same vein, the method of code/decoding for the information industry is another battleground between advanced countries. What we need are global rules and standards, but they must be reached equitably and be transparent. Therefore, the process must be achieved by mutual consultation, and not only by the great powers, that is, MNCs or certain advanced countries.

Business models

In the USA, there is a rush to register IT-related business models under the framework of industrial ownership. E-commerce has produced new types of business that were unimaginable before such systems as Amazon.com's one-click service.[1] These new business models are registered and protected by intellectual property rights. First come, first served. But, is this right? Late comers, like developing countries, cannot run such new business models unless they pay royalties. This seems somewhat unfair. To give a rather esoteric comparison: if a *sumo* wrestler registered a special winning technique and collected a royalty when others used it, then *sumo* would not stay in existence for long as a competitive sport. Rules must be defined in order to create a level playing field, not to give one team – developed countries or MNCs – home advantage. All can fight using the same techniques without paying royalties in the same marketplace.[2]

Intellectual property rights should be esteemed but some modifications are necessary to control business model monopoly, such as shortening the period of protection and applying negligible royalty payments, because the Internet world is principally based on an open architecture philosophy.

Problems of the information age

Cyberspace creates new problems such as the so-called amplifier effect, technical interchangeability of systems, the protection of privacy, pirates or hackers (crackers), harmful information (pornography, bomb-making, cyber terrorism, etc.), and general criminal conduct (harassment, leakage, data falsification, fraud, etc.). In addition, in e-commerce, the protection of consumers and taxation issues are specific problems. Employment and relocation are also an issue. Here, four main points are discussed.

Amplifier effects

On Black Monday (October 19) 1987, computers automatically sent out selling orders for stocks when they reached pre-set baseline prices, which then engendered a further fall in stock prices. This was a classic case of mechanical or programming error that highlighted how networks can amplify and spread pessimism or panic. Thereby, a vicious circle is easily created. The Asian monetary crisis, in a sense, has been negatively influenced by this network amplifier effect, forcing exchange rates and stock prices downward.

A machine is not human. It cannot stop the pre-set programmed procedures. Regular surveillance and human interaction are necessary.

Security

In the cyberworld, high-tech wrongdoing easily occurs. Viruses can enter computer systems and privacy can be violated, so in order to secure commercial information or privacy through the Internet, coding and decoding systems are necessary. Usually keys are used to code and decode transmitted data. There are two systems: the common key and the open (or public) key. The former uses common keys where both the sender and the receiver have the same key to open and close the code, whilst the latter uses an openly-registered key for coding but an individual key for decoding data. In e-commerce, other factors such as guaranteed information (received information should correspond exactly to the sent information) and identification or confirmation of senders are also of importance.

New systems or institutions are needed for these new developments. For example, an attesting office which administers private passwords, registered digital signatures, cryptographic certificates, and registered open keys is necessary for electronic commerce.

Furthermore, electronic money may create complications such as money laundering, tax evasion and other financial crime, if payment records are encrypted. New control and settlement facilities are also needed if issued by companies other than existing banking and credit card companies.

Taxation in the borderless age

Taxation is another problematic issue. Trade can easily cross national borders, therefore the question arises, how can tax authorities impose and collect taxes?

When and where? Value-added tax (VAT), income tax, and taxes for e-commerce activities. How are these items to be considered?

For instance, who should be charged VAT, the final sellers, consumers, or credit card companies? By the same token, online commerce poses the question on the corporate income tax level. Usually, corporate income tax is based on a business establishment or a physical presence. However, it is very difficult to trace the location of a company in cyberspace. The idea of taxing the data stream over the Internet rather than the transaction itself has been floated, but, so far, there is no consensus about this 'bit tax.'

Employment

E-commerce directly links producers and consumers. This means that traditional intermediaries are no longer necessary. In the case of parts procurement, producers can utilize electronic data interchange (EDI) systems to purchase worldwide so that hierarchical subcontracting systems are no longer needed. This creates drastic industrial structural changes, leading to unemployment. However, the unemployed have to be absorbed in other places, possibly service industries.

Recent phenomena demonstrate that e-commerce without a physical foundation does not work well. Amazon.com, for instance, realized that it had to establish its own warehouses and distribution systems to better fulfil consumer satisfaction. This is called a 'click or brick' decision. A mixture of e-commerce and traditional businesses may guarantee more employment. In any case, re-education and relocation of those displaced is necessary. Computer literacy education for the weak (unemployed, older generation, and disabled) is thus indispensable.

Providing for a new age

Information infrastructure

Following US Vice-President Al Gore's declaration to support the super information highway project, enormous investment in information infrastructure is expected to be made. The construction of trunk and feeder lines of optical fiber networks will require extra public expenditure, but it will also create multiplier effects for information-related industries.

Because computer and telecommunications technologies are converging, major investments are foreseen in the software and hardware industries, space industries (satellites), as well as in telecommunications (switching, relay, terminals, and cellular phones). Moreover, as digitalization advances, broadcasting, photographic and cinematographic industries will join the multimedia age – forming giant information and entertainment conglomerates.

The digital divide and computer literacy

Income disparity brings about digital disparity, that is, what we call the 'digital divide.' It is reported that in the USA,

"Among the 5.5 million White, Asian, and Pacific Islander families with an income of at least US$75,000, living in metropolitan areas, headed by someone with at least a college education and aged 30 to 55, 87 percent had computers at home, and 68 percent had Internet connections. At the other extreme, the 1.2 million Black and Hispanic urban households with incomes below US$15,000, in which all adults lack a high school diploma or GED, and headed by someone aged 30 to 55, only 7 percent had computers at home and only 2 percent had Internet service." US Department of Commerce 2000, pp. 69–70

This observation can also be applied to countries on a developed/underdeveloped divide.

Understanding the importance of education and the training of people for the new computer age is vital for a nation's competitive edge. Retraining in order to relocate workers is also necessary. The ability to handle PCs is akin to language skills. Increasing computer literacy is, therefore, indispensable. Developing countries have to be assisted by advanced countries through official development assistance (ODA) in this field.

Cyber police

Physical programming errors such as the year 2000 problem could be solved, although the process was costly, by changing programs. However, virus-related crimes which require vaccines or antivirus tools are increasing.[3] The more sophisticated computer technologies become, the more difficult it is to control computer-related crimes. These include hacking (intrusion to secret and private information and the theft, falsification, or destruction of such data; interception of messages and credit card numbers; harassment and hate mail; etc.), financial crimes (the use of false credit cards and electronic money, money laundering, tax evasion, etc.), harmful information (pornography, how to make bombs, etc.), and the violation of intellectual property rights. In order to avoid such computer-related crime, a high-tech police force is urgently needed.

The dangers related to cyber terrorism and hacker attacks are more clearly understood. Cyber attacks on atomic-powered electricity generation plants and the US Defense Department are well documented. It is said that cyber attacks such as that on Iraqi air-defence systems by the US military, Yugoslavian defence headquarters by NATO, and the Japanese government's home pages by Chinese hackers did really happen.

Global cooperation

The WTO is generally seeking liberalization in trade and services (World Trade Organization 1998). The General Agreement on Trade in Services (GATS) is the first multilateral trade agreement on services. GATS covers eleven main service sectors: business; communication; construction; distribution; education; environment; finance; health; tourism; sports and recreation; and transport. The crucial obligations under GATS are transparency and most-favoured-nation (MFN) treatment (the latter should not extend beyond ten years). GATS is relevant for e-commerce, because many transactions through the Internet cover these service activities.

The WTO's Singapore Ministerial Conference in 1996 declared that the objective of the Information Technology Agreement (ITA) was to maximize freedom of world trade in IT products and encourage continued technological development on a worldwide basis. Another important agreement under the WTO framework is Trade-Related Aspects of Intellectual Property Rights (TRIPS). This aims to ensure the adequate protection and effective enforcement of intellectual property rights. Within the framework of e-commerce, the protection of copyright, trademarks, and domain names is of great importance. As far as copyright is concerned, two important treaties were provided by the World Intellectual Property Organization (WIPO) in 1996, namely, the WIPO Copyright Treaty and the WIPO Performances and Phonograms Treaty.

For online transaction security, a standard for secure electronic transactions (SET) was developed in 1997, at the instigation of private credit card companies. SET addresses the security of Internet purchases by credit cards and related payment authorization and money transfer.

Another important consideration is regional cooperation. For instance, APEC has the Asia-Pacific Information Initiative that promotes information facilities between member countries. Recently, the government of Japan proposed a network-forming project utilizing a telecommunications satellite to be launched in 2003, with free access for users for remote medical diagnosis, as well as emergency communication measures for natural disasters. The Kyushu-Okinawa Summit in 2000 also declared a Charter that will be described later.

The IT revolution in Japan

Japan lags behind Asian newly industrialized economies (NIEs) in terms of Internet use (see Table 2.1). In 1999, 1,447 people in every ten thousand used the Internet in Japan, but equivalent figures for Singapore, Hong Kong, and Korea were 2,946, 2,519, and 1,468, respectively. Japan is also slow in the diffusion of broadband telecommunications. The digital subscriber line (DSL) is used by around 2 million in the USA and 1 million in Korea, but there

Table 2.2 *IT-related legal infrastructure in Japan*

2000	April	Introduction of official electronic certification system (amended the Commercial Registration Act)
	July	Basic electronic specification on certification for government applications and notices
	August	Guidelines for government administration information plans
	October	Action plan for MOF-related procedures relating to tax, tariff, and statistics
		Revision of inspection standards for computer software on industrial ownership for business models
		Start to examine amendments of the Civil Law, the Commercial Law, and the Crime Law regarding IT
2001	January	Basic Act for High-degree Information and Technology Network (Basic IT Act) effective from this month
	March	Announcement of the 'e-Japan' project
	April	Act for Electronic Signature and Certification (Electronic Signature Act) effective from this month
	May	Act for Information Disclosure effective from this month

Source: Japan External Trade Organization.

were only two thousand users in Japan in the middle of 2000. Reasons for this include the language barrier, expensive access charges, slow infrastructure development, and monopolistic markets.

The Japanese government felt the need to catch up with the recent progress in IT, and several measures were undertaken, such as legal preparation, establishment of IT plans, infrastructure building, and education. At the same time, the private sector is also quite active in promoting IT-related industries; as examples, this chapter describes a unique idea in the software field called the "TRON" project, and a newly developed cellular phone that can connect to the Internet.

Legal infrastructure

New laws and acts are needed as cyberspace transcends time and location. E-commerce requires systems and mechanisms for the registration of digital signatures, identification, attesting, and certification. Industrial property rights for new ideas should be established. E-government also needs a framework for digital databases, electronic procedures, and specifications. Recently, the government has enthusiastically provided and strengthened this legal infrastructure (see Table 2.2).

The Basic Act for High-degree Information and Technology Network (Basic IT Act) was effective from January 2001. It aims to promote e-commerce and IT use in government administration (e-government). It also endorses utilization of information and telecommunications technologies in the public sector. A related law covering government accountability and transparency (the Act for Information Disclosure) was effective from May 2001. This aims to promote disclosure of government documents and stipulates rights for request and procedures.

The Mori administration set up the IT Strategic Committee in July 2000 to encourage the IT revolution in Japan. Moreover, the Telecommunications Council released *The Information and Telecommunications Vision for the 21st Century* in March 2000 and the Economic Council published *The Policy Direction of Economic Rebirth (IT Revolution)* in June 2000.

Government plan for IT and the Okinawa Charter

In November 2000, the IT Strategic Committee, which advises the prime minister published the draft of the "National IT Strategies for 2005." The target is to realize an environment where 30 million households can access high-speed Internet facilities using DSL and/or cable TV and an additional 10 million can be connected to super high-speed Internet by optical fibers within five years (by 2005). There are some 43 million households in Japan so it is intended that almost all households will be able to access the Internet through broadband lines. The aim is to propel Japan into most advanced nation status within five years with four priority fields (*Nihon Keizai Shimbun*, 6 November 2000):

1 Infrastructure building:
    * construction of optical fiber networks for 10 million households
    * universal service for isolated places and islands
    * support for R&D activities
2 Realization of e-government:
    * electronic database for administration matters by 2003
    * information disclosure through the Internet
3 Promotion of e-commerce:
    * legal preparation for e-commerce by 2002
    * market size to be ten times that of 1998 in 2003
4 Human resource development:
    * the Internet diffusion rate to be over 60 percent by 2005
    * the number of Ph.D. and Masters degree holders relating to IT to surpass that of the USA by 2005
    * acceptance of around 30,000 foreign IT engineers and researchers by 2005

The Japanese government intends to promote the IT revolution externally, too. In the G8 Kyushu-Okinawa Summit in July 2000, "The Okinawa Charter on Global Information Society" was declared following enormous coordination efforts by the Japanese government. It emphasised: (a) seizing digital opportunities; (b) bridging the digital divide; and (c) promoting global participation. The Charter proposed to establish a Digital Opportunity Taskforce ("dot force") to pursue the following objectives (Government of Japan 2000a):

1 Actively facilitate discussions with developing countries, international organizations, and other stakeholders to promote international co-operation with a view to: (a) fostering policy; (b) regulatory and network readiness; (c) improving connectivity, increasing access, and lowering cost; (d) building human capacity; and (e) encouraging participation in global e-commerce networks.

2 Encourage the G8's own efforts to cooperate on IT-related pilot programs and projects.

3 Promote closer policy dialogue amongst partners and work to raise global public awareness of the challenges and opportunities.

4 Examine inputs from the private sector and other interested groups such as the Global Digital Divide Initiative's contributions.

5 Report its findings and activities to each government's personal representatives before the next meeting in Genoa.

In response to the Charter, the government of Japan prepared a comprehensive cooperation package to address the international digital divide. It committed ODA and non-ODA funds of US$15 billion over five years. The Special Action to implement this package included: (a) raising awareness of IT opportunities and contributing intellectually to policy and institution building; (b) developing and training human resources; (c) building IT infrastructure and providing assistance for network establishment; and (d) promoting the use of IT in development assistance (Government of Japan 2000b).

Original ideas by the private sector

Although Japan seems to have been slow on the uptake with regard to IT preparation, there are now several unique and interesting ideas around. One is the TRON project, a made-in-Japan OS, and the other a wireless Web phone, i-Mode.

The TRON project

The TRON project started in 1984, headed by Professor Ken Sakamura, to establish a new architecture for loosely coupled distributed information processing systems. TRON stands for The Real-time Operating system Nucleus.

The project produced TRON operating chips and new OS languages such as BTRON, ITRON, and CTRON. The basic idea behind the project is "computing everywhere." For example, an experimental TRON-concept intelligent house has roofs, floors, bathrooms, air-conditioning systems, alarm systems, and electronic appliances such as TVs, refrigerators, telephones, and fax machines with their own chips and/or sensors which can operate like a microcomputer and communicate with the owner. The concept is "computing everywhere" or establishing a "ubiquitous computing" society (Sakamura 1999).

Tenets and characteristics of the project are as follows:

1   The TRON program is open-source language like 'Linux' so that everybody can download and use it.
2   TRON chips are very compact and small so that handy and portable machines such as mobile phones can embed them.
3   Human interface is emphasised, what is called "enableware." The whole concept is quite user-oriented so that everyone can use TRON-operated machines.
4   Regional culture is not forgotten. For example, a new program called "Cho-Kanji" (Super Chinese Character) based on BTRON can use 130,000 letters which greatly widens the use of Chinese characters and other Asian languages such as Korean, Thai, Hindi, etc.

The first point is very interesting. The Internet world is characterised as individualistic but with participation concepts. Everybody can participate in and add to its content. Knowledge is shared among participants. This is far from egoistic, profit-seeking business activities such as Microsoft engages in. The TRON language is open for everybody and famous companies in Japan such as Nippon Telegraph & Telephone Corp. (NTT) and Toyota Motor Corp. use it freely, leaving Professor Sakamura not quite as rich as Bill Gates.

The second point also addresses the current situation where heavily equipped PCs are becoming out of date for Internet purposes because mobile phones can connect to the Internet. Networks of PCs are no longer needed as mobile phones can be substituted for them.

The third point emphasises that TRON is user friendly. The concept, "enableware," aims to develop generalized technologies to enable equipment to be used in a variety of circumstances, that is, it finds and corrects mismatches between individual circumstances and their environments.

The fourth point is of different but equal importance. Chinese characters are used by more than 1.2 billion people in the world (one in five persons) but Chinese characters allotted to the present Western computer standards number only 7,000 letters. Cho-Kanji can present rich and deep Chinese as well as Japanese literature using the original letters, such as a sutra, a Chinese masterpiece, "The History of Three Nations," and one Japanese classic, "The Tale of Genji."

According to Sakamura (1999, pp. 13–15), OS languages have three varieties: ITRON, BTRON, and CTRON. ITRON (Industry TRON) defines an operating system for machine-embedded control systems, "designed to serve at the very core of the entire TRON Project." ITRON has three specifications, according to its development stages. ITRON1 is intended for 16-bit MPUs, ITRON2 for 32-bit MPUs and μITRON for 8-bit microcontrollers. These are used in automotive engines, mobile telephones, fax/copy machines, digital cameras, and LAN connections. BTRON (Business TRON) defines an operating system for the human–machine interface. It is designed to offer system-level support for video and other multimedia equipment. Its features also include multilingual support and a standard interface for the disabled (such as a special keyboard and computer designed for handicapped persons). Cho-Kanji is programmed by BTRON. CTRON (Communications and Center TRON) is OS software for communication equipment, especially for multitask, real-time processing. It is used in electronic switching systems, PBXs, and fault-tolerant computers. A further variety, JTRON, released in November 2000, is a combination of Java and ITRON. Java language, which was invented by Sun Microsystems, suits the networks while ITRON has real-time merits. Thus JTRON is good for cellular phones. The Japanese domestic operator J-PHONE has already decided to produce JTRON-loaded next-generation mobile phones.

According to the TRON Association, a questionnaire survey done between November 1999 and January 2000 (out of 911 received, 896 are valid) shows that ITRON used in OS designs in various products averaged over 60 percent of the field of consumer-related products (home appliances, communication terminals, entertainment/education equipment, audio visual equipment, and personal information appliances) (see Table 2.3).

Indeed, it is worth stressing here that it is a unique project from an exceptional person, Professor Sakamura, that has produced original OS languages based on concepts different from Western-dominated computer logics. Japan already had the advantage of mass producing home appliances and communication-related machines, and this, combined with the unprecedented rapid dissemination of cellular telephones throughout the country, has enabled frequent utilization of OS language in such equipment. Thus, Professor Sakamura's contribution has been truly great.

i-Mode mobile telephone

NTT DoCoMo first sold a new model of mobile telephones called "i-Mode" on February 22, 1999. The model was quite different from other mobile telephones of that time. It had four functions: (a) telephone; (b) Internet; (c) e-mail; and

Table 2.3 *ITRON OS use and application fields (only systems using an OS),
1999/2000 (percent)*

Application fields	ITRON	Commercial OS	In-house
Personal information appliance	47.6	42.9	9.5
Communication equipment (network facilities)	37.5	42.2	20.3
Communication equipment (terminal)	65.3	29.3	5.3
Home appliance	81.3	18.8	0.0
Entertainment/education equipment	66.7	33.3	0.0
Audiovisual equipment	61.2	30.6	8.2
Electrical equipment	35.7	57.1	7.1
Transportation-related equipment	43.2	29.5	27.3
Industrial control/factory automation	36.4	38.4	25.3
Personal computer peripheral	42.1	34.2	23.7
Medical equipment	45.5	40.9	13.6
Miscellaneous commercial systems	38.9	44.4	16.7
Miscellaneous measuring instruments	26.9	61.5	11.5
Others	50.0	36.4	13.6

Source: TRON Association (http://www.itron.gr.jp).

(d) online information services. The basic idea behind it was one-phone functions like a "concierge" service at a hotel. The last function included mobile
banking, mobile trade, restaurant and station guide, ticket reservation, news
information, and games. This hit product sold 1 million after only five months
on the market and reached 5 million after one year. Currently, it is said that
there are more than 10 million i-Mode users.

The name i-Mode came from information service counters in international
airports that have the sign of a minuscule letter "i" (Matsunaga 2000). The
distinguishing feature of this mobile phone is that i-Mode can work as a small
computer terminal. Current PCs are well equipped with multifunctions but ordinary people rarely use all functions: word processing, e-mail, and Internet
access are the main uses. The mobile phone is cheap, small, light, and portable.
Offering popular requirements such as e-mail Internet functions, this new mobile phone is therefore more convenient than bulky computer terminals. For
example, i-Mode can send and receive e-mail with 250 letters, which is sufficient to communicate with friends and loved ones.

i-Mode phones use the packet telecommunications method to send and
receive information data. This method imposes a monetary charge depending
on the volume of data exchanged, not on the time spent on-air. Since Japan's

telephone charges are time-based, the new charge is lower than the old one (basic charge for one month 300 yen + one packet 0.3 yen/128 byte + contents charge if charged). Another feature is its access language. i-Mode uses compact hyper-text markup language (C-HTML), which is basically the common language of the Internet, so that i-Mode can easily access information and content for a user to build their own home page. There is another language called WML in the Wireless Application Protocol (WAP) which is being promoted by Nokia, Ericsson, Motorola, etc. as a world standard. However, another reason for its success has been the use of well-circulated languages instead of adopting a new world standard.

Mobile phones for i-Mode are manufactured by four companies: NEC, Panasonic (Matsushita), Fujitsu, and Mitsubishi Electric. They are called the DoCoMo family. As explained in the previous section, these phones are loaded with TRON chips. After the emergence of i-Mode, competitors J-PHONE and IDO[4] also went into the same business. As of April 2000, the total number of mobile phones in use in Japan had reached around 52 million, with market share as follows: NTT DoCoMo (58 percent), KDDI (27 percent), and J-PHONE group (15 percent). It is estimated that the number will reach 79 million by the end of 2005.

Related issues: new address allocation IPv6

Users of the Internet must have their own, unique address. At present, addresses are allocated according to IPv4 (Internet Protocol Version 4). However, this version can handle only about 4.3 billion terminals and is now almost exhausted. The next version called IPv6 can cover 2^{128} addresses, that is, more than will ever be needed. This gives rise to the possibility of countless microcomputer accesses and networks. Online networks can be established between mobile phones, PC terminals, home appliances (TV/video, refrigerator, cooking range, bath, air conditioning, etc.), door locks, and car navigation. If these machine items have their own addresses, we can communicate with them. Is this a nightmare or progress?

Some problems

Phone companies competing with each other for world standards offer wireless telecommunications methods. The next or third-generation cellular phone will roam worldwide. This international roaming service is necessary, but getting agreement on a standard for wireless telecommunications has been hard to realize at the International Telecommunications Union in Geneva. US operators and KDDI of Japan are promoting the cdma2000 method, while Europe may be pushing the EDGE method, and NTT DoCoMo and J-PHONE group of Japan are promoting W-CDMA. Which one is adopted is vitally important to each company. NTT DoCoMo's virtual monopoly may be lost if its standard is not adopted.

The idea of ubiquitous computing is good and we can enjoy a convenient lifestyle with microcomputers and chips in every electronic item. However, it also puts personal privacy at risk. If every mobile phone has a function for position identification, we can be monitored at all times. In addition, it is easier to intercept wireless transmission so that phone-tapping opportunities widen. Surely, we do not want such a life. Another scary factor is incidents of computer-equipped malfunction in a machine-to-machine world. The wrong radio signals could result in fires, explosions, and/or plane crashes. We have already had accidents involving the malfunctioning of heart pacemakers, and cockpit problems caused by mobile phones.

Monopoly is problematic in terms of prices and services. NTT has long been criticized for its high access charges that caused delay in the development of the Internet in Japan. It is said that the present charge, 5.6 yen per three minutes, is ten times that of the USA. Recently the Fair Trade Commission has been investigating NTT's hindrance to broadband ventures by intentionally delaying its preparation for DSL. These are cases of impediment by monopoly. A further break-up of NTT is again being discussed. (The original NTT was divided into three companies in July 1999: NTT East Japan, NTT West Japan, and NTT Communications. Together with NTT Data and NTT DoCoMo, five NTT companies form a holding company and reign over Japan's telecommunications markets.)

As explained, multinational telephone companies are competing with each other to set the world standard and gain market hegemony. Strategic alliances have been forming between multimedia MNCs. NTT DoCoMo is pursuing the same course and recently announced plans to form a strategic partnership with America Online in September 2000, and with AT&T in November 2000. However, the widespread deployment of i-Mode type cellular phones in the US market is questionable for several reasons: (a) PCs are popular in the USA and Internet access is usually done through PCs; (b) text-based wireless Internet services are easier to use when commuting by public transport rather than when driving to work; and (c) tiny screens with tiny keys make it not worth the effort for many Americans.

Concluding remarks

Technologies nowadays have been changing very rapidly. This is called "dog year" progress. Changes are also noncontinuous. Leapfrogging may bring about instant happiness to developing countries. For example, the lack of telephone line infrastructure caused surprisingly rapid expansion of mobile phones in some developing countries. However, due to enormous gaps in information technologies and facilities between advanced and developing countries, the digital divide is obvious. Several measures and efforts should be taken to narrow the gap, especially in the fields of education and IT skills. Those displaced must be cared for, too.

Competition amongst private companies will bring us a better life in terms of convenience, cost, time, and amenity through new products. But the monopolistic tendencies of MNCs should be restricted. The determination of world standards for new products should be transparent and made with due consideration for people's welfare in developing as well as in advanced countries.

Finally, the fundamental thought behind the Internet world is what Illich called conviviality (Illich 1973). Individual participation and joint ownership of new concepts and ideas are of great importance in the new global information age. Based on this philosophy, both advanced and developing countries have to re-engineer their society for the twenty-first century. However, the special considerations of developing countries should not be forgotten by the developed world as we enter into cyberworld.

Notes

1. The Japanese version of Amazon.com's one-click service was temporarily rejected by the Patent Agency in May 2001.
2. The original Japanese *sumo* had forty-eight winning wrestling techniques. Now it has been expanded to seventy.
3. Internet viruses such as Melissa and Loveletter are famous. At present, the newest virus called MTX is playing havoc with cyberspace. In November, the total number of complaints reached 2,203, the highest reported number per month registered in the grievance office (IPA) in Japan, out of which 894 were MTX infections. The number of complaints was 3,675 in 1999 and jumped to 8,331 in January–November 2000. (*Nihon Keizai Shimbun*, December 8, 2000) (see also http://www.ipa.go.jp).
4. Later, IDO and DDI Cellular merged to form KDDI in October 2000 and its mobile section is now called "au."

References

Government of Japan 2000a, *The Okinawa Charter on the Global Information Society*, July 22, 2000, Tokyo.

    2000b, *Japan's Comprehensive Co-operation Package to Address the International Digital Divide*, July 14, 2000, Tokyo.

Illich, I. 1973, *Tools for Conviviality*, London: Calder and Boyars.

Kagami, M. 1998, New strategies for Asian technological development: problems facing technology transfer and backward linkage, in M. Kagami, J. Humphrey, and M. Piore (eds.), *Learning, Liberalization and Economic Adjustment*, Tokyo: Institute of Developing Economies, JETRO, pp. 1–32.

Matsunaga, M. 2000, *i-Mode Affair* (in Japanese), Tokyo: Kadokawa Shoten.

Piore, M. and Sabel, C. 1984, *The Second Industrial Divide: Possibilities for Prosperity*, New York: Basic Books.

Sakamura, K. 1999, *ITRON: An Open and Portable Real-time Operating System for Embedded Systems (Concept and Specification)*, Los Alamitos, CA: IEEE Computer Society Press.

US Department of Commerce 2000, *Digital Economy 2000*, Washington, DC, June 2000.

World Trade Organization 1998, *Electronic Commerce and the Role of the WTO*, Geneva.

3 The IT revolution and telecommunications infrastructure

Masatsugu Tsuji

Introduction

The traditional Japanese economic systems of employment, production, and corporate organisation provided a strong basis for growth from the 1960s to the 1980s. However, these systems have not adapted well to the IT revolution and, as can been seen from Internet penetration ratios, Japan has lagged behind both Western and other East Asian countries. As a result, the government has set up a task force charged with devising a plan to encourage: (a) the deployment of broadband optical fiber infrastructure; (b) the promotion of so-called cyber government; (c) the promotion of e-commerce; and (d) the development of human resources for IT.[1]

After the oil crisis, the US manufacturing sector was in danger of collapsing, but in the 1990s it was revitalised by the adoption of IT. Not only software, but Internet hardware such as the ATM or server, were for the most part monopolized by US manufacturers.[2] Industrial transformation changed the market structure in such a way that online businesses such as Amazon.com and Charles Schwab surpassed the performance of existing market leaders. This new economy is based on its competitive and market-oriented characteristics.

In this paper, we attempt to analyze Japan's true position in the IT revolution. We focus on telecommunications infrastructure and the application of IT, especially the Internet, to economic and business activities. These are the key factors for promoting the development of IT, since the former is the basis for high-speed transmission of digital information and the latter the basis for various business uses. We also undertake an international comparison. Based on these discussions, we propose a possible strategy for the Japanese economy, a business strategy to fully utilize the Japanese advantage. A business model will be presented which transforms the e-economy to an m-economy, with mobile equipment a major means of communication.

In what follows, we first describe Internet access in Japan and show the extent to which Japan lags behind other countries. We then discuss the current telecommunications infrastructure and focus on the deployment of optical fiber networks. Finally, we consider the best strategy for the Japanese IT revolution. By focusing on Japanese advantages, such as telecommunications infrastructure and the high penetration rate of mobile phones, we discuss examples of business models and make policy recommendations to build on these advantages.

The telecommunications market and Internet access: current postion

The telecommunications market has been transformed as a result of technological development and deregulation. New competitors have been entering the local call market, which was once monopolized by NTT before it was split up in 2000 and, since then, by NTT locals such as NTT East and NTT West.

The current situation of the local call market

It is evident that the telecommunications market has been changing at a much greater rate than expected. It is said that the Internet evolves at the speed of a dog year, that is, four times faster than real time. The local call market was monopolized by NTT, with a market share as high as 98 percent, but a new charge settlement between NTT and the new common carriers (NCCs) dramatically lowered charges. The new interconnection charges were based on total elements long-run incremental costs (TELRIC)[3] which is based on the assumption that facilities for interconnections are utilized efficiently, rather than on historical costs. As a result, interconnection charges dropped to 4.50 yen/three minutes from 10.64 yen/three minutes. Since NTT locals (NTT East and NTT West) charge 10 yen/three minutes for local calls, even allowing for interconnection charges, NCCs are able to compete with NTT. NCCs (which are long-distance NCCs such as KDDI and JT) have announced that they will enter the local call market with the rate of 8.80 yen/three minutes, and NTT will follow suit.

Other entrants are local telecommunications carriers established by power companies such as TTNet and QTNet. They have their own telecommunications networks and need not depend on that of NTT, and they can set charges lower than those of their rivals. TTNet has set its charges at 8.70 yen and QTNet at 8.60 yen for three minutes, and TTNet has been attracting more subscribers in the Tokyo Metropolitan area. One interesting entrant is a venture business named Fusion Communications which utilizes the Internet Protocol (IP) network. Through this technology, it will provide both local and long-distance service at the same rates, namely, 20 yen/three minutes. Thus, the Japanese local call market will be more competitive than ever before.

Although discussions have previously been held and deregulation, such as price caps, been imposed to generate competition in this market, none has been successful so far. A year ago, no one would have expected this.[4]

Table 3.1 *International comparison of Internet charges, December 1999 (US$)*

City	Tokyo	New York	London	Paris	Dusseldorf	Geneva
Telecommunications charges	23	19	24	24	26	24
Internet access charges	24	21	20	12	32	11
Total	47	30	44	36	58	35

Source: MPT.

Internet penetration in Japan

The IT revolution has been inspired by the Internet which has penetrated into all areas of life, not only those related to business and economics. In order to analyse the IT revolution in Japan, we will first examine current use of the Internet.

There is no definite figure for the number of Japanese Internet users. According to the Ministry of Posts and Telecommunications (MPT), it is estimated to have been about 27 million at the end of 1999, compared to the USA's 163 million, and the EU's 70 million. Nordic nations such as Sweden, Norway, and Finland show the highest Internet penetration ratio of more than 40 percent. The USA is about 40 percent, ranked fifth, and the UK 24 percent. Japan, on the other hand, is 21.4 percent and ranked thirteenth. This number is almost the same as that of Korea. Other statistics give a total of about 20 million users with a penetration ratio of about 24 percent.[5] These figures seem to be rather high, compared with other Asian countries.

Internet access charges

It has been suggested that the low penetration ratio in Japan is due to high telecommunications charges. The current international comparison of Internet access charges is shown in Table 3.1, and the difference seems to be smaller than it used to be. However, dial-up charges for a 24-hour flat rate in Tokyo (NTT's ISDN) was still 1.8 times higher than that of New York (Bell Atlantic) in November 1999 (see Table 3.2). Before the flat-rate system was started in Japan, Tokyo was ten times higher than New York. In both cases, therefore, the price difference has fallen.

Types of Internet access

Let us briefly examine how the Japanese access the Internet. MPT's data shows the number of subscribers to different types of Internet access (December 2000):

Table 3.2 *Comparison of flat rates for Internet access,*
November 1999 (US$)

City	Tokyo	New York
Basic fee	$28	$11
Telecommunications charges	$45	$15
Internet access charges	$20	$24
Total	$93	$50

Source: MPT.

dial-up is 1.58 million, cable modem 625,000, and DSL (Digital Subscriber Line) 9,700. Dial-up includes ISDN, mostly INS64, and other statistics show that ISDN accounts for about half of dial-up, namely about 800,000.[6] These figures show that the majority of individuals still choose low-speed access to the Internet. Let us look at the situation and characteristics of different access measures in more detail.

ISDN

In recent years, NTT has promoted its ISDN service and, as a result, subscriptions increased sharply, reaching 5.077 million in September 1999. It operates at 64kbps, up to 128kbps at best, and uses existing copper lines so all subscribers with fixed telephones throughout most of Japan can have it easily installed. ISDN, however, is technologically suited to the telephony service, because telephones and facsimiles, for instance, can be used at the same time on one single line. But for Internet access, its speed is rather low and it has become obsolete technology.

In order to promote sales and respond to consumers' desire for lower charges, NTT started a flat-rate ISDN service in November 1999 at a monthly charge of US$70. In May 2000, NTT started a new service called "FLETS ISDN," at a monthly charge of US$40. NTT East and NTT West together currently have about 300,000 subscribers. In order to cope with increasing competition from other high-speed and broadband accesses, NTT will lower its monthly charge to US$25 in 2001.

CATV

The current number of subscribers via the CATV modem at the end of December 2000 was about 625,000, and 188 CATV companies are Internet service providers (ISPs). As a means of accessing the Internet, CATV has become increasingly popular, largely because of its flat-rate charges. It costs about US$50–60 per month in addition to an initial fee of US$300, which is still far cheaper for heavy Internet users than the current dial-up. CATV is also provided at higher speeds, such as 30Mbps, and with a larger volume. Because of these characteristics, the number of Internet users via the CATV network is expected to grow.

Each CATV company has access to a higher layer called zone access quality (ZAQ) that connects the companies to the Internet. If the cables connecting ZAQ and the companies have a smaller capacity, congestion results and speeds are greatly reduced. In addition, since the CATV network consists of arcs where each subscriber connects to the network, the more subscribers that connect to a particular arc, the slower the speed of connection.

Due to the 1993 deregulation of CATV, as well as technological development, CATV operators have been expanding their business activities into such areas as CATV telephony services, preparing for digitalization and full service. Nevertheless, interconnections between different CATV networks remain quite unsatisfactory. Each CATV network is an important local information infrastructure, but they are still separate from each other, and have not yet achieved national coverage.[7]

New technology for Internet access

Advances in telecommunications technology have facilitated broadband access to the Internet, creating the so-called "broadband age," but unfortunately Japan has failed to adopt it.

Digital subscriber line (DSL)

This is an Internet service, also called SDSL, HDSL, ADSL, etc., that has broadband characteristics but utilizes the current telecommunications network. An existing copper wire has a capacity of 1147kHz, of which the telephone service occupies only a quarter, that is, 26kHz. DSL technology uses the other three-quarters for Internet access. Depending on the transmission method, it enables high-speed interconnection to the Internet of 1.5–2Mbps. In addition, since DSL uses a different band from the telephone, it is possible to have 24-hour connections to the Internet. DSL has a hybrid fiber/copper makeup that can fulfil customer demand for high speed, but it is thought to be a transitory technology until carriers commit themselves to the more expensive construction of optical fiber networks.

Several venture businesses started this service in early 2000, and after a slow start with only 10,000 users in December 2000, it has grown rapidly, as shown in Figure 3.1.

NTT traditionally placed priority on the strategy of expanding ISDN to subscribers. At the early stage of DSL technology, DSL use caused negative effects to the sound quality of ISDN communication so NTT claimed that its facilities

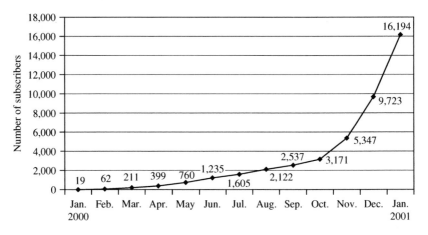

Figure 3.1 Growth of DSL subscriptions, 2000–2001 (Source: Ministry of Posts and Telecommunications)

were not suited to DSL. Thus, NTT was reluctant to allow other DSL operators to use its wireline for the same reason. However, due to recent technological progress and NTT's new strategy of placing emphasis on DSL, local NTTs have now started their own service and attracted many subscribers. In addition to NTT locals, other NCCs such as KDDI and JT will begin DSL services. Thus, DSL is becoming a possible means of broadband access to the Internet throughout Japan.

In the USA, since December 1999 when line sharing with DSL was approved, the number of subscribers has been increasing rapidly, and it is forecast that at the end of 2000 it will reach 1 million. Korea had 330,000 DSL users by March 2000, and was expected to have half a million at the end of 2000. This is because many high-rise apartments and condominiums were constructed during the high growth era, and DSL carriers installed the DSL facilities next to the telephone distributors of those buildings. By installing equipment near to its subscribers, DSL carriers can both expand their subscriber base, and maintain the quality of transmission.[8]

Fixed wireless access (FWA)

This type of access replaces subscribers' cables with wireless local loops. This system thus saves the cost of deploying subscriber lines and is expected to play a role in realizing fibre to the home (FTTH). It still faces some technological difficulties for extensive use, and the possibility of sending data to large office buildings and condominiums is currently at the experimental stage. This experimental Internet access service via FWA has already started for large business users.

Internet access via power lines

Every house has lines connected to the electricity supply which could be used for broadband Internet access. The speed is expected to be 1–3Mbps. Power companies have already deployed optical fiber networks, and their total mileage is close to that of NTT, so that this technology will solve the issue of the "last one mile" for FTTH. However, electricity lines carry noise from electric appliances, and success depends on how this noise can be erased. Experimental projects have already been started by power companies.

Optical IP communication network

The Optical IP Communication Network service is the provisional name for an NTT system based on IP protocol. This service makes it possible to re-alise the FTTH dream, that is, each house is connected directly to the optical fiber network. NTT locals started this service in parts of Tokyo and Osaka at the end of 2000. The speed is currently about 10Mbps, and will possibly reach 100Mbps, facilitating the transmission of motion pictures and music via the Internet. It costs about US$150 per month, which is rather expensive in comparison to DSL, so that small office and home office (SOHO) or busi-ness firms, not individuals, are thought to be the main subscribers at this time. Even with this service, all subscribers do not necessarily enjoy a speed of 10Mbps, because not only is there little content currently available, but the backbone network by which each ISP accesses the Internet does not necessar-ily meet this speed. Although this network still has technological and content problems, Internet usage leads to many other economies, and the "gigabyte age" is within reach. Therefore, this network should be an open platform for all carriers and ISPs, although NTT locals own it. KDDI will start the same broadband Internet access service by using the optical communication net-work. In order to secure fair interconnection, a regulatory scheme should be implemented.

Internet access via mobile phone

Internet access via mobile phones is called i-Mode by NTT DoCoMo, J-Sky by J-Phone, and EZweb by au and Tu-ka. Since i-Mode was started in February 1999, the growth in mobile access has been remarkable (see Table 3.3.); at the end of 2000, there were about 58 million mobile and cellular subscribers, nearly half with access to the Internet.

Of the carriers, i-Mode has 17.2 million subscribers (60.1 percent), EZweb 5.2 million (19.4 percent), and J-Sky 4.5 million (16.7 percent). Internet access via Personal Handy-Phone System (PHS) is available only from KDDI, with about 4 million subscribers in the same period. Thus, DoCoMo is now the biggest ISP in Japan. In 1999, the number of mobile phones exceeded that of fixed telephones, and now it is the largest Internet access tool. The success of

Table 3.3 *Growth of Internet access via mobile users, 2000 (thousands)*

	January	March	June	September	December
Number of users	4,593	7,499	12,723	19,679	26,866

Note: Numbers indicate total of i-Mode (DoCoMo), J-Sky (J-Phone), and EZweb.
Source: MPT.

DoCoMo indicates that mobile and cellular phones will be the major means of accessing the Internet in future.

The success of DoCoMo's i-Mode is based on the following factors: (a) Internet Protocol; (b) Web language HTML; (c) packet switching; (d) shorter connecting time; (e) reasonable charges based on amount of data; and (f) stability of communication.[9] Because of these characteristics, i-Mode directly targets general users, not computer specialists or engineers. It bears full possibility not only for future applications, but also for content.

Prediction of broadband Internet access

It is expected that Internet access will become increasingly high speed and broadband, and that by 2005 optical fiber will serve 20 million DSL users and 10 million CATV users. (Figure 3.2 provides a further example.) The FCC also predicts that in 2004 the number of subscribers via DSL and CATV in the USA will be 1.3 million and 1.5 million, respectively. Thus, broadband service will be fundamental to numerous applications.

Issues of Internet access

There are several major issues concerning Internet access in the broadband age, a few of which are summarized below.

Fair connection

Networks such as CATV and those of other carriers operate in a fair and competitive market; the large difference in their market shares is the result of network competition. But telecommunications carriers who have to utilize NTT's subscriber lines claim that NTT's dominance and the bottleneck monopoly are still major issues. Let us take DSL as an example. All carriers that wish to provide DSL service have to use NTT's subscriber lines and other facilities to connect to individual subscribers. They claim that NTT does not give them fair treatment and the issue of co-location arises. They also claim that NTT deliberately rejects applications to use NTT facilities and charges higher fees than those

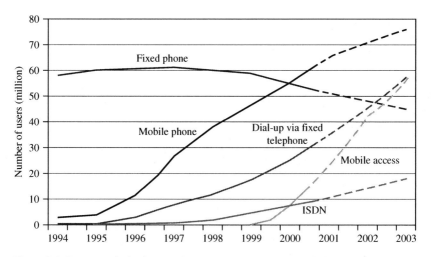

Figure 3.2 Forecast of telephone and Internet access, 1994–2003 (Source: NTT)

of its affiliates. The MPT has been working to implement fair access rules. These are the same issues that have been under discussion on how to maintain fair competition in the telecommunications market.

Re-restructuring of NTT

The giant NTT was split into two locals, one long-distance, and a holding company, but NTT still maintains allocation of funds and human resources across the four companies. There has been some progress towards the complete separation of these companies to promote competition among them. However, the business boundary between NTT locals and NTT Communications (long-distance carrier) is not clear, nor is it necessary in the age of the Internet.[10]

NTT locals want to start a new Internet access service called "L-mode," which is an i-Mode version for fixed telephones, that is, installing the PC function inside telephones to simplify Internet access. The issue is that since the Internet can connect distance servers, this violates the current regulation that NTT locals cannot engage in long-distance services. NTT locals want to expand into new areas to increase profits, but current regulation prohibits this. Thus, the real issue is that regulation based on traditional telephony service does not meet the needs of the Internet age.

These are some suggestions for promoting increased competition in the telecommunications market: (a) NTT locals enter the long-distance and international market; (b) NTT Communications provides local service; (c) NTT locals enter each other's regional markets; and (d) further deregulation is implemented to open NTT's local subscriber line.

Technology management

Another issue that has delayed Japanese Internet access is the technology management of carriers. Technology investment is both risky and costly when innovation is occurring so rapidly. A huge amount of accumulated investment results in becoming sunk costs as new technology becomes available. NTT's ISDN and DSL are typical examples. When ISDN subscribers want to change to DSL, they have to bear the extra costs of equipment as well as service charges to convert from the digital to the analog system.[11]

Even under such uncertainty, carriers and providers have to proceed with investment to meet the demand of consumers. As a business decision, carriers are required to predict the trend and direction of technology.

Telecommunications infrastructure: a comparison with the USA

Telecommunications infrastructure provides the basis for the IT revolution; without it, there can be no revolution. Here we summarize the current state of telecommunications infrastructure, and make a comparison between Japan and the USA.

Deployment of optical fiber networks

Optical fiber networks for telecommunications are, in general, classified into two categories: trunk lines and subscriber lines. Long-distance carriers, NTT, and other NCCs have already established their fiber networks linking all their nodes (branches) throughout Japan. NTT alone has established about 180,000km of trunk fibre cables. For subscribers, there are different agents such as: (a) local NTTs (NTT East and NTT West); (b) local NCCs such as TTNet, CTK, OMP, and Qnet, which were established mainly by electric companies; (c) CATV companies; and (d) cellular phone and mobile phone companies.

The total length of optical fiber networks in subscriber lines is summarized in Table 3.4. This table shows that NTT's share is always less than 50 percent. This seems to imply that in this market NTT is not dominant and NCCs have the advantage. However, NCCs include companies other than telecommunications carriers, such as CATV and power companies, and not all of their networks necessarily connect to telephones or PCs.

Intense competition between different companies in the deployment of optical fiber indicates that carriers, NTT as well as NCCs, recognize optical fibers as being the basis of competitiveness in the future. Table 3.5 indicates the areas covered by NTT optical fibers. This table shows that most of the business areas of big cities are already covered by optical fibers.

Table 3.4 *Length of optical fiber subscriber lines, 1993–1999 (thousand km)*

	1993	1994	1995	1996	1997	1998	1999
NTT	15	20	25	40	50	60	80
NCCs	25	30	45	70	105	120	140
Total	40	50	70	110	155	180	220

Source: MPT.

Table 3.5 *Percentage of areas covered by NTT's optical fibers, 1994–1999*

	1994	1995	1996	1997	1998	1999
Business areas[a]	30	50	70	90	93	95
Residential areas[a]	7	8	9	10	20	30
Average	10	15	18	20	25	35

Note:
[a] Business and residential areas are in large cities with a population of 300,000 or more.
Source: NTT.

Table 3.6 *Length of optical fiber installed by six major power companies, 2000 (thousand km)*

Tohoku Electric Co.	18	Kansai Electric Co.	40
Tokyo Electric Co.	45	Chugoku Electric Co.	6
Chubu Electric Co.	18	Kyushu Electric Co.	20

Source: MITI.

Optical fiber networks of power companies

Table 3.6 shows the total length of optical fiber installed by major power companies in Japan. Electric companies own power plants, distribution networks, and other facilities, and the purpose of the networks is to control and operate their systems of generation, transmission, and distribution, and to secure a stable supply. In addition, their networks automatically measure electricity usage. These networks require a certain level of quality and reliability and can be utilized as the public switched network of telecommunications carriers. The characteristic of this network is that it can act as subscriber lines, which is why electric companies have started providing telecommunications services.[11]

Tokyo Electric Company, for instance, currently owns 45,000km of optical fiber network, and plans to extend this to 80,000km in five years. The purpose of this expansion is not only to promote its telecommunications services operated by its affiliated company, TTNet, but also to set up a new company with Softbank which will begin a new business in 2000 providing Internet services at a fixed rate. The existing network is too small to supply fiber to the curb (FTTC). Tokyo Electric Company will install 8,000km of optical fibers in the Tokyo Metropolitan area, and will expand to cities with a population of more than 100,000 by the end of 2004.

TTNet

TTNet was established by Tokyo Electric Company, and has been providing a leased circuit for business companies; it started a local service in 1998. The basis of its telecommunications services lies in the optical fiber networks originally created for the power company. The total network length in 1999 consisted of 60,590km of optical fibers and 8,955km of metal cables, and the network is mainly located in the Tokyo Metropolitan area.

TTNet's services consists of telecommunications (47 percent), leased circuit (22 percent), services of other carriers such as international, mobile and cellular (18 percent), and Internet connection (13 percent). The characteristics of TTNet can be summarized as: (a) the density of optical fiber network, which is the same as NTT in the Tokyo Metropolitan area; (b) technology and know-how of maintenance, operation, and construction of network; (c) many large-sized corporate customers; and (d) the bland image of Tokyo Electric Company, which is the largest in Japan.

TTNet has been making an effort to construct optical subscriber lines on its own and providing various services based on them, including telephone as well as Internet services. In the Tokyo Metropolitan area, TTNet's density of optical fiber network is the same as that of NTT. In addition to this, TTNet can interconnect to NTT's subscriber lines at a location very close to the consumer.

OMP (Osaka Media Port)

OMP was established in 1985 as a joint venture of Kansai Electric Company (25.6 percent), Osaka City (25.0 percent), and Osaka Gas (6.5 percent) and other stakeholders, and started local call services, such as leased circuit, for businesses located in Osaka City in 1987. Currently, OMP owns 16,000km of optical fibre network and plans to construct an additional 40,000km.

OMP has placed its future strategy on providing high-speed Internet service via the CATV network, since one of OMP's affiliate firms provides a service for interconnecting CATV companies to the Internet. Thus, OMP's network enables Internet connection at 10Mbps using a flat-rate charging system, for example US$60 per month. Twenty-three CATV companies have received this

Table 3.7 *Length of trunk optical network in the USA: totals of all long-distance carriers, 1992–1998 (thousand km)*

1992	1993	1994	1995	1996	1997	1998
3,563	3,666	3,930	4,136	4,704	5,470	5,890

Source: FCC.

Table 3.8 *Average areas covered by optical fibers of local carriers in the USA, 1993–1998 (percent)*

Carrier	1993	1994	1995	1996	1997	1998
Ameritech	37.3	38.6	42.5	45.2	47.7	50.2
Bell Atlantic*	56.4	59.4	60.8	61.7	59.2	61.7
BellSouth	27.7	30.3	33.1	35.9	38.1	40.2
NYNEX*	47.0	48.2	49.6	50.9		
Pacific Telesis	38.2	38.8	39.5	40.4	41.5	42.0
SBC	35.1	38.2	41.8	43.7	46.7	48.8
US WEST	35.3	35.7	38.5	41.8	42.2	42.3
RBOC Total	38.3	40.7	43.0	45.4	47.4	49.4
GTE	16.9	17.5	22.3	24.4	25.6	26.3
Sprint	15.6	18.1	21.4	23.5	28.7	39.6
Total	33.3	35.3	32.6	34.2	35.7	45.3

Note: *From 1997, Bell Atlantic data includes NYNEX. Some other companies, due to mergers, also no longer exist.
Source: FCC.

service so far and they had 50,000 subscribers by June 2000. OMP is currently the largest CATV Internet provider.

OMP thus aims to be an Internet provider instead of a local telecommunications carrier. The difference between TTNet and OMP lies in the fact that the density of population in the Osaka area is much smaller than the Tokyo Metropolitan area, so OMP has shifted to Internet services for CATV companies by making use of its optical fiber network.

Comparison with the USA

Let us compare the optical fiber networks with those of the USA. Statistics on the trunk network are provided in Table 3.7. The difference between Japan and the USA reflects the difference in land area, and it is natural for the USA to have much longer links. On the other hand, Table 3.8 shows an interesting

Table 3.9 *Penetration ratio of mobile phones, September 1999 (percent)*

Finland	Sweden	Hong Kong	Korea	Japan	UK	Taiwan	USA	Germany
64.9	54.9	54.4	45.1	41.0	33.8	31.5	27.6	23.8

Source: MPT.

comparison for optical subscriber lines. In the USA, Regional Bell Operating Companies (RBOCs) cover nearly 50 percent of the region with optical fiber networks. This figure seems to be larger than that of NTT, as shown in Table 3.5. Japanese data, however, does not include other local carriers. Since NTT's share is about half of the total of non-NTT local carriers, areas covered by local carriers must be, approximately, doubled.

Strategy for the Japanese IT revolution

In the previous section, we made an international comparison of optical fiber infrastructure, and concluded that Japanese infrastructure does not necessarily lag behind that of the USA. Now, based on this discussion, we analyze a strategy for making use of Japanese advantages.

Japanese advantages in IT

Relative Japanese advantage in the IT revolution lies in its optical fiber infrastructure, and in the penetration rate of mobile communication. The penetration rate of mobile and cellular phones in the major economies is shown in Table 3.9. Nordic countries have the highest ratio, while developing economies tend to have a high rate due to poor infrastructure for fixed telephones. According to Table 3.8, the Japanese rate is higher than that of the USA. As mentioned earlier, the number of mobile phones was about 58 million at the end of 2000. In addition to this, all mobile phones are now digitalized. This is an important characteristic when considering business applications.

Mobile phones and telecommunications infrastructure are not separate concepts but are related to each other. Without the deployment of the latter, the penetration rate and applications of the former cannot be fully developed. Broadband infrastructure serves as the common platform for the application of mobile phones. If the infrastructure capacity is small, then mobile communications can easily be disrupted. A large capacity of broadband infrastructure can handle numerous accesses concurrently. Anyone can access the Internet at any time, anywhere, without inconveniencing others.

Characteristics of the mobile phone in e-commerce

Characteristics of i-Mode were described earlier. In this section, some other advantages are discussed, namely: (a) packet communication; and (b) ubiquity. Since it utilizes packet switching, it is charged by the packet. This makes charges far lower than those of telephony which are based on communication time. This is of great benefit to e-commerce. In addition, exchange of information between machines without direct human operation becomes possible, unlike voice telephony which requires human operation. Examples of its application include management of inventories, home and office security, and automobile navigator systems. PCs at the office can monitor inventories in remote vending machines, and mobile phones attached to machines send data 24 hours a day; houses or offices can be remotely monitored via mobile phones. This notion has led to "Internet electrical appliances," which are operated from outside the home. A navigation system inside the car can automatically receive real-time information on parking garages, hotels, and restaurants. In addition to this, mobile services are ubiquitous, that is, they are ready to transmit and receive any kind of information at any time and anywhere.

It might be thought that mobile phones are too small to contain all the functions required for various types of e-commerce. This will be solved in the near future by the development of the application service provider (ASP). Currently, for users' PCs or servers all necessary application software and data are contained on a hard disk as well as in its memory. Eventually, it will not be necessary to store them in users' PCs or mobile phones, but to download from the ASP when necessary. Thus, small mobile phones will be able to do the same tasks as today's PCs.

Prerequisites for wider application

We have discussed the possibility of further applications of mobile phones, but there are other conditions which first must be satisfied, namely reallocation of the radio wave spectrum, and further R&D application.

High-speed wireless Internet and telecommunications services require radio waves. This is a scarce resource, so efficient use of radio waves is a necessary condition for the IT revolution. The recent rapid increase of radio wave usage by mobile phones has become an obstacle to its further application, so reallocation is urgent. The current scheme of radio wave allocation protects the right of incumbent agents. In order to cope with this, a radio wave spectrum auction should be introduced.[13] Spectrum auctions have been widely accepted worldwide, particularly for wireless communications. The disadvantage of this type of auction is that bidding rises too high for small agents to win, but it also has many merits and the experiences of Western economies show it to be generally successful.

For high-speed wireless Internet access to be realised, further R&D for applications such as Internet Protocol version 6 (IPv6) is required. This technology will make Internet electrical appliances a reality, and mobile phones will be able to control and operate this equipment from remote places.[14]

Conclusion: from e-economy to m-economy

In this paper, we try to analyze Japan's advantage for future high-speed and broadband wireless Internet access, and conclude that it has relative advantages in its optical fiber network and the penetration rate of mobile phones. They are the two key factors for the future. In addition to these, further R&D such as the next generation Internet Protocol is required.

It is commonly recognized that Japan has a relative advantage in hardware but is rather weak in application software. An urgent requirement is to create business models and new markets by making full use of broadband wireless Internet access, for example: (a) online transactions such as "online shopping," "mobile banking," "mobile trade," and "reservation of tickets," (b) acquisition of information such as news, weather forecasts, and stock prices; (c) entertainment such as TV games, music, and *Karaoke*; and (d) databases such as transportation, restaurants, dictionaries, recipes, and telehomecare. Another example is the i-Mode automobile navigation system. Because of its characteristics this is the most suitable on-board communication device for use in cars.

Thus, in the near future, broadband Internet access will solve the fundamental constraints of information acquisition, namely the amount of information, and physical and geographical restrictions.

Notes

1. This is common to all East Asian economies. For factors which are obstacles to e-commerce in the East Asian economies, see Gatfild, Yang, and Ping 2000.
2. Since the so-called "net bubble" burst in 1999, when stock prices of Internet-based companies plummeted, the notion of the new economy has been fading away. This is also another point in contrast with the Japanese economy, where the strategy of the IT revolution is just being adopted.
3. For a discussion of TELRIC, see Tsuji 2000d, for example.
4. Another factor to inspire local competition is 'priority connection' which will begin in April 2001, called "My Line." In contrast to the USA, Japanese consumers can choose different carriers for local, semi-local, long-distance, and international calls. This new scheme has motivated all carriers to enter the local call market.
5. Ministry of Posts and Telecommunications 2000, p. 13.
6. Japan Internet Association 2000, p. 53.
7. For more details on the recent deregulation of CATV and other related issues, see Tsuji 2000b.

8. Quality of DSL depends on how far the subscriber is located from DSL equipment, which is usually installed at local switches. In Korea, a high density of population and huge apartment complexes therefore make the development of DSL easy.
9. Currently its capacity cannot meet the huge demand so problems such as disruption of service have often been reported.
10. For further details, see Tsuji 2000a, 2000c.
11. In some cases, they have to change telephone numbers.
12. There are ten electric companies in Japan, and the Tokyo and Kyushu Electric Companies have already entered the local call market. In addition, most electric companies engage in cellular and PHS services.
13. A research group also recommends this spectrum auction; see Oniki 2001.
14. The government will spend about US$100 million over the next two years for its R&D project, since it is thought to be a key technology for the next stage of the Internet.

References

Federal Communications Commission (statistical data), http://www.fcc.gov./ccb/stat.

Gatfild, T., Yang, C., and Ping, X. 2000, An empirical analysis of the Internet business in China, *Proceedings of the International Conference on Economic Globalization*, Shanghai, China, pp. 269–283.

Japan Internet Association (eds.) 2000, *Internet White Paper 2000* (in Japanese), Tokyo: Impress.

Ministry of Posts and Telecommunications (telecommunications), http://www.mpt.go.jp/joho_tsusin.html.

Ministry of Posts and Telecommunications (ed.) 2000, *Telecommunications White Paper 2000* (in Japanese), Gyousei, Tokyo.

Oniki, H. 2001, New allocation of radio wave by auction, *Nihon Keizai Shimbun* (in Japanese), February 1, 2001.

Telecommunications Carriers Association (statistical data), http://www.tca.or.jp/japan/daisu/yymm/0101matsu.html.

Tsuji, M. 2000a, Deregulation in the Japanese telecommunications market: new regulatory schemes, in M. Kagami and M. Tsuji (eds.), *Privatization, Deregulation and Economic Efficiency*, London: Edward Elgar, pp. 22–49.

2000b, 'Infrastructure-building in the Japanese telecommunications sector: from public–public partnership to public–private partnership, in Bin S. Berg, M. Pollitt, and M. Tsuji (eds.), *Private Initiatives in Infrastructure: Priorities, Incentives, and Performance*.

2000c, An analysis of local competition in the Japanese telecommunications market, paper presented at the ICFC Conference, Seattle, USA, September 2000.

2000d, The new direction of regulation and deregulation in the converging Japanese telecommunications market, in Bohlin et al. (eds.), *Convergence in Communications and Beyond*, Amsterdam: Elsevier Science.

4 International division of labor in East Asia's IT industry

Hiromi Ohki

Introduction

Estimates of worldwide IT commerce based on the customs statistics of twenty-six countries,[1] compiled by the Japan External Trade Organization (JETRO), highlight East Asia's (Asia NIEs, ASEAN4, China) role as a major supply base. PCs, a key element of IT infrastructure, have become dramatically cheaper, a development supported from the supply side by the East Asian IT industry.

During the 1980s, East Asia was a base for the supply of video recorders and other visual equipment, but during the 1990s there was a shift to computer-related equipment. In the late 1980s and early 1990s Taiwanese companies superseded Japanese companies as the main players, and production expanded from ASEAN into China. The USA maintained its 1980s role of main absorber by taking 40.6 percent of East Asia's IT exports. But the international division of labor in the IT industry of the 1990s, based on the supply of low-price PCs, reached a new stage in 2000. The rules of the game were changing. East Asian countries were moving from low to high value-added fields, and industrial concentration in China was increasing.

How will the IT market share shift between East Asia and Japan, the USA and Europe? Japanese and US companies in the computer and semiconductor industries shifted their resources from hardware towards services and content, whilst the manufacturing sector began to rely increasingly on outsourcing. They increased specialization in fields with high value added and, on the production front, are likely to strengthen their reliance on East Asia.

World IT production and trade

World IT production

According to estimates by the Organisation for Economic Co-operation and Development (OECD 2000), the global market for IT amounted to US$1.8 trillion

56

in 1997. This was split between computer-related equipment (computers, peripherals, printers, modems, and connectors) which accounted for 19%, communications (including both telecommunications equipment and telecommunications services) accounting for 43%, and computer software and services, 38%. Market shares were 36% for the USA, 27% for the EU, and 17% for Japan.

In this OECD estimate, the share of IT-related equipment is just 19 percent. The reason is that IT equipment is limited to computer-related finished products and does not include semiconductors and electronic parts. Increased demand for IT finished products stimulates the production of related intermediary goods such as semiconductors and other electronic parts, measuring equipment for testing semiconductor products, semiconductor manufacturing devices, and capital goods. According to *The Emerging Digital Economy II*, a report issued by the US Department of Commerce (1999), computer and hardware production value, that is, intermediate goods and capital goods in addition to computer finished products, accounts for 31.8% of the IT production value in the USA. When telecommunications equipment (5%) is added, the figure rises to 36.8%.

The Japan Electric Industry Development Association (JEIDA) has estimated the value of IT hardware production in the world from a survey of six IT industries in thirty leading countries. According to this survey, the value of IT production in the world reached US$990.15 billion in 1998: computers and peripherals accounted for 27%, telecommunications equipment for 21%, and electronic parts for 33%. The USA produced 34% of the total (see Table 4.1).

World IT trade

The value of IT hardware in world trade amounted to US$924.8 billion (import base) in 1999 and accounted for 16% of total world trade (see Table 4.2). The IT contribution to world trade expansion between 1996 and 1999 was 39.6%. Computers, peripherals, and parts accounted for 31.6% of IT trade; electronic parts for 40.7% (24.4% semiconductors and other electronic parts, 16.3% miscellaneous electronic parts), and telecommunications equipment for 11.0%.

In 1999, the value of trade in semi-finished goods and components was US$492.2 billion, exceeding the value of finished goods which reached US$432.5 billion. Computers made up a large proportion of the finished goods, and many of the semiconductors and other electronic parts went into computers and peripherals. The highest growth rate was in telecommunications equipment. Within this category, mobile phones (cell phones) grew most and video equipment grew the least.

Table 4.1 *World IT production, 1998 (US$ billion)*

	Japan	USA	Europe[a]	Asia[b]	World[c]
Computers and peripherals	41.15	86.93	57.80	75.07	275.62
Computers	23.91	60.23	34.92	41.76	170.98
Peripherals	17.24	26.70	22.88	33.31	104.64
Telecommunications equipment	28.67	4.85	68.66	19.11	212.85
Wired telecommunications equipment	14.93	38.68	30.00	9.95	100.50
Mobile phones	13.74	46.18	37.66	9.15	112.35
Electronic device parts	69.88	129.53	45.32	74.48	330.76
Semiconductors and other electronic parts	44.65	68.25	19.21	40.23	175.08
Miscellaneous electronic parts	25.22	61.28	26.11	34.25	155.67
Measuring equipment	4.80	32.88	29.13	2.10	72.37
Audiovisual equipment	16.19	7.19	14.74	37.82	79.96
Office equipment	5.83	5.11	3.82	3.16	18.59
Total	166.52	266.49	219.47	211.74	990.15

Notes:

[a] Europe: fourteen countries.

[b] Asia: China, Hong Kong, Indonesia, Malaysia, the Philippines, South Korea, Singapore, Taiwan, Thailand, and Vietnam.

[c] World includes Japan, the USA, Europe, Asia, and others (Australia, Brazil, Canada, and South Africa).

Source: Compiled from Japan Electric Industry Development Association (JEIDA) 2000.

Global IT trade expanded between 1996 and 1999, with exports reaching US$155.7 billion and imports US$154.3 billion. Of the increase in exports, 41.8% went to the USA and EU combined, and 42.5% to East Asia. In the case of imports, the figures were 54.8% for the former and 25% for the latter. In other words, East Asia was the main exporter and the USA and EU the main importers.

The countries or regions that achieved most striking growth in IT trade (exports) were those located around the large consumer markets of Japan, the USA, and Europe. Significant growth in exports was also seen in China, Finland, Ireland, Korea, Mexico, and Taiwan.

Computers and peripherals (hereafter referred to as "computers") are the biggest items in IT trade. Exports reached US$292.4 billion in 1999, an increase of 8.3% on the previous year (see Table 4.3). Imports amounted to US$292.4 billion, up 10.8%. US imports expanded at an average annual rate of 9.5% from 1996 to 1999, whilst the US contribution to the increased value of world imports was 30.8%, trailing only the EU (eleven countries) at 35.2%. The top suppliers

Table 4.2 *World IT trade (imports), 1996 and 1999*

	1996			1999			1996/1999	
	Value (US$ bn)	Share of world trade (%)	Share of IT trade (%)	Value (US$ bn)	Share of world trade (%)	Share of IT trade (%)	Average annual growth rate (%)	% contribution to world trade
Total value of world imports	5,373,700	100.0	–	5,763,500	100.0	–	2.4	–
IT products (total)[a]	770,439	14.3	100.0	924,779	16.0	100.0	6.3	39.6
Computers and peripherals	230,475	4.3	29.9	292,364	5.1	31.6	8.3	15.9
Computers	49,195	0.9	6.4	59,198	1.0	6.4	6.3	2.5
Peripherals	95,887	1.8	12.4	117,295	2.0	12.7	6.9	5.5
Parts	85,393	1.6	11.1	115,960	2.0	12.5	10.7	7.8
Office equipment	17,939	0.3	2.3	15,317	0.3	1.7	–5.1	–0.7
Telecommunications equipment[b]	67,200	1.3	8.7	101,424	1.8	11.0	14.7	8.8
Wired	41,546	0.8	5.4	56,864	1.0	6.1	11.0	3.9
Mobile	19,427	0.4	2.5	36,787	0.6	4.0	23.7	4.5
Others[c]	6,228	0.1	0.8	7,772	0.1	0.8	7.7	0.4
Semiconductors and other electronic parts	188,449	3.5	24.5	225,940	3.9	24.4	6.2	9.6

Table 4.2 (cont.)

	1996			1999			1996/1999	
	Value (US$ bn)	Share of world trade (%)	Share of IT trade (%)	Value (US$ bn)	Share of world trade (%)	Share of IT trade (%)	Average annual growth rate (%)	% contribution to world trade
Miscellaneous electronic parts	134,301	2.5	17.4	150,812	2.6	16.3	3.9	4.2
Video equipment	41,853	0.8	5.4	43,230	0.8	4.7	1.1	0.4
Audio equipment	26,902	0.5	3.5	24,922	0.4	2.7	−2.5	−0.5
Measuring and testing devices	63,279	1.2	8.2	70,641	1.2	7.6	3.7	1.9
Finished products	362,425	6.7	47.0	432,539	7.5	46.8	6.1	18.0
Parts	418,014	7.6	53.0	492,240	8.5	53.2	6.5	21.6

Notes:

[a] The value of trade in IT products is for: the USA, Canada, EU11, Switzerland, Europe (fifteen countries including Hungary, Poland, and the Czech Republic), Australia, New Zealand, Japan, China, Middle East (fifteen countries including Israel and Turkey).

[b] Telecommunications equipment comprises telephones, answering machines, fax machines, switchboards, etc.

[c] "Others" includes radar, wireless devices, etc.

Source: JETRO, from International Financial Statistics (IMF) and national statistics.

Table 4.3 *Computer trade by economy, 1996 and 1999*

	Exports					Imports				
	1996		1999			1996		1999		
	Value (US$ m)	Share (%)	Value (US$ m)	Share (%)	Average growth (%)	Value (US$ m)	Share (%)	Value (US$ m)	Share (%)	Average growth (%)
USA	43,957	18.3	46,686	16.0	2.0	60,634	26.3	79,695	27.3	9.5
Japan	28,776	12.0	26,331	9.0	−2.9	18,534	8.0	19,504	6.7	1.7
China	5,380	2.2	11,810	4.0	30.0	3,029	1.3	7,085	2.4	32.7
Asia NIES	65,501	27.2	76,454	26.2	5.3	30,247	13.1	39,092	13.4	8.9
Taiwan	18,631	7.7	24,531	8.4	9.6	2,885	1.3	8,497	2.9	43.3
Singapore	32,415	13.5	29,799	10.2	−2.8	14,628	6.3	13,905	4.8	−1.7
ASEAN4	15,881	6.6	26,498	9.1	18.6	5,280	2.3	6,013	2.1	4.4
Malaysia	10,195	4.2	16,961	5.8	18.5	3,392	1.5	3,652	1.2	2.5
Philippines	871	0.4	4,183	1.4	68.7	794	0.3	1,415	0.5	21.2
EU11	68,540	28.5	82,012	28.1	6.2	86,125	37.4	107,937	36.9	7.8
Eastern Europe	504	0.2	2,922	1.0	79.7	2,131	0.9	3,313	1.1	15.9
Hungary	367	0.2	2,661	0.9	93.5	389	0.2	1,090	0.4	41.0
Latin America	4,219	1.8	11,787	4.0	40.8	5,950	2.6	8,236	2.8	11.4
Mexico	3,826	1.6	9,348	3.2	34.7	1,994	0.9	3,967	1.4	25.8
World	240,594	100.0	291,749	100.0	6.6	230,475	100.0	292,364	100.0	8.3

Source: Japan External Trade Organization (JETRO).

were Japan, Singapore, and Taiwan, which accounted for 43.0% of total US imports in 1999, although compared with 1996, their combined share dropped. Instead, imports from such countries as China, Costa Rica, Malaysia, Mexico, and the Philippines increased sharply.

Trade in electronic components accounted for 40.7% of IT trade (1999, imports). Of this, semiconductors and other electronic parts accounted for 24.4%, and miscellaneous electronic parts (capacitors, resistors, printed circuits, switches, fuses, etc.) for 16.3%, with an average annual growth rate of 3.9%.

Looking at semiconductor exports by country, we see that the USA produced about one-quarter of the total, followed by the Asian contingent of Japan, Korea, Malaysia, Singapore, and Taiwan (see Table 4.4). Together, these six countries accounted for about 80% of the total. Looking at average annual growth rates from 1996 to 1999, we see that Taiwan (up 15.3%), Korea (up 8.1%), and Singapore (up 5.2%) have greatly increased their exports.

IT trade transaction ratio and degree of penetration

Table 4.5 shows the trade transaction ratio (the ratio of trade value to production value) for IT hardware using 1998 data. The ratio of world trade to world gross domestic product was 18.1%. Compared to the figure of 33.3% for automobiles, the trade transaction ratio for IT hardware was high, but the figure is misleading because the data for production value covered more countries and more products than data for trade values. Furthermore, products that are re-exported from Hong Kong and Singapore – that is, products that are manufactured in China and Malaysia, shipped to Hong Kong and Singapore and then exported from there – are double counted. Nevertheless, the trade transaction ratios for computers, peripherals, semiconductors, and other electronic parts can be assumed to be fairly accurate, because the surveyed products are almost in agreement and because producing regions are centered on Japan, Europe, the USA, and Asia.

The high level of the trade transaction ratio for IT hardware and the upward trend of this ratio can be affirmed by the degree of import penetration of IT-related goods, namely import value/(production value – export value + import value), the degree of export dependence in the USA and Japan, and the increasing ratio of IT exports and imports to GDP in East Asian countries. In 1999, the degree of import penetration in the USA was 38.3% for computers and peripherals and 34% for electronic parts. Laptop computers accounted for about 40% of the US$11.3 billion computer exports in 1998, hard disk drives accounted for 40%, or US$13.2 billion, of the US$32.8 billion peripherals imports, and displays for US$8.1 billion. Japan showed an even higher degree of trade dependence than the USA. The degree of export dependence and the degree of import penetration exceeded the figures for the USA for computers, peripherals and electronic parts. Japan's import penetration ratio, which was

Table 4.4 *Semiconductor trade by economy, 1996 and 1999*

	Exports					Imports				
	1996		1999			1996		1999		
	Value (US$ m)	Share (%)	Value (US$ m)	Share (%)	Average growth (%)	Value (US$ m)	Share (%)	Value (US$ m)	Share (%)	Average growth (%)
USA	37,554	20.2	49,351	21.3	9.5	38,080	20.2	38,564	17.1	0.4
Japan	35,785	19.3	32,713	14.1	-2.9	13,295	7.1	13,464	6.0	0.4
China	1,477	0.8	3,711	1.6	35.9	4,685	2.5	13,397	5.9	41.9
Asia NIES	53,743	29.0	68,986	29.7	8.7	58,402	31.0	70,427	31.2	6.4
Korea	17,305	9.3	21,843	9.4	8.1	11,460	6.1	16,893	7.5	13.8
Taiwan	9,554	5.2	14,635	6.3	15.3	14,017	7.4	17,208	7.6	7.1
Hong Kong	7,133	3.8	9,481	4.1	10.0	11,906	6.3	14,225	6.3	6.1
Singapore	19,751	10.6	23,026	9.9	5.2	21,019	11.2	22,101	9.8	1.7
ASEAN4	20,017	10.8	36,040	15.5	21.7	20,745	11.0	29,876	13.2	12.9
Malaysia	16,405	8.8	17,233	7.4	1.7	16,303	8.7	19,549	8.7	6.2
Philippines	2,022	1.1	16,759	7.2	102.4	1,368	0.7	7,309	3.2	74.8
EU11	30,930	16.7	34,706	14.9	3.9	36,797	19.5	37,323	16.5	0.5
Germany	7,402	4.0	9,150	3.9	7.3	9,322	4.9	10,474	4.6	4.0
UK	7,826	4.2	6,633	2.9	-5.4	10,720	5.7	8,228	3.6	-8.4
France	6,159	3.3	7,461	3.2	6.6	5,381	2.9	6,598	2.9	7.0
Italy	2,719	1.5	2,217	1.0	6.6	3,881	2.1	3,138	1.4	-6.8
Ireland	1,787	1.0	2,841	1.2	16.7	1,385	0.7	2,385	1.1	19.9
Latin America	1,980	1.1	2,606	1.1	9.6	7,339	3.9	12,265	5.4	18.7
Mexico	1,878	1.0	2,344	1.0	7.7	5,577	3.0	10,093	4.5	21.9
World	185,506	100.0	232,187	100.0	7.8	188,449	100.0	225,940	100.0	6.2

Source: Japan External Trade Organization (JETRO).

Table 4.5 *Trade transaction ratios for IT hardware, 1998*

	Trade (*a*) (US$ million)	Production (*b*) (US$ billion)	$\frac{a}{b}$ (%)
Computers and peripherals[a]	160,673	275,620	58.3
Computers	51,153	170,980	29.9
Peripherals	109,520	104,640	104.7
Office equipment	16,431	18,590	88.4
Telecommunications equipment[b]	78,619	212,850	36.9
Wired	49,032	100,500	48.8
Mobile	29,587	112,350	26.3
Semiconductors and other electronic parts	194,157	175,080	110.9
Miscellaneous electronic parts	139,304	152,000	91.6
Measuring and testing devices	66,470	72,370	91.8
Total	894,946	990,150	90.4
Automobiles (1,000 units)[c]	17,614	52,842	33.3
World	5,330	29,492	18.1

Notes:

[a] The world trade value for computers and peripherals was calculated by adding the trade values for computer machines themselves and peripherals.

[b] The world trade value for telecommunications equipment was calculated by adding the trade values for fixed-line telecommunications equipment and mobile phones (cell phones, etc.).

[c] Automobile imports are to the sixteen leading countries. Exports, from the ten leading countries, total 20.982 million units, an export/production ratio of 39.7 percent.

Source: Figures for IT trade are estimated by the Japan External Trade Organization (JETRO 2000). Production values are compiled from Japan Electric Industry Development Association (JEIDA) 2000.

37% in 1991, declined slightly from 57% in 1995 to 52.4% in 1999, but this was because imports of computers increased. The import penetration ratio for computers stood at only 0.5% in 1991 but then rose to 18% in 1996, to more than 20% in 1997, and to 24% in 1999. This was due to an expansion in the import of PCs. The ratio of IT trade to GDP increased in East Asian countries, exceeding 50% in Singapore and Malaysia.

Factors supporting IT division of labor

There are a variety of reasons for the briskness of trade transactions in computer peripherals, semiconductors, and other electronic parts. The Internet has caused a worldwide expansion of demand for PCs, whilst the standardization of PC products enables peripheral equipment, parts, central processing units, and hard disk drives to be procured at advantageous prices from the international market. In addition, the division of processes in companies aiming for optimum worldwide production is proceeding on a global scale.

Redefinition of value added and division of labor

As a result of the IT revolution, companies are re-examining their competitiveness and redefining the source of their industry's added value. The PC industry is a typical example. The global PC industry is controlled by two elements, operating systems and microprocessors, the so-called "Wintel" (Windows + Intel) set-up, and through this computer production achieved dramatic structural change as value added shifted from assembly to parts. The PC industry therefore differs from the automobile industry where value added arises on the final assembly line. Moreover, even among PC parts, value added differs according to the degree of technological complexity. For example, the core parts, the CPU and OS, are Wintel, the liquid-crystal panel and batteries are high-tech, the hard disk drive (HDD) and CD-ROM are mid-tech, and the keyboard and display are mature products (see Figure 4.1).

Meanwhile, leading US PC makers such as Dell, which have increased profits through the direct sale of PCs, have control over distribution by excelling in brand, sales route, and management ability. Under the Wintel–Dell set-up, US

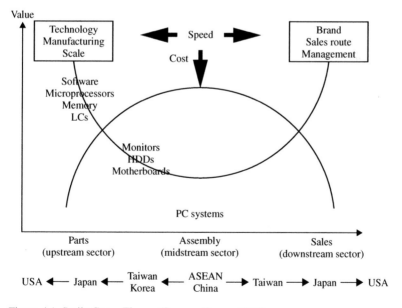

Figure 4.1 Smile Curve Theory (Source: Hwang 1996)

companies have developed a firm grip on the field of high value added in core parts, whilst in East Asia value added differs according to the technological level of each country and investment by foreign companies. There are high-tech sectors such as liquid-crystal panels and batteries in Taiwan and Korea, mid-tech sectors such as HDDs and CD-ROM drives in Singapore and Malaysia, and mature-product sectors such as keyboards and displays in China. Overall, East Asian countries are striving to achieve higher levels of value added.

In Singapore, production is largely centered on foreign companies, and here two trends have emerged. First, US HDD makers are shifting production from Singapore, the world's largest HDD manufacturing country, to neighboring countries. With major limitations in the size of its labor force, Singapore provides little scope for expanding production, so US makers are setting up new production centers in neighboring countries. Cases are arising which clearly show that Singapore's dominance as a production centre is on the decline.

Second, the role of subsidiaries in Singapore is changing. Apple and Compaq have set up production and distribution centers in Singapore to service the Asia-Pacific region, excluding Japan, whilst Dell and Gateway have established corresponding centers in Malaysia. But with the increase in outsourcing, there is a strong possibility that the production functions at these centres could be pared down. Factors behind this are intensifying price competition and rising labor costs. The need for regional production and distribution control by subsidiaries is decreasing due to the spread of build-to-order (BTO) and the strengthening of distribution services by Taiwanese manufacturers, which are major original equipment manufacturing (OEM) suppliers.

Acceleration of outsourcing in the IT industry

There are a number of factors behind the outsourcing of IT hardware:

1   The product cycle is much shorter (ten years ago the cycle for high-tech products was four or five years, now it is about six months).
2   Leading makers are putting priority on product development and marketing, and have no leeway for manufacturing in terms of labor, finance, or time.
3   Digital home appliance products are connected to other information equipment and networks, and are used in conjunction with them, making the timing of product launching most important.
4   Technology-oriented venture companies, which play the leading role in the IT industry, put priority on development.

Until now, outsourcing in the manufacturing industry generally consisted of OEM (the placement of external orders in the assembly section for production only) or original design manufacturing (ODM) (the design of products in accordance with the contractor's specifications). Since the early 1990s, however, there has been an increase in the number of specialized order-receiving companies handling specific processes, such as material procurement, production, distribution and other supply chain roles, design, prototype manufacture, or testing processes. Electronics manufacturing services (EMS) companies have emerged, unifying these tasks, adding functions besides manufacturing, and managing the distribution of finished products.

In the PC industry, the major brand makers, various Japanese firms as well as IBM, Dell, and Gateway, are concerned not only with shifting low value added production and sales to OEM manufacturers, but also with gaining management control over factory operations, product costs, technology and development trends, and production facilities at home and abroad. Taiwanese and Korean OEM and EMS firms are generally more directly competitive with each other. As the main IT-related companies go ahead with building tripolar supply-chain set-ups covering North America, Europe, and Japan, the EMS companies are also establishing production centers in these regions. As finished product makers turn more and more to outsourcing, the scale of the EMS market is expanding.

Products handled by EMS companies are diverse and include computers and peripherals, cell phone handsets, telecommunications equipment, semiconductors, and medical equipment. By having a number of clients, they bring out the merits of scale, raise the operating ratios of their plants, and increase their cost competitiveness by, for example, lowering costs through the mass procurement of parts and materials. It is notable that many US IT companies are consigning tasks to EMS firms.

Semiconductors: from vertical integration to horizontal division of labor

Special foundry companies, especially in Taiwan, have appeared and attract much attention for their high earnings. A "foundry" refers to a type of business or a company specializing in commissioned manufacture for the semiconductor industry. They deliver pre-processed products in wafer shape to order. In some cases, they accept consignment production for the whole process. Fabless semiconductor companies, which do not have manufacturing plants, handle circuit and layout design for products, while foundries handling consigned production involving pre-processing have emerged. Looking at the sales of special foundry companies, we see that the scale of the global foundry market in 2000 reached an all-time high of US$11.9 billion, an increase of 80.1 percent on the previous year.[2]

In the 1990s, there were dramatic changes in the structure of the semiconductor market that led to the emergence of the foundry business. In-house design and production of integrated circuits was no longer efficient. Vertically integrated companies are less competitive than specialized producers, so semiconductor

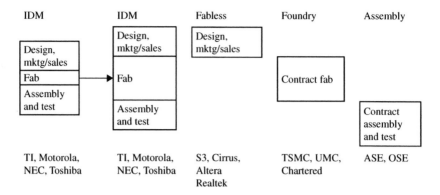

Note: Integrated device manufacturing (IDM) is a vertically integrated company.
Figure 4.2 Vertical integration and horizontal specialization in the semiconductor industry (Source: JETRO 1999)

production has shifted from vertical integration to horizontal integration, bringing together parts manufactured by companies specializing in specific processes or sectors (see Figure 4.2).

Global logistics manufacturing systems

The production of PCs is now based on the assembly of finished products in consuming countries, but the parts are manufactured elsewhere. This has begun to eliminate inefficiencies in global logistics manufacturing systems in terms of the delivery time for components, half-finished goods, and finished goods. PC OEM assemblers determine the quality, capabilities, manufacturing status, raw material supply, production time, and delivery lead-time of their component suppliers, and they can accurately estimate their delivery times and quantity produced. To further lower costs, these companies must thoroughly understand the components, half-finished goods, and finished goods' production sites, freight, delivery time, and storage conditions (see Table 4.6).[3]

The global logistics manufacturing system developed by Taiwanese companies breaks down in the following way. Goods whose prices change only about once a year such as cases, connectors, and power packs, are manufactured in China. These are assembled into a semi-finished product (a "bare bones kit"[4]) that includes the electrical supply device, cables, and speakers in the PC case. This package is shipped to the final production site. Products with high value added like CD-ROMs, modems, and motherboards are shipped by air so they can respond more rapidly to changes in price. High-cost goods like CPUs and HDDs that are subject to sharp swings in price are procured by assemblers in their own countries.

Table 4.6 *Delivery schedules in global logistics manufacturing system*

Component	Origin	Delivery method	Delivery time	Safety stock
CPU	Marketplace	Surface	●	◎
Hard disk	Marketplace	Surface	●	◎
CD-ROM drive	Production site	Air freight	◎	◎
Modem	Production site	Air freight	◎	◎
Memory	Production site	Air freight	◎	◎
Fan	Production site	Air freight	◎	◎
Heat sink	Production site	Air freight	◎	◎
Motherboard	Production site	Air freight/ sea freight	◎/○	◎
Case	Production site	Sea freight	○	○
SPS	Production site	Sea freight	○	○
Disk drive	Production site	Sea freight	○	○
Speakers	Production site	Sea freight	○	○
Keyboard	Production site	Sea freight	○	○
Monitor	Production site	Sea freight	○	○mostly/◎less

Note: ● less than three days   ◎ three to seven days   ○ more than seven days.
Source: Asia IT Report, September 2000.

The ascendancy of Taiwanese companies is due not only to their manufacturing skills, but also to the shipping and after-service functions they undertake as service providers. For example, the Taiwanese computer company, Arima, which is supplying Compaq's Presario notebook PC, set up a plant in Houston in 1998, the first production base it had established outside Taiwan. Arima is involved in not only the manufacturing of the computer, but also its design and specification. It also provides a just-in-time delivery service. Arima markets the computer by bypassing the maker and shipping it directly to retail outlets and consumers, and offers services to users through e-mail. Taiwanese companies are moving from being subcontractors for manufacturing to full service providers that can handle product development, specifications, production, and delivery.[5]

Production and supply of computers, peripheral equipment, and semiconductors in East Asia

Industry specialization in East Asia

Global PC manufacturing logistics shape the division of labor and scatter production and assembly sites around the world. Figure 4.3 shows the structure

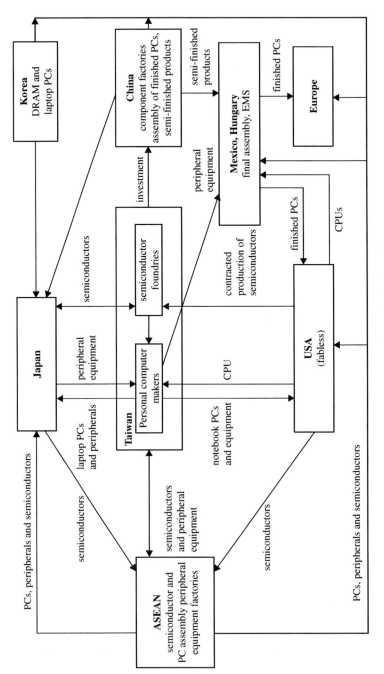

Figure 4.3 Specialization of the semiconductor, PC, and peripherals industries in East Asia

of the division of labor between East Asia and Japan–USA–Europe for PCs and semiconductors. The main points are:

1   Orders from PC manufacturers in Japan, the USA and Europe: OEM was received mainly from companies in Japan, the USA and Europe.
2   Procurement of semiconductors: if supply is not available within the region, raw materials such as wafers are imported from Japan and the USA. The supply of semiconductors is reliant on Japan and the USA.
3   Peripheral equipment and PCs are assembled after semiconductors have been incorporated at a company's own facilities or a co-operating plant in East Asia. Taiwanese companies' share of the global production of PCs, peripherals and electronic components in 1999 was 91% for scanners, 75% for cases, 66% for keyboards, 64% for motherboards, 52% for monitors, 56% for mice, 54% for modems, 49% for laptop computers, and 19% for desktop computers. Moreover, 58% of the scanners supplied by Taiwanese companies, 78% of the cases, 92% of the keyboards, 40.5% of the motherboards, and 73.3% of the monitors are produced outside Taiwan. In addition, 47.3% of the IT hardware produced by them is manufactured offshore, and 33.2% of that overseas production is done in China.

Aside from Taiwan, half of the worldwide market for HDDs is supplied by Singapore, where the bases of many of the main HDD makers are concentrated. Floppy disk drives (FDDs) are being produced in the Philippines, where many Japanese-related companies are relocating their FDD production, and keyboards are being made in Thailand, Malaysia, and China, where production is increasing significantly.
4   Peripheral equipment and PCs are assembled in the countries in which they will be used, or in Mexico, Hungary and other neighboring countries. Production in the country of use is carried out through build-to-order (BTO) arrangements. Installation of MPU and other parts in the final assembly process is still handled in the final market countries. This system makes it possible to produce PCs to local customers' specifications.

Dominance of Taiwanese companies and movement of IT firms into China's Chu-Chiang Delta

Rapid rise of Taiwanese companies

The reason that Taiwanese companies have become major world players in the manufacture of PCs is their OEM strengths (see Table 4.7). The proportion of

Table 4.7 *PC makers procurements from Taiwan, 1998–2000*

	Value (US$ billion)			Taiwanese suppliers
	1998	1999	2000	
Compaq	5.6	>7.1	9.5	Mitac International, Arima Computer Corp., Inventec Corporation, Giga-Byte Technology, Gvc Corp., Hon Hai Precision Industry, Ouant Computer Inc., Advanced Datum Information, Lite An Technology Corp., Tatung, Taiwan Litean Electronic Co., Ltd., Delta Electronic Inc., Enlight Cor Silitek Corp., Chicony Electronics, Compec Manufacturing, Gold Circuit Electronics, Unicap Electronics Industrial, Unitech Printed Circuit Board
IBM	1.5–2.5	4.0–4.5	about 5.0	Acer Inc., Universal Scientific Ind., Hon Hai Precision Indusry, Taiwan Semiconductor Manufacturing, Gold Circuit Electronics, Vertex Precision Electronics, Lite An Technology Corp., Tatung, Acer Peripherals Inc., Taiwan Litean Electronic Co., Ltd., Delta Electronic Inc., Ouant Computer Inc., Chicony Electronics
Dell	–	3.5	4.3	Ouant Computer Inc., Compal Electronics Inc., Hon Hai Precision Industry, Taiwan Litean Electronic Co., Ltd., Delta World Wiser Electronics, Gold Circuit Electronics, Compec Manufacturing, Silitek Corp., Chicony Electronics, Aopen
HP	1.5	2.5–3.5	–	First International Computer, Mitac International, Compal Electronics Inc., Asutek Computer Inc., Hon Hai Precision Industry, Ouant Computer Inc., Enlight Corp., Macromix International Co. Ltd., Wus Printed Circuit Co., Compec Manufacturing, Gold Circuit Electronics, Tatung, Alpha Top, Silitek Corp., Chicony Electronics, Umax Data Systems Inc.
Apple	–	1.5–2.0	–	Alpha Top, Wus Printed Circuit Co., Adanced Datum Information, Silitek Corp., Chicony Electronics, Ouant Computer Inc.
Gateway	–	0.5–1.5	–	Ouant Computer Inc., Mag Technology, Delta Electronic Inc., Micro Star International
Intel	–	5.0–1.5	–	Taiwan Semiconductor Manufacturing, Advanced Semiconductor Engineering Inc., Orient Semiconductor El., Compec Manufacturing, Nanya Technology, Unicap Electronics Industrial, Hon Hai Precision Industry, Acton Technology
Top twenty companies	18	23.04	30.0	

Source: *Dempa-shimbun*, November 6, 2000.

OEM (production volume) in total production of PCs and peripheral equipment manufactured by Taiwanese companies was 64.8% in 1998, with an 86% share of notebook PCs, 67% of monitors, and 67% of desktop computers (see Table 4.8).

At the beginning of the 1980s, Taiwan's IT hardware production mainly centered around the OEM production of terminals by foreign-capital companies, and monitors by domestic firms. During the latter half of the 1980s, however, many foreign-capital companies left Taiwan because of the appreciating Taiwanese dollar, leaving it to the small domestic companies to drive subsequent growth.

The beginning of the 1990s proved an opportune time as fierce competition lowered prices in the global PC market. As a result of outsourcing by large overseas plants, beginning with the production of motherboards, Taiwanese companies were contracted for OEM hardware. During the latter half of the 1980s, they competed with Korean companies over quality and, as a result of international criticism that they were merely imitators, they steadily improved their technology. Korean companies, their capital backed by the introduction of technology from abroad, built production facilities and began exporting computers. However, as they could not keep up technologically with the short product cycles in the PC industry, they were dragged down by competition over prices and withdrew from the market.[6]

Until 1993, procurement from Taiwan was the exclusive preserve of IBM but, after Compaq set up an international procurement office (IPO) in Taipei in 1995, it became by far the largest company in terms of value of purchases, reaching US$7 billion in 1999. Dell Computers had been doing well with production to order and its direct sales business models whilst, before its 1995 restructuring, Compaq had fared poorly.

The strength of Taiwanese companies lies in the fact that these mainly small and medium-sized companies can respond to orders for small quantities and a range of specifications, whilst still maintaining low margins. This melds well with the PC business, which seeks to mass produce low-margin products with little investment in facilities and to increase product turnover rates. This is in contrast to South Korea, where large companies try to achieve efficiency by manufacturing products in bulk.

Increasing concentration of PC makers in China

Taiwanese PC makers have already shifted 95 percent of their production of desktop computers to China, centering around the Chu-Chiang River Delta region. Taiwanese companies in China produce 35% of the world's motherboards for desktop computers, 80% of the CD-ROMs, 60% of the keyboards, 50% of the power packs, and 30% of the monitors (see Figure 4.4). Taiwanese PC makers have kept up their competitiveness by relocating more of their production

Table 4.8 *Taiwanese PC and peripheral production, 1998*

Product	Total production (US$ million)	OEM production volume (US$ million)	OEM proportion (%)	Proportion of OEM products manufactured domestically and overseas (%) Domestic	Overseas	Number of units sold (1000)	Ratio of units sold in each market (%) USA	Europe	ASEAN	Japan
Laptop PCs	8,423	7,244	86.0	100	0	609	43.7	21.1	9.9	5.2
Monitors	7,523	5,040	67.0	28	72	4,991	41.2	35.4	14.6	2.5
PCs	6,464	4,331	67.0	55	45	–	–	–	–	–
Motherboards	4,310	1,323	30.7	62	38	5,322	32.1	34.1	17.0	3.9
SPS	1,498	1,468	98.0	9	91	5,873	38.8	34.2	12.8	5.4
CD-ROMs	1,388	428	30.8	47	53	3,066	37.0	33.0	13.0	
Cases	1,201	504	42.0	25	75	6,193	43.6	31.8	15.7	
Scanners	818	351	43.0	62	38	1,524	41.0	35.3	6.8	7.4
Graphics cards	588	135	30.0	35	65	–	–	–	–	–
Keyboards	498	350	70.3	9	91	6,051	39.1	30.1	4.5	8.1
UPS	320	230	71.8	75	25	–	–	–	–	–
Mice	170	118	69.4	11	89	5,690	32.2	30.1	13.7	6.1
Sound cards	133	78	58.6	35	65	1,406	36.0	41.0	9.0	
Video cards	40	18	45.0	82	18	–	–	–	–	–
Total	33,374	21,618	64.8							

Source: Market Intelligence Center/Institute for Information Industry (MIC/III), September 2000.

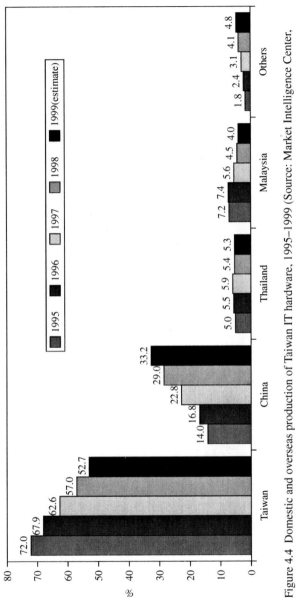

Figure 4.4 Domestic and overseas production of Taiwan IT hardware, 1995–1999 (Source: Market Intelligence Center, *Asia IT Report*, September 2000)

of computer peripherals to the Chu-Chiang River Delta in southern China. They began producing PC-related equipment in the region in the 1990s when the competition over low-priced PCs began. Establishing a foothold to produce OEM hardware for US computer makers, the Taiwanese IT hardware industry soon began moving en masse to Shenzhen and Dongguan in Guangdong Province. Guangdong Province has become a huge base for IT manufacturing, with approximately 10,000 Taiwanese-related companies located there, approximately 2,500 of which are in Dongyuan.

Future developments

There are a number of changes occurring in the IT industry that are shifting the international division of labor. Namely, changes in the rules of the game; a shift from low value added to high value added fields by East Asian IT companies; and the impact of China as a domestic market and its increasing role in electronics production. These changes are so significant that some in Taiwan suspect that they herald the twilight of this once-booming industry.

Changes in the rules of the game

The IT revolution has caused many industries and companies to question their own *raison d'être*, re-examine their competitiveness, and redefine the source of their value added. As a result, companies are reviewing their core businesses with an eye to higher value added fields. The outcome of these moves is more division of labor, more outsourcing, and increased segmentation of processes leading to the emergence of highly specialized companies. The PC industry is facing a redefinition of its added value or a re-examination of its competitiveness.

Falling profit margins of PC firms

As the commercialization of PCs continues to gather momentum, computer manufacturers are finding it increasingly difficult to make a profit from selling only computer terminals. IDC data show the average prices for desktop PCs in 1999 fell 14.8% from 1998 levels. In contrast, laptop PC market prices fell only 4.5% from 1998, but this was due in part to LCD and other component shortages.

The key factor in this price fall has been competition for OEM orders. As more large OEM firms compete, prices are bound to fall further. PC firms have suffered from continually falling profit margins and stock prices. Migration of production facilities to China continues, and large firms are exploring new business areas.

Opportunities for selling computers

Computers have become tools for e-mail and e-commerce, and manufacturers are discovering new sources of revenue in the provision of these services packaged with their hardware. Opportunities for selling computers are open to all companies, so PC buyers can include e-commerce firms such as America Online. The PC configuration needs of these firms and their purchasing behavior differs markedly from that of the traditional PC vendor. Industry players must be aware of how trends develop and must respond accordingly.

Analog era vs. digital era

The definition of IT competition is also being revised in the Japanese home appliance industry. In the analog era, competition in industry involved increasing production capacity by reinforcing plant lines and, thereby, boosting product supply capacity. Makers which lost their competitiveness responded by lowering manufacturing costs by consignment production or offshore production in Asia, and by maintaining product line-ups in appliance retail stores.[7] In the digital era, however, more value will be created in software than in manufacturing, so the key to ensuring competitive strength will lie in increasing the number of software development engineers. Almost all core parts with high profit ratios will be made overseas.

The move toward domination by the top ten PC firms

Currently, the largest firms possess overwhelming advantages. Although the scramble to gain orders is primarily among these top ten firms, this means OEM manufacturers that work with these firms will have opportunities to grow with them. By contrast, SME manufacturers are feeling the heat of increased international competition and are suffering from contracting sales channels, shrinking orders, and even fiercer competition for orders.

These conditions all suggest that the rules of the game are changing. Under the old rules, Taiwanese IT vendors definitely enjoyed the upper hand, but the emergence of new trends or a resurgence of the free PC market will turn this advantage into a burden. Vendors must adjust their business strategies and ordering behavior. Also, OEM producers must adjust their production and supply models.

The moves from low to high value added fields

The question has become how to maintain, and even improve, performance under the new rules. Generally, there are two ways in which to expand global market share. The first is to take market share from competitors, and the second is to create and capitalize on new demand.

Looking at the international division of labor in the IT industry from the viewpoint of value added, East Asian countries are striving to achieve higher levels of value added.

Development of next-generation products

The strategy of developing next-generation products is designed either to expand existing markets or for entry into new marketplaces. Although the PC product market will remain for a while longer, the industry's fast-paced maturation and the growing number of low-cost products are forcing manufacturers to look to new markets and roll out new products, such as networking, wireless communications, and smart appliances. Only then can enterprises hope to pass through the growth bottleneck. Taiwanese firms are focusing on cost reduction by expanding their firm grip on upstream industries through investment in core parts, such as thin film transistor (TFT), LCDs, magnesium alloys, and lithium batteries. Also, Korea firms are increasing their role in the global IT industry by developing more IT products. They have an impressive share of global output for CDMA mobile phones, DRAM, cathode ray tubes (CRTs), and LCDs. In 1999, the world CDMA market stood at 280 million phones, of which Korea produced 31.5 million, that is, 12 percent of the market. In addition, online Internet users have already passed the 33.7 million mark, and the country was also the first in Asia to have more domestic cellular phone users than fixed-line users. Plunging IT product prices, together with the ever-rising popularity of the Internet, have heightened competition in the field of global IT manufacturing.

Southeast Asian companies' shift to high value added fields

The foundry business is a particularly promising field in the semiconductor industry. Foundry sales were estimated to account for approximately 9 percent of total semiconductor production in 2000. Growth in the foundry industry can be explained on the basis of two points.

The first is the diversification of uses for semiconductors. The growth in demand for semiconductors for communications equipment and digital home appliances has contributed to the rapid growth of companies that do not possess wafer production facilities and specialise exclusively in design.

Secondly, there has been a vast expansion in the amount of capital investment required for the construction of factories as a consequence of the increasing sophistication of semiconductor production techniques. Because of the need to spread business risks, integrated production companies making semiconductors are gradually increasing the quantity of their orders to foundries.

China's rising production capacity

The scale of production in the Chinese electronics industry is expanding astonishingly fast and is affecting not only home appliances and audiovisual equipment, but also information equipment. China's production of electronic components and PC-related products is increasing, especially in Guangdong Province. This has been due, in particular, to the transfer of production of PC-related materials by Taiwanese companies to China. Taiwanese investment is now moving from Huanan to Shanghai and Suzhou.

Investment by European and American companies is also becoming increasingly common as China prepares for entry into the WTO. Now that China's path into WTO membership has been cleared, previously reluctant foreign manufacturers in IT-related fields (information and telecommunications) have begun channelling their funds into capital investment there. Additional investment from US and European companies, on top of funds flowing in from Taiwan (the main source of investment), will augment the production capacity of China's IT industry. Manufacturers of communications equipment, in particular, are setting up factories to produce mobile telephones. The IT industry is gradually expanding from PCs into communications.

Chinese companies are increasingly emerging. It seems likely that production in the IT industry in 2000, including production of PCs and peripheral equipment, along with software development, amounted to an annual 250 billion yuan (approximately 3.25 trillion yen), and is estimated to have grown around three times during the five years from 1996. Experts in the industry reckon that production of PCs in 2000 will top the 8 million unit mark, which is approaching the Japanese figure of 10 million. According to the American survey company IDC, sales of PCs in China in 1999 are likely to amount to 4.94 million units, placing China in second place behind Japan in terms of volume of unit sales. The largest Chinese PC company, Lianxiang, acquired a 9.1 percent share of the Asian market outside Japan in 1999, and now occupies the top position in this market, having overtaken IBM and Compaq.

Conclusion

Outsourcing by Japanese, US and European IT companies is reinforcing their dependence on Asia. As a consequence of the shift in competition in the PC and appliance industries from manufacturing to services and software development, outsourcing and other divisions of function are proceeding in low value added sectors. Outsourcing is usually the result of reviewing a business and reconsidering processes such as management, cost, and quality, determining which internal resources should be utilized, and then endeavoring to strengthen competitiveness by effectively utilizing external resources.

This can be seen in the strategies of US computer manufacturers to diversify their focus away from computers alone, and in accelerated outsourcing by Japanese electronics manufacturers which are now more dependent on electronic parts than on the sale of finished products.

Companies in developed countries are faced with intensifying international competition and have to cut costs as a result. One way of achieving this is outsourcing. Outsourcing is expected to expand as these companies focus their core businesses on high value added. The range of work that can be outsourced is expanding not just in manufacturing, but in the service industries as well. Dramatic cuts in communication costs mean that some services, such as customer support and data inputs, can now be contracted out. For example, data input work can be outsourced to English-speaking workers in countries such as India and the Philippines where labor costs are low, then sent to American customers via electronic communication.

Transfer of the axis of production to China seems likely to have an effect on the division of labor in the IT industry in East Asia. There has been no change in the role of East Asia as the world's main source of IT hardware, but it is possible that China will become the center of production. The rise of the Chinese electronics industry, largely attributable to China's increased production capacity, is expected to throw down the gauntlet to ASEAN products and lead to greater penetration by Chinese products, not just into the US market, but ASEAN markets as well.

Notes

1. Customs clearance data on IT-related trade was collected from Australia, Brazil, Canada, China, Colombia, Finland, France, Germany, Hong Kong, Indonesia, Ireland, Italy, Japan, Malaysia, Mexico, New Zealand, the Philippines, Portugal, the Republic of Korea, Singapore, Spain, Sweden, Switzerland, Taiwan, the UK, and the USA.
2. Estimates from Intercoverage, a semiconductor market survey company. *Nikkei Sangyo Shimbun*, October 10, 2000.
3. *Asia IT Report*, September 2000.
4. Hon Hai was the first company to move into "bare bones" production. Hon Hai was originally a large maker of connectors, with four factories in China. In 1996, it built a PC housing case factory and expanded by buying small housing case makers and acquiring more employees. The company now supplies its products to Compaq, Dell, and Apple. Rethinking its OEM purchases, Compaq, which bought Digital Equipment in 1999, divided up the production of its US$499 PC into four areas – motherboard, subsystem, housing case, and final assembly – and it made Hon Hai its main supplier. (Mizuhashi 1999, p. 169).
5. "Service provider: Taiwan changing its high-tech foundation," *Nikkei Sangyo Shimbun*, November 14, 1999.

6. Mizuhashi 2000.
7. "Acceleration of specialization in digital appliance industry," *Nihon Keizai Shimbun*, August 30, 2000.

References

Hwang, C.-Y. 1996, *Electric Brain Superpower* (in Japanese), Tokyo: ASCII Corporation.

Japan Electric Industry Development Association (JEIDA) 2000, *The Electronic and Information Industry Vision for 2010* (in Japanese), Tokyo.

Japan External Trade Organization (JETRO) 1999, *Report on Semiconductor Industry in Southeast Asia*, July 1999.

2000, *White Paper on International Trade 2000*, September 2000.

Market Intelligence Center, *Asia IT Report*, various issues.

Mizuhashi, Y. 1999, Taiwan: Founded on Electronics, *W-Net*, December 1999.

2000, Taiwan's rush into IT hardware trade, *Report on Structural Problems in Economic Trade*, JETRO, July 2000.

OECD 2000, *OECD Information Technology Outlook 2000*, Paris.

US Department of Commerce 1999, *The Emerging Digital Economy II*, Washington, DC, June 1999.

5 Electronic industry in Asia: the changing supply chain and its effects

Yasushi Ueki

Introduction[1]

In this chapter, I focus on the electronics industry, an industry that is rapidly introducing IT into its business operations. Companies in the sector face intensive global competition, continual price erosion, shortening product lifecycles, and the uncertainty of fluctuations in demand. Their customers insist on just-in-time delivery, and they need to decrease supply chain inventories.

To cope with this, companies must share information on supply, demand, and inventories with their partners over the Internet. Step-by-step interactions should be replaced by parallel, simultaneous interactions across the entire supply chain. To this end, multinational companies are introducing computer-aided management systems such as supply chain management (SCM), electronic commerce and outsourcing.

US companies gather materials, parts, and products from all over the world, especially from Asia. They often outsource the manufacturing process and concentrate their own resources on R&D and sales activities. As an example, Mexico, encouraged by the formation of NAFTA, imports and assembles parts for export to the US market.

Companies in Asia, including Japan, are trying to respond to these changes. Recession in the 1990s forced them to increase productivity, cultivate new markets, and change the structure of their division of labor so as to absorb the benefits of IT and meet their customers' demands.

Supply chain management, electronic commerce and outsourcing in Asia

Supply chain management in Asia

Supply chain management by Dell Computer in Asia

This example will help to explain the international division of labor that emerged in Asia and Japan during the 1990s.[2]

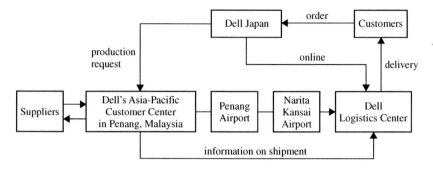

Figure 5.1 Production and distribution flow of Dell Computer (Source: *Nikkan Kogyo Shimbun*, July 25, 2000)

Dell Computer is famous for its direct model and build-to-order (BTO) system; they can accept orders directly from customers and deliver customized products quickly, without the need for finished goods' inventories. Products ordered from Japan are manufactured, customized and, with software installed at the Asia Pacific Customer Center (APCC) in Malaysia, flown to Japan. Dell has links with FedEx and other transportation companies. Computers arriving in Japan are transported to a Dell Logistic Center (DLC), where peripherals procured in Japan can be added. They are then delivered to customers (see Figure 5.1).

As a result of siting Kansai DLC close to Kansai International Airport, Western Japan in 2000, 90 percent of customers will receive ordered products within two days of shipping from Malaysia, compared to 67 percent before it was opened.

This shortening of delivery lead-time was realized by information sharing between the company's offices and partners. In Malaysia, the APCC and suppliers of parts and peripherals share information on production and delivery plans. They can decide on how many products to produce and when they must be delivered to Dell's sites. Each ordered product is identified by a code and controlled on the computerized system, from preparation to shipment. Customers can monitor the state of their products in real time. In Kansai DLC, vendor managed inventory (VMI) was introduced. In this system, peripherals are delivered to Dell's warehouse but are still owned by the vendors until the PCs, with their peripherals, are shipped. Dell's inventories become close to zero.

In China, Dell introduced the direct model to nine main cities, including Beijing and Shanghai, in 1998. It also introduced direct sales on the Internet and this became the first electronic commerce (e-commerce or EC) in mainland China. In Xiamen, Dell has established the China Customer Centre (CCC) to duplicate the manufacturing and professional functions found at the APCC.

Supply chain management by Japanese firms

The twin pressures of recession at home and worldwide demand for reduced delivery times has encouraged Japanese firms to introduce enterprise resource planning (ERP) and other computer-aided management systems.

A snapshot of the situation is shown by a survey of articles on IT that have appeared in newspapers, magazines, the Internet, etc., compiled by the Electronic Commerce Promotion Council of Japan (ECOM). According to the survey, business-to-business (BtoB) e-commerce is increasing rapidly: 33 companies in fiscal year 1997, 175 in 1998, 295 in 1999, and 126 from April to July 2000.

By classifying the cases into some fifty categories, we can confirm that electronic data interchange (EDI), SCM, the Internet and the Web increased explosively in 1998 and are now mainstream. The e-marketplace is growing rapidly (see Figure 5.2).

Electronic data interchange and electronic commerce in Asia

Electronic commerce in Asia

Through its ability to make the supply chain more efficient, it is expected that the use of BtoB e-commerce will further increase dramatically. In 1999, according to the Gartner Group forecasts, the worldwide BtoB e-commerce market was US$145 billion of which the North America region accounted for 63% with revenue of US$91 billion. The Asia-Pacific market was US$9.2 billion (6.3%) and Japan was the third largest market at US$11.1 billion (7.7%) (see Table 5.1).

By 2004, worldwide BtoB e-commerce is projected to surpass US$7.29 trillion. The North America region will remain the largest market but with a decreased overall share of 39% and revenue of more than US$2.84 trillion. The Asia-Pacific market will grow at an annual rate of 155% reaching US$992 billion and accounting for 13.6% of the market. The Asia-Pacific region will surpass Japan by 2002.

The growth of e-commerce is based on BtoB systems that replace paper-based transactions. Many companies in Asia have already entered into the BtoB business. In Singapore, companies such as Singapore Network Services Pte Ltd (SNS), SESAMi.com, BeXcom, and ECnet offer a number of BtoB services. They provide a marketplace where participating firms make deals. They also provide transaction-related services such as logistics and accounting.

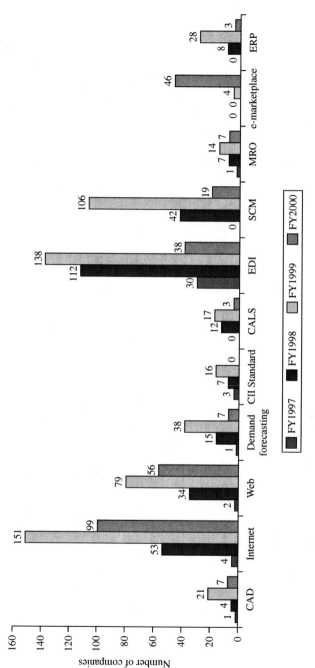

Note: [a] The cases of FY2000 were collected from April 1 to July 31, 2000.
[b] CII = Center for the Informatization of Industry; CALS = commerce at light speed; MRO = maintenance, repair and operation.

Figure 5.2 Number of IT-related articles classified by category, 1997–2000 (Source: ECOM 2000)

Table 5.1 *Business-to-business e-commerce, 1999 and 2004 (US$ billion)*

	World	Japan	Asia-Pacific	North America	Latin America	Europe
1999	145	11	9	91	1	32
(share)	100.0%	7.7%	6.3%	62.8%	0.7%	21.9%
2004	7,290	861	992	2,840	124	2,340
(share)	100.0%	11.8%	13.6%	39.0%	1.7%	32.1%
Annual growth	118.9%	138.7%	155.0%	99.0%	162.2%	136.2%

Source: Gartner Group 2000.

Table 5.2 *Introduction of BtoB e-commerce for parts, materials, and products in ASEAN5, 2000 (percent)*

	Number of respondents	Already introduced	Not yet	Planning
Total	335	17.3	71.3	11.3
Indonesia	64	9.4	78.1	12.5
Malaysia	85	30.6	56.5	12.9
Philippines	29	17.2	69.0	13.8
Singapore	28	35.7	35.7	28.6
Thailand	129	8.5	86.0	5.4
General machinery	11	0.0	90.9	9.1
Assembly of electric and electronics products	77	33.8	49.4	16.9
Electric and Electronics parts	106	19.8	67.9	12.3
Assembly of automobiles	14	0.0	85.7	14.3
Automobile parts	80	8.8	86.3	5.0
Precision instruments	5	20.0	80.0	0.0
Others	42	7.1	81.0	11.9

Note: The number of respondents was used for calculation of share as denominator.
Source: Japan External Trade Organization (JETRO) 2000.

EDI/SCM and procurement of parts by Japanese firms in Asia

In 2000, the Japan External Trade Organization (JETRO) conducted a survey of Japanese electronics and automobile firms in Indonesia, Malaysia, the Philippines, Singapore and Thailand (ASEAN5). This showed that 17.3% of companies had already introduced BtoB e-commerce and a further 11.3% were planning to do so (see Table 5.2).

Table 5.3 *Contents of BtoB e-commerce in ASEAN5, 2000 (percent)*

	Number of respondents	Upload of electronic catalog	Upload of procurement plan	EDI within industry	Developed SCM
Total	50	14.0	10.0	60.0	20.0
Indonesia	5	0.0	0.0	60.0	20.0
Malaysia	23	8.7	13.0	73.9	21.7
Philippines	4	0.0	25.0	0.0	50.0
Singapore	10	40.0	10.0	50.0	0.0
Thailand	8	12.5	0.0	62.5	25.0
General machinery	0	0.0	0.0	0.0	0.0
Assembly of electrical and electronics products	22	13.6	4.5	63.6	27.3
Electrical and electronics parts	18	11.1	16.7	72.2	11.1
Assembly of automobiles	0	0.0	0.0	0.0	0.0
Automobile parts	6	0.0	16.7	33.3	33.3
Precision instruments	1	100.0	0.0	0.0	0.0
Others	3	33.3	0.0	33.3	0.0

Note: The number of respondents was used for calculation of share as denominator.
Source: Japan External Trade Organization (JETRO) 2000.

The ratio of "doing" e-commerce was high in Singapore (35.7%) and Malaysia (30.6%). The sum of the ratio of "doing" and "planning" was highest in Singapore (64.3%), followed by Malaysia (43.5%) and the Philippines (31.0%). In the industrial sectors, the ratio of "doing" e-commerce was extremely high in the assembly of electrical and electronic products (33.8%), "planning" was high in the electronic sector and the assembly of automobiles, and the sum of "doing" and "planning" in electronics was extremely high.

Asked about the types of BtoB systems they were using, 60% of the fifty firms that responded said they had introduced EDI, whilst 20% had introduced SCM (see Table 5.3).

Thus, some Japanese firms in ASEAN5 have already introduced BtoB e-commerce, mainly EDI, but a smaller number have introduced SCM. Asia Matsushita Electric in Singapore (AMS) is now connecting its internal network to networks of suppliers through EDI vendors such as SNS. Matsushita set up an organisation, Asia Matsushita EDI, which is organised through twenty production bases, to support their introduction of EDI for the procurement of parts and materials.

Outsourcing of manufacturing

Roles of contract manufacturers

As we have seen, EDI/SCM in outsourcing makes the supply chain more efficient. PC manufacturers, such as HP, sold their factories to contract manufacturers (CMs) and are using CMs or electronics manufacturing service (EMS). The introduction of IT made it possible to share information with external enterprises as if they are integrated into one company.

CMs are contracted to produce proprietary products, to distribute products and to design and handle after-sales services. Customers of EMS enjoy the benefit of reduced production costs and avoid the risks inherent in owning production facilities. They develop worldwide networks and concentrate their resources on development, sales, and activities such as R&D that make more efficient use of their assets. The lifecycles of IT products are very short; the difference in sales between a top seller and the rest is very large, but lifecycle and sales are difficult to predict with accuracy. Technologies are also progressing very rapidly; more value added is acquired from R&D activity, but the resources necessary for R&D and production facilities are very great.

CMs reduce costs and investment risks by contracting with many firms. This enables CMs to reduce the burdens of fixed costs by enjoying economies of scale, to recoup initial investment in the facilities in a shorter period, and to increase purchasing power in procuring parts.

CMs are now expanding their services to cover more of the supply chain from design to distribution. Some of them are becoming original design manufacturers (ODMs), contract manufacturers with product design capabilities. ODMs can reduce development time for new product models by creating "ready-to-go" products for their customers. ODMs with technologies to be integrated into advanced products can produce new products soon after their customers recognize the need for them.

Activities by contract manufacturers in Asia[3]

According to Manufacturers' Services Limited (www.msl.com), the market size of the worldwide EMS industry was US$73 billion in 1999, US$88 billion in 2000, US$106 billion in 2001, and growing at a two-digit growth rate annually (see Table 5.4). At the time of writing, North America accounted for 47% of worldwide EMS industry revenues, Europe 24%, Japan 18%, other Asia 8%, and the rest of the world 3%. Reed Electronic Research forecast that, in 2000, global output of electronic products would be split 32% from the USA, 24% from Europe, 19% from Japan, and 20% from Asia-Pacific.

Table 5.4 *EMS industry forecasts, 1998–2003 (US$ billion)*

	World electronics market	EMS market	EMS market share
1998	633	60	9.5%
1999	672	73	10.9%
2000	711	88	12.4%
2001	759	106	14.0%
2002	813	126	15.5%
2003	873	149	17.1%

Source: Manufacturers' Services Limited, http://www.msl.com (originally Technology Forecasters, 2000).

There seems to be increasing room for the EMS market in Asia. Several Asian companies are world class: NatSteel Electronics, which will be acquired by Solectron, JIT Holdings, acquired by Flextronics International, and Universal Scientific Industrial Co., Ltd. from Taiwan. These were included among the top fifty CMs.[4]

Major CMs have already been operating in Asia. SCI Systems is in Malaysia, China, Singapore, and Thailand. Solectron has operations in China, Japan, Malaysia, Singapore, and Taiwan, and will extend this to Indonesia with its acquisition of NatSteel (which also operates in China and Malaysia). Celestica has manufacturing and design facilities around the world, including in China, Hong Kong, Malaysia, Thailand. Flextronics International, headquartered in Singapore, has manufacturing centres in China and Malaysia, and a design center in Taiwan. These companies are among the top six CMs in the world.

Changing Japanese firms
Historically, Japanese firms have had a manufacturing section to produce at least their key products. But some Japanese firms have already begun outsourcing production to CMs. Mitsubishi Consumer Electronics America transferred its wireless telephone assets to Solectron and contracted out the manufacturing (*Nikkei Business*, October 16, 2000). Japanese firms are changing and the market for electronic management services is growing.

The Japanese electronics management services industry can be broadly classified into three types:

1 Subsidiaries created by parent companies:[5] Sony[6] is redesigning its Engineering, Manufacturing and Consumer Services (EMCS) systems; the production system can be differentiated by product categories and by Sony Group company. In 2001, Sony will integrate domestic manufacturing facilities for the final assembly of electronics

products into a new EMCS platform company, tentatively named Sony EMCS AV/IT.[7] Sony has also agreed with Solectron to cooperate in electronic manufacturing. It will transfer two manufacturing facilities in Japan and Taiwan to Solectron, and will contract out the electronics management services from these facilities to respond to fluctuations in demand and product cycles.

2   Foreign companies: in 1999, Solectron opened a New Product Introduction (NPI) center in Japan, becoming the first US-based electronics management services company to establish a manufacturing presence in Japan. In October 2000, Celestica announced the official opening of an office in Japan.

3   Independent companies: for example, Kyoden aims to become a Total Solution Provider (TSP) in electronics and offers services such as design of printed circuit board (PCB) and box, ODM, prototyping, procurement of parts, mass production, logistics, and maintenance. This company is growing very rapidly.[8] It is building an EMS factory in Japan to meet growing demand and the emerging new market of digital consumer electric appliances.

Large Japanese firms are spinning off their own manufacturing facilities and exposing them to competition from outside manufacturers, whilst using EMS to strengthen their manufacturing facilities and concentrate their resources on R&D, services, and devices. Some of them have an advantage in key devices that form the largest proportion of the production costs of IT products and will generate more value added.

Singapore: e-commerce hub and the crossroad of Western and Japanese manufacturing systems

EDI, e-commerce and EMS provide supporting services for constructing Supply Chain Management. In this section, we describe the development process of indigenous CMs with case studies of EDI/e-commerce vendors in Singapore. This will help us to examine the effects of IT on the electronics sector in Asia, and to understand the roles of services for Supply Chain Management.

Electronics industry and contract manufacturers in Singapore

Singapore is a world centre for the production of electronics goods; more than 7 percent of global electronics data processing equipment, including computer equipment, was produced in Singapore in 1998 (Reed Electronics Research 2000).

Foreign direct investment (FDI), especially from the USA and Japan, played an important role in developing Singapore's electronics industry, with US firms dominating the rapid growth of investment in computer-related products from the mid-1980s,[9] followed by Japanese investment in computer and related peripherals manufacturing from the mid-1990s.

The growth of the electronics manufacturing industry stimulated investment and growth in the electronics supporting industries, particularly printed circuit boards (PCBs) and their assembly (PCBA). Japanese key components manufacturers, US CMs and Singapore's indigenous companies provided the new investment. US firms outsourced to local electronics supporting industries which, in turn, encouraged local acquisition of know-how and the expansion of the range of services they could offer. Outsourcing was extended to logistics and warehousing, design services, etc. As a result, a number of local firms succeeded in supplying to Japanese firms in Singapore (Wong 1998).

Today, indigenous CMs, for example NatSteel Electronics, Venture Manufacturing, JIT Holdings, Omni Electronics, CEI and PCI, and the Philippines-based Ionics, are listed on the Singapore Stock Exchange. Some of these firms are now amongst the world's top fifty CMs.

Thus, the electronics industry in Singapore has evolved within an environment of competition and cooperation with the production networks of US and Japanese electronics firms.

E-commerce in Singapore

Following the success of the electronics industry, the Singapore government promoted a national IT master plan, "IT2000", to make Singapore an "intelligent island." "The Infocomm21 Strategic Plan,"[10] a new master plan on information and communication technology (ICT) based on a BtoB e-commerce survey conducted by the then National Computer Board (NCB), now reorganised into IDA (National Computer Board 1999), aims to position Singapore as an e-commerce hub.

The survey investigated more than 1,000 companies from eight industrial sectors.[11] 73.3% of companies had corporate Internet access and 33.4% owned corporate websites. About 9% of the companies were using Internet based BtoB e-commerce and some 28% expressed an interest in doing so within the next six months.

Usage of BtoB was highest among electronics product manufacturers, followed by freight forwarding companies. Of the electronics product manufacturers, 14.9% were already trading on the Internet and 28.9% were interested in BtoB. In the case of freight forwarding companies, the corresponding proportions were 9.2% and 26.0%.

Case studies of electronic data interchange and e-commerce

SNS

SNS[12], which renamed as CrimsonLogic in 2002, was incorporated in 1988 and financed by government organizations such as the Trade Development Board (TDB) to operate the trade-related EDI "TradeNet" service.

SNS diversified the service. EDIMAN was a service for manufacturers that linked buyers and suppliers in the procurement process from order to delivery by EDI. Six hundred companies, fifty of which were Japanese, and included Hitachi, Aiwa, and Sony, as well as Motorola, Compaq, HP, and Phillips, used this service (Center for the International Cooperation for Computerization [CIIC] 2000).

SNS spread its activities worldwide, setting up joint ventures or affiliates in Canada, China, India, Malaysia, Mauritius, the Philippines, Taiwan, and South Africa to transfer technologies and know-how (Center for the International Cooperation for Computerization [CIIC] 2000).

ECnet[13]

ECnet was founded in Singapore, in 1995, under the name Advanced Manufacturing Online (AMO), but is now headquartered in the USA. It began to make its e-supply chain management services or ECnet available in 1998. To augment its services, it allied with Oracle, Sun Microsystems, DHL, FedEx, HP, and others.

The services were created exclusively for high-tech sectors such as electronics components and semiconductors, contract manufacturing, computer and peripherals, communications and networks, and consumer electronics. They cover supply chain management processes, including order management and inventory management. Some sixty-five multinational companies are deployed, mainly as buyers, and more than 1300 companies operated as suppliers on ECnet in August 2000. Customers include AMD, Epson, Siemens, Phillips, Sharp, Hitachi, Motorola, Seagate, and JIT. The company offers its services in China, Hong Kong, Japan, Korea, Malaysia, Mexico, Singapore, Thailand, and the USA, and is planning to spread its activities to Ireland and the Netherlands. In Malaysia, eighty factories, including JVC, Matsushita, and Sony, were linked to the ECnet system in 1999 (Asia and Pacific Internet Association 1999). In China, ECnet allied with Capinfo Company Limited, one of the Internet and EC enterprises backed by the government.

Many multinationals in high-tech sectors operating in Asia already exchange documents electronically through EDI-VAN (value added network) systems, but Asian firms find it more difficult to invest in expensive proprietary software.

ECnet services make participation easier and cheaper. They can be offered by connecting existing EDI or ERP/MRP systems. It translates between such standards as EDIFACT and XML, to automatically share data between systems. This is realized through a standardized Internet browser that enables the system to deploy rapidly and to eliminate time-consuming and error-prone manual processes.

ECnet is also offering ECnet Exchange, an Internet-based marketplace for electronics components. Registered buyers can participate in the marketplace but, in order to guarantee the source and quality of the components, sellers are limited to registered manufacturers of finished products, OEMs, component manufacturers, authorised distributors, and trading companies. ECnet Exchange ensures financial transaction security by offering an escrow service and also a logistics service. This service was started in February 2000 and more than 600 companies have already registered.

NatSteel Electronics and ECnet[14]

NatSteel Electronics Ltd., founded in Singapore, was one of the world's top ten contract manufacturers, but in 2000 it was announced that Solectron would acquire a 33 percent stake of the company. NatSteel Ltd., the parent company of NatSteel Electronics, decided to sell because of the weak PC sales of its major customer, Apple Computer. In 1999, the group turnover was S$3,230 million: Apple accounted for 49%, HP for 18% (more than 60% in 1995), IBM for 14%, Compaq for 9%, and others 10%.

NatSteel started to address the introduction of e-commerce in 1999 by linking its existing ERP system to ECnet. The company started the e-commerce implementation process by developing a system for its 200 suppliers. At the beginning, three kinds of messages were used: Purchase Order (PO) and Delivery Forecast for the order process, Advance Shipping Notification for the logistics process, and Invoice, Credit/Debit Notice and Payment Advice for accounts payable trade. Some 100,000 documents per annum were transferred to electronic data.

Before introducing ECnet, documents were sent from NatSteel's procurement section to suppliers by mail, telephone, and fax. NatSteel's logistics section arranged transportation forwarders by telephone and so on. After the introduction of ECnet, selected messages were sent or accepted through ECnet electronically.

As a result of the introduction of ECnet, the percentage of suppliers connected with NatSteel online increased within three months from 9% in the EDI-VAN environment, to 32%. Order lead-time was reduced by two to three days. The company also succeeded in reducing the cost of paperwork for PO by 50% and on accounts payable trade by 35%.

Table 5.5 *World share of production in Asia and China, 2000 (percent)*

	Asia	China
Color TVs	57.2	24.0
DVD players	92.9	19.2
Mobile phones	42.4	8.7
Desktop PCs	43.0	9.6
HDDs	97.1	7.5
VTRs	76.0	21.2
Air conditioners	78.4	40.5

Note: Unit base, estimates in 2000.
Source: Nihon Keizai Shimbun, July 15, 2000.

China: global production base built into networks

China's growth

Asia is the world manufacturing centre for IT goods. Today, China is attracting investments from all over the world, especially Taiwan which is encouraging relocation of manufacturing to the mainland. China has grown to be the world production centre for IT and electronic products. *Nihon Keizai Shimbun* (July 15, 2000) reported that China is catching up with Japan in the production of new products such as DVD players and mobile phones.

Moreover, China's world share of unit production of IT-related products is growing rapidly. Its share of desktop PC manufacturing is already second to Taiwan and expected to rise from 8.7% in 1999 to 9.6% in 2000 (see Table 5.5). Another survey by the Institute for Information Industry (III) in Taiwan said that the production value of PC-related products in mainland China will surpass that of Taiwan in 2000 (*Nihon Keizai Shimbun*, November 24, 2000).

China will also rank third in the world behind Korea and Japan in terms of mobile phone manufacturing. Its share will increase from 7.6% in 1999 to 8.7% in 2000. Furthermore, China's share of audiovisual products is even higher than its share of IT products, holding the top position by producing about 25% of the world's colour televisions and more than 20% of its VCRs. China is becoming one of the world's manufacturing centres of DVDs, following Japan (46%) and Malaysia (22%) in 2000.

In addition to its growing large domestic market, cheap labor cost, and economic liberalization in preparation for its entry to the WTO, accumulation of industry, especially around Guangdong and Shanghai, is acting to invite further foreign direct investment.

China and the global supply chain network

The networks of contract manufacturers in China

As mentioned above, major CMs also operate in China. In addition to the shift of PC manufacturing from Taiwan to China, analysed by Ohki in this volume (Chapter 4), multinational CMs have acquired facilities or are making alliances with existing companies in China.

Jabil Circuit Inc. ventured into China for the first time with the acquisition of Hong-Kong-based GET Manufacturing. Sanmina Corp. acquired Chinese contract electronics manufacturer Ocean Manufacturing Ltd., which has a factory in Shenzhen, administrative offices in Hong Kong, and a branch procurement office in Taiwan.

In the case of Flextronics, acquisition and merger agreements announced in 2000 will expand its services in Asia including China: the acquisition of the Dii Group will improve its PCB business in China; the merger agreement with Li Xin Industries will expand plastic operation in Northern China; and the merger with JT Holdings will provide Flextronics with manufacturing operations through JIT's new operations in Tianjin and Shanghai.

Cyber network embracing China

In addition to China's attractions as a manufacturing base, it has great potential for e-commerce development. It has the largest number of Internet users in Asia and the most rapidly increasing numbers of users. The number of computer hosts is exploding, up from 542,000 in July 1998 to 6.5 million in July 2000, and the number of Internet users was 16.9 million in July 2000, up from 1.175 million in July 1998 (China Internet Network Information Centre [CNNIC] 2000).

The Chinese government is actively participating in the development of e-commerce by cooperating with private and even foreign companies. ECnet, allied with Capinfo, is being backed by Chinese governmental organisations.

Hong Kong acts as a "portal" for companies embarking on e-commerce business in mainland China. It can offer such services as finance, telecommunications infrastructure, and logistics, and native Chinese companies can also offer advice on entering mainland markets. Some e-commerce companies operating in China are headquartered in Hong Kong.

Alibaba.com is one such company. It was founded in mainland China, but has its international headquarters in Hong Kong, offices in Beijing, Shanghai, Hangzhou, London, and Silicon Valley, and a joint venture in Seoul, Korea. It offers BtoB marketplace focusing on small and medium-sized enterprises (SMEs) to over 400,000 registered members from over 200 countries, and with more than 170,000 members in China in 2000.

The transportation company Tradelink[15] is one of the largest e-commerce service providers in Hong Kong. The company, incorporated in 1989, is a joint venture between the Hong Kong Special Administrative Region (HKSAR) and the private sector offering EDI service. It handles tens of millions of transactions annually, servicing 53,000 companies. Tradelink participated in a regional alliance with Singapore and Taiwan government-backed e-commerce facilitators: SNS and Trade-Van Information Services Co. of Taiwan. The total membership of the three networks at the time of the agreement exceeded 90,000 organisations: 51,000 from Tradelink, 25,000 from SNS, and 14,000 from Trade-Van. These three companies aim to expand the alliance to cover the whole region, and have already decided to invite KTNET of Korea and InfoShare Information Technology Development (IITD) of China to join them.[16] Such networks will closely connect mainland China and the Asian region with the global trade network and system of international division of labor.

Effects of information technology on ASEAN

For this section, Singapore is not included in ASEAN unless specifically mentioned.

Losing competitive advantage

As a part of ASEAN's development strategy, member countries invited companies from more developed countries to set up factories. This led to higher value added production, a development pattern described as flying geese. However, it is noticeable that some ASEAN countries are now losing their comparative advantage (see Table 5.6). China's labor costs are lower than ASEAN's, especially Thailand's and Malaysia's. Industries in these new growing middle-income countries need to shift to higher value added products. More automation and skilled labor will be needed to promote this shift, but capital and skilled labor are scarcer in these countries than in more advanced countries such as Singapore.

Changing developing patterns

Two additional factors are now affecting the flying geese development pattern.

Current characteristics of business location

Recent location trends indicate that firms producing cutting-edge goods favour information-oriented localities well endowed with R&D networks and universities, such as Silicon Valley, that are close to large markets. Companies need to update information on changing demands, to deliver products rapidly with fewer inventories and at lower costs, and use sales and R&D information efficiently. But ASEAN has a shortfall in telecommunications infrastructure and highly

Table 5.6 Assessment of investment conditions in selected Asian economies (A = most favorable conditions)

	China	Korea	Malaysia	Singapore	Taiwan	Thailand	Indonesia	Philippines	Vietnam
Supply of labor	A	C	C	D	D	B	A	A	A
Quality of labor	C	B	C	B	A	C	D	B	D
Cost of labor	A	C	C	D	D	B	A	A	A
Infrastructure	C	C	B	A	B	C	C	C	D
Domestic market	A	C	C	D	B	B	C	C	C
Local supplier	C	C	B	B	A	B	D	D	D
Incentives	B	B	A	A	C	A	C	B	C
Competitiveness ranking 1998 (WEF)[a]	28	19	17	1	6	21	31	33	39
Competitiveness ranking 1998 (IMD)[b]	24	35	20	2	16	39	40	32	n/a

Notes:
[a] WEF (World Economic Forum).
[b] IMD (Institute of Management Development).
Source: OECD 2000.

skilled engineers, and markets in individual countries are not large compared to China (see Table 5.6). The accumulation of industry, especially key components and materials, is not enough, and ASEAN countries are at a disadvantage in attracting foreign direct investment.

Prevailing outsourcing

The outsourcing of IT and manufacturing, which has already spread in Asia, has led to the construction of more efficient and flexible global supply chains. Users of these services can build SCM by using outsourcing even if they lack adequate internal resources to do so. This will also affect ASEAN.

Japanese firms have led the way in transferring their manufacturing operations to ASEAN, but they pave the way for outsourcing in Singapore and Japan. In parallel with this process, firms will integrate, abolish, scrap-and-build, and change the roles of existing operations or relocate operations.

These trends create business opportunities for the multinational CMs which are spreading their activities in Asia. This will, in turn, affect relationships between Japanese and Asian local firms.

Production outsourcing will release multinationals from some of their existing operations. As IT transcends national and companies' boundaries, it will become easier for multinationals to transfer business to more competitive countries. Furthermore, the fact that supplies of key components and materials in ASEAN mainly depend on imports will work in their favor. Spreading e-commerce will also support outsourcing to build global SCM.

The need for ASEAN indigenous companies to change

ASEAN is losing competitiveness as local companies have been mainly been engaged in relatively labor-intensive processes. Thailand is a production base for labor-intensive HDDs, but foreign companies dominate the supply of HDD parts. Indigenous suppliers are not interested. The Board of Investment (BOI) of Thailand analysed the reasons as follows (Panichapat and Kanasawat 1999):

1   HDD is a very volatile industry.
2   HDD firms are mainly American and not concerned about long-term relationships. Thai suppliers are accustomed to long-term relationships and feel more comfortable with Japanese firms in the automobile and electrical appliance industries.
3   Large Thai conglomerates with technological strength found HDD parts less attractive than petrochemical, automotive, electronics, electrical appliances, and so on.

4 Thai SMEs did not have enough technical and financial strength to supply HDD parts.

These characteristics are not limited to the HDD industry, they also force multinationals, including Japanese firms, to introduce SCM or outsourcing. Cooperation between multinationals, including electronics manufacturing service and EDI vendors, is deepening.

Faced with all this, indigenous firms need to increase their scale of production or shift to higher value added products such as electronics parts. Simultaneously, they need to promote the introduction of IT and IT-based services so as to increase productivity, improve services to customers, and seize new business opportunities. In the current situation of scarcity in human and capital resources, IT will enable them to make flexible use of outsourcing, and concentrate on businesses with competitive advantage.

Conclusion

The development of supply chain management gives companies greater flexibility in choosing their operating location, depending on the competitive advantage of each company and country. As ASEAN loses competitiveness, China is emerging as a production centre and market for IT-related products. It is possible that China will follow the developmental process and division of labor already seen in Singapore.

In addition, ASEAN firms' readiness for IT, production scale and purchasing power for components, seem to be inferior to that of multinational CMs. CMs can contract or form a partnership to retain SCM services and use e-commerce to optimize their procurement, production, and delivery processes. Thus, indigenous ASEAN firms will be forced to increase their scale of production, shift to higher value added products, and introduce IT and IT-based services to improve productivity and services, and to seize new business opportunities. IT also makes it possible to extend market reach and reveal global niche markets. This will provide business opportunities for developing countries.

Current obstacles to developing IT – cost, security issues, infrastructure, etc. – will be overcome by technology and the diffusion of IT itself. As seen in the case of NatSteel, transfer to Web-based EDI increased registration on the system. Actual experience of the Web will help firms in developing countries to introduce IT, with advanced firms, already accustomed to the business practices of the region, playing an important role. They can transfer their IT-related know-how to other firms.

IT, with its economies of scale and scope, will push developing countries into globalization. Multinationals promote globalization and closer connections within and between Asia and the rest of the world; liberalization of investment and trade on a bilateral and multilateral basis complement these trends.

However, it must be remembered that the introduction of IT and globalization sometimes forces countries into industrial restructuring, which in turn increases unemployment. Companies will integrate, abolish, scrap-and-build, and change the roles of existing operations or relocate operations in response to the changing business environment. This can generate opposition to deregulation and globalization and will reduce the benefits of IT. It will be strategically important for global cooperation and negotiation on trade and investment liberalization to include discussion on IT in order to support a social safety network.

Notes

1. Cases of companies in this paper mainly depend on information from each company's website and newspapers, such as *Nihon Keizai Shimbun*, *Nikkei Sangyo Shimbun*, and *Nikkan Kogyo Shimbun*.
2. Ohki's paper in this volume (Chapter 4) detailed the international division of labor in PC manufacturing.
3. See Kagami and Kuchiki 2000 for information on CMs in Mexico.
4. See top fifty contract manufacturers for 1999 at Manufacturing Market Insider's website (http://www.mfgmkt.com/top_50.html).
5. Except for the examples mentioned in this paper, Matsushita announced the FY2001–2003 business plan that include the spin-off of manufacturing facilities. The aims are: (a) identification of revenue and expenditure of manufacturing department; (b) shifting to large-scale and high-efficiency factories through the integration of small factories; and (c) creation of a professional body with high-efficiency manufacturing like EMS, proprietary devices and modules, and ultimate assembly technologies.
6. In addition to Sony's press release on July 26, 2000, see *Nikkei Business*, October 16, 2000.
7. The new company will be responsible for the domestic engineering and manufacturing processes of all electronics products. That includes mass production design and prototyping, materials procurement, production planning, manufacturing technology, and mass production. Inventory control, logistics, and customer services will also be included, with the aim of creating speedy, flexible, and high quality manufacturing.
8. Consolidated sales of Kyoden have more than tripled from 17.6 billion yen in March 1997 to 66.5 billion yen in March 2000. This was a result of the growth of the EMS market and this company's aggressive merger and acquisition strategy. Kyoden made Sotec, a PC maker, affiliate in 1998.
9. On the history of the growth of the electronic industry in Singapore, see Wong 1998.
10. About the Infocomm21 Strategic Plan, see IDA 2000.

11. The eight industrial sectors were: manufacturing of electronics products, chemicals and chemical products, manufacturing of aircraft and spacecraft, logistics services, freight forwarding, storage and warehousing, courier other than postal, and publishing.
12. See SNS's website, Schware and Kimberley 1995, and Burn and Martinsons 1997.
13. The case mainly depended on information from ECnet's website and materials obtained from ECnet Japan.
14. The case of NatSteel and ECnet depended on information from NatSteel's website, Teo, Kam, and Lim 2000, and materials obtained from ECnet Japan.
15. In addition to Tradelink's website, see Burn and Martinsons 1997.
16. This alliance is named the Pan-Asia e-Commerce Alliance and grew to seven members with the participation of TEDI of Japan and DagangNet of Malaysia as of May 2002.

References

Asia and Pacific Internet Association (APIA) 1999, Supplier hubs: EDI over the Internet in the Asia Pacific, *APIA Newsletter*, No. 3, October–November 1999.
Burn, J. M. and Martinsons, M. G. 1997, *Information Technology and the Challenge for Hong Kong*, Hong Kong: Hong Kong University Press.
Center for the International Cooperation for Computerization (CICC) 2000, *Report on Information Technology Policy and Industry in Asian Countries*, Tokyo, July 2000.
China Internet Network Information Centre (CNNIC) 2000, *Semiannual Survey Report on the Development of China's Internet*, July 2000.
Electronic Commerce Promotion Council of Japan (ECOM) 2000, Recent trends of BtoB EC in Japan (in Japanese), September 11, 2000.
Gartner Group 2000, Gartner Group says business-to-business e-commerce transactions becoming more global, Press Release on February 16, 2000.
Infocomm Development Authority of Singapore (IDA) 1999, *Key Findings of ICT Usage Survey 1999 on the ICT Adoption of Business in Singapore*, Singapore.
2000, Singapore paves the way as trusted global e-commerce hub, Press Release on August 1, 2000, Singapore.
Japan External Trade Organization (JETRO) 2000, *Questionnaire Survey of Japanese Companies Residing in ASEAN on Outlook of Production and Trade* (in Japanese), conducted May/June 2000.
Kagami, M. and Kuchiki, A. 2000, Silicon Valley in the South: new management networks emerging in Guadalajara, paper presented at the international workshop on "A Study on Industrial Networks in Asia," Institute of Developing Economies, JETRO, January 2000.
National Computer Board (NCB) 1999, *Key Findings of NCB Survey on Internet-Based Business-to-Business Electronic Commerce in Singapore*, Singapore, January 1999.
OECD 2000, *Knowledge-Based Industries in Asia*, Paris.

Panichapat, C. and Kanasawat, Y. 1999, *Hard Disk Drive Industry in Thailand*, Bangkok: Thailand Board of Investment (BOI).

Reed Electronics Research 2000, *The Yearbook of World Electronics Data 2000/1*, Sutton, UK.

Teo, T., Kam, W. P., and Lim, V. 2000, *Issues and Challenges in E-Commerce: A Casebook*, New York: McGraw-Hill.

Schware, R. and Kimberley, P. 1995, Information technology and national trade facilitation, World Bank Technical Paper No. 316.

Wong, P. K. 1998, *Globalization of US–Japan Production Networks and The Growth of Singapore Electronics Industry*, National University of Singapore.

6 IT diffusion in Southeast Asia: the cases of Singapore, Malaysia, and Thailand

Norihiko Yamada

Introduction

In Southeast Asia, there is increasing awareness, particularly at government level, of the importance of the IT revolution through its likely impact on development. Since the 1997 economic crisis, commitment to IT has increased and, though government is not the sole key player, its policies on information infrastructure, the telecommunications sector, and education are central to the future of the information society. Today, the region is attracting multinational corporations (MNCs) from all over the world and, whilst there is an undeniable sense that the word "IT" has wings, nonetheless it brings a new dynamism to the region.

Singapore has achieved the reputation of being one of the most successful IT countries in the region, and even in the world. Table 6.1 shows that Singapore is well endowed with information infrastructure which spreads into every area of society. Malaysia and Thailand come next, but the other countries, Philippines, Indonesia, and Vietnam, are still at a very early stage.

This is just the start of IT diffusion in the region but, already, much is expected of it. The literature has tended to focus on the convenience, efficiency, technological innovation, and its other positive aspects. However, here I would like to discuss the issue from the point of view of the general public: does national IT development meet with the needs/demands of the public, and do they really exploit it?

Because of its leading role and dominance in IT, Singapore is the main country considered here. Its experience can be a model for other countries in the region. I also briefly look at Malaysia and Thailand to examine their current situation and at the lessons they can learn from Singapore.

Table 6.1 *Diffusion rates of information infrastructures, 1999*

	Penetration (%)				
	Main telephone lines	Cellular mobile phones	Internet users	PCs	GDP per capita, 1998 (US$)
Japan	55.70	44.94	14.46	28.69	30,105
Indonesia	2.91	1.06	0.19	0.91	605
Malaysia	20.30	13.70	6.87	6.87	3,333
Philippines	3.88	3.66	0.67	1.69	898
Singapore	48.20	41.88	29.45	52.72	21,413
Thailand	8.57	3.84	1.31	2.27	1,859
Vietnam	2.68	0.42	0.12	0.89	335

Source: ITU Telecommunication Indicators,
http://www.itu.int/ti/industryoverview/index.htm.

Singapore

Background

Since independence, Singapore has achieved rapid economic growth despite its small domestic market and geographical area.[1] This can be partly attributed to an efficient and pragmatic government that has provided the infrastructure base for MNCs to undertake manufacturing and service operations.[2]

In the early 1980s, the government began promoting the application of IT; the policy-makers saw it as a key strategic factor in restructuring its economy from a manufacturing and service operation center to a higher value added economy. The overriding aim was to increase the sophistication of the industrial structure and to keep its competitiveness in global markets.

IT policy of Singapore

The spearhead of IT in Singapore was the establishment of the National Computer Board (NCB) in 1981 to implement the National Computerization Plan (NCP) of the previous year. The NCB was the center of IT development until the establishment of the Infocommunication Development Authority (IDA) in 1999.

During this period, the government mainly focused on the diffusion and exploitation of computer technology. Under an NCB initiative, a Civil Service Computerization Program (CSCP) was implemented in 1981 to demonstrate the benefits of computerization.

In 1986, NCB, cooperating with Singapore Telecom, the Economic Development Board, and the National University of Singapore, launched a National

IT Plan (NITP). It was aimed at nurturing an export-oriented IT industry and at increasing the productivity and competitiveness in all economic sectors. The government shifted its focus towards encouraging integrated strategies between hardware manufacturing, telecommunications and software services, and manpower development.[3]

During the 1980s, as an outcome of CSCP, online services such as TradeNet, SchoolLinks, and LawNet,[4] were begun. IT manpower increased from 850 to 14,300 in 1991. As for infrastructure, companies in Singapore were able to make direct international calls to more than 160 cities around the world using a 100 percent automated and touchtone phone. In 1989, optical fiber cable networks were laid, and Singapore became the first country in the world to offer nationwide commercial ISDN services.[5] Singapore had created the basic foundation for IT during the 1980s, and this paved the way for the next stage.

In 1992, the NCB issued a Masterplan, *IT2000: A Vision of an Intelligent Island*. Its aim was to transform the country into an intelligent island where IT is exploited to the fullest to enhance people's quality of life.[6] The plan was based on the recognition that Singapore needed to have a new information infrastructure if it was to keep its competitiveness as a regional hub.

A key element was the construction of the National Information Infrastructure (NII). In 1996, Singapore ONE (One Network for Everyone) was launched to build the world's first broadband multimedia network covering a whole country.[7] As of October 2000, Singapore ONE is accessible by more than 99 percent of homes, all schools, and a number of public facilities. There are 250,000 users with 300 application providers. Even people without computers can access the system at kiosks located in public places such as street corners and shopping malls.

IT2000 and Singapore ONE have laid a solid foundation. Today, Singapore is moving into a new stage with its ICT21 Masterplan. It is expected to lead Singapore into the position of the information and communications technology (ICT) hub of the new economy by 2010.

Details of the Masterplan were announced in 2000 (see Table 6.2). As a first step, the government completely liberalized the telecommunications market in April 2000, two years ahead of the original schedule. As of September, 140 companies were granted licenses. International call fees have already been reduced to half. The government felt that it had to liberalize ahead of schedule in order to keep up with rapid technological innovation and to survive global competition.

Initial conditions

It has therefore been twenty years since the government implemented IT policies. The government has gradually laid a solid basic foundation and adjusted its policy as required so that Singapore did not experience a supply side bottleneck.[8]

Table 6.2 *Key components of the ICT 21 Masterplan*

Aim	Policy
1 a Full liberalization of the telecommunications industry	• On April 1, 2000, telecommunications sector in Singapore was fully liberalized ahead of originally schedule of April 1, 2002.
• To be a leading ICT hub in the Asia-Pacific, the telecommunications market must be liberalized while attracting new investments and players who bring innovative, high quality, and cost-effective services.	
b ICT industry development	• Jumpstarting the interactive broadband multimedia industry
• To double the size of the ICT industry by 2005, especially to focus on new growth areas such as e-commerce application software and services, broadband applications, content hosting and development, mobile and wireless communications, mobile Internet services, and embedded software in information appliances and smart devices.	• Building new capabilities and leveraging on innovation for new Internet economy
	• Fostering strategic partnership and alliances overseas to help local companies regionalize and globalize
2 Dot.com the people's sector	• Improving the affordability of PCs and accessibility to the Internet for low-income households.
• Income, language, and mindsets are three main causes of the digital divide and possible barriers to new subscribers. Even though the gap is narrowing today, the rapid pace of development and emerging new technologies may possibly leave them behind in the future.	• Working with industry and community groups, IDA to make available more locally relevant contents in other Asian languages.
	• Implementing e-Ambassadors program, whereby volunteers teach late adopters in the use of ICT appliances, to narrow the gap between them.

3 Developing manpower
- Manpower shortage in the ICT sector is a problem in every country in the world. In 2010, Singapore will need 250,000 workers in the sector. In order to meet demand, Singapore must not only develop its own talent, but also prepare to accept international manpower.

  - Co-operating with industry and the institutions of higher education, IDA provides the appropriate training to students and workers to nurture a talent pool that is knowledgable on the Internet
  - Making policy to attract and retain international talent
  - Building up e-learning and becoming its hub in the region

4 Dot.com the public sector
- The public and business can reach, communicate, and interact with the government electronically to obtain government information and utilize government services while on the move.

  - Pushing the envelope of electronic service delivery
  - Building new capability and new capacity
  - Innovating with infocomm technologies
  - Anticipating to be proactive, sensing to be responsive
  - Developing thought leadership in e-government

5 Dot.com the private sector
- To enhance e-commerce by leveraging its strength in e-commerce infrastructure.

  - Laying a robust foundation for e-business
  - Catalyzing the digital transaction
  - Spurring consumer demand
  - Branding Singapore as a trusted global "dot.com" hub and an e-business thought leadership centre
  - Attracting top talents
  - Fostering an e-lifestyle and bridging the digital divide

Source: Infocomm 21, http://www.ida.gov.sg.

However, we should keep in mind that Singapore had beneficial initial conditions:

1   Singapore had a high GDP per capita so could invest in the project.
2   There exists an electronics industry cluster of MNCs.
3   Its small size and population made for easy penetration.
4   Strong and effective leadership can adjust policy to fit the circumstances.
5   There were basic social infrastructures.

Singapore has manipulated these given factors skilfully. Today, IT is spreading into every area of society, and PCs and the Internet are widely diffused among the people. However, whether the people really share the fruit of IT is a different matter. Many challenges remain.

IT in society

PCs and the Internet

According to the IT Household Survey 1999 conducted by NCB,[9] only 11% of households had PCs in 1987, rising to 41% in 1997. Today, the PC penetration rate of Singapore households is 59% (see Figure 6.1) and 57% of Singaporeans have access to the Internet.[10]

The survey demonstrates that PC penetration varies with household type. Some 78% of private households have at least one computer compared to 55%

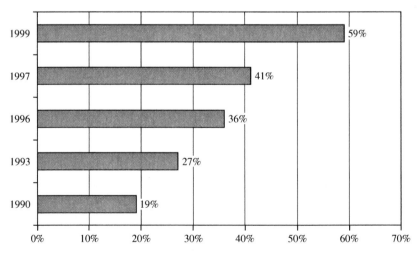

Figure 6.1 Ownership of computers in Singapore households, 1990–1999 (Source: National Computer Board 2000)

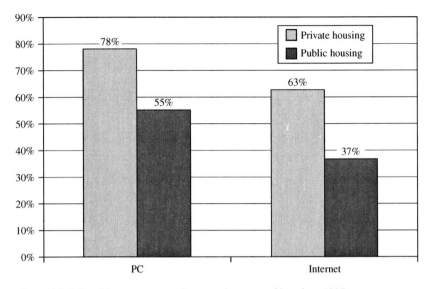

Figure 6.2 PC and Internet penetration rates by types of housing, 1997
(Source: National Computer Board 2000)

of those in public housing (see Figure 6.2). Within public housing, 78% of executive flats/maisonettes have PCs compared to 64% of 4–5 room flats and 41% of 1–3 room flats (see Figure 6.3).

The same trend applies to Internet access: 63% in private housing and 37% in public housing (see Figure 6.2). Within public housing, residents in executive flats have higher access rates than those in 1–3 rooms (see Figure 6.4). Today, the GDP per capita of Singapore is about US$22,000, and NII is accessible to all households. Even so, the degree of IT penetration is affected by income differences.

IT usage by the public
High IT penetration rates do not mean that usage is sophisticated. According to the survey, most people use PCs and Internet for e-mail, games, and information retrieval. On the other hand, online banking, distance learning, online shopping, and online government services, which were expected to be the main usages in the IT era, are the least used (see Figures 6.5 and 6.6).

At present, the Singapore government provides 130 kinds of online services, such as selling government publications, providing real-time traffic information, bookings for driving tests, and submitting various application forms. However, only 21.5% of Internet users have ever accessed online government transactions.

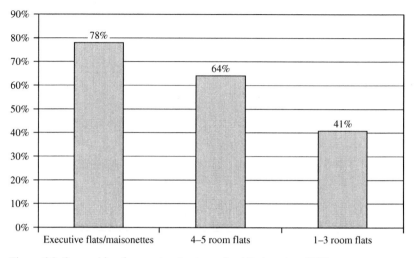

Figure 6.3 Ownership of computers by type of public housing, 1997
(Source: National Computer Board 2000)

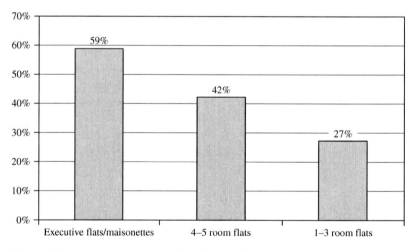

Figure 6.4 Internet access by type of public housing, 1997 (Source: National
Computer Board 2000)

Figure 6.7 shows the types of online government transactions and Figure 6.8 shows the main reason for not accessing online government services. IT is expected to bring efficiency and benefits, but interestingly, many people still prefer to handle the process in the old-fashioned way so that the new online services do not always meet public requirements.

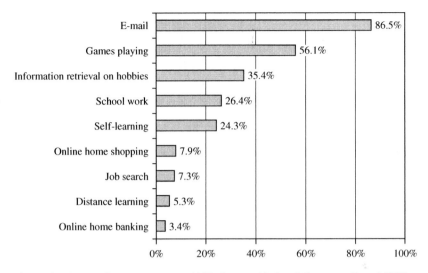

Figure 6.5 Types of computer usage, 1997 (Source: National Computer Board 2000)

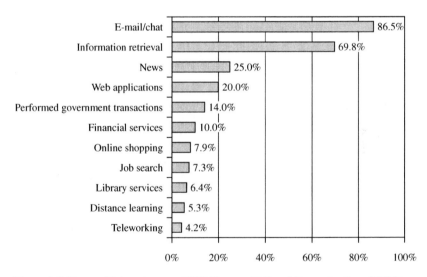

Figure 6.6 Types of Internet usage, 1997 (Source: National Computer Board 2000)

IT in education
The government launched its Masterplan for IT in Education in 1997 and the introduction of computers into secondary schools began in 1981. Since then, all schools have been gradually computerized. At present, the curricula for

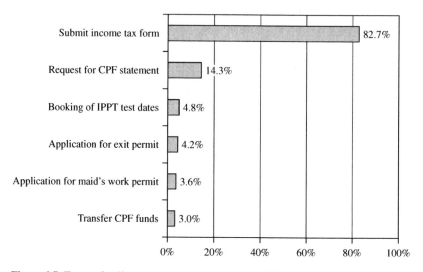

Figure 6.7 Types of online government transactions, 1997 (Source: National Computer Board 2000)

primary and secondary schools require 10 percent and 14 percent use of IT respectively. The student:computer ratio is 5:1 in secondary schools and 6:1 in primary schools. Also, all schools are connected to Singapore ONE, and each school has at least two PCs connected to it.[11] What is significant is that after primary school, pupils have basic computer literacy. IT education at primary level expands IT literacy, and reduces the divide between "haves" and "havenots". The government says that all school leavers will be IT literate by 2003.

The gap between government and people

Judging from the supply side, Singaporeans are certainly enjoying the fruits of IT. There are information infrastructures accessible to all households, a variety of online services and applications, and higher IT education. From the demand side, it seems that the supply is not really meeting their needs. The survey shows that there is a gap between government and society; a high diffusion rate is not always accompanied by sophisticated usage. Also, even in an egalitarian society like Singapore, we see that income affects the degree of IT diffusion. Therefore, it is interesting to note what the Singapore experience tells us. Even though the country has largely achieved an information society and, from the beginning, the government has paid attention to both economic and social development so that IT education and literacy is widespread, the fact remains that the sophistication of IT is centering on the supply side first, and the fruits of IT have not yet ripened amongst the public.

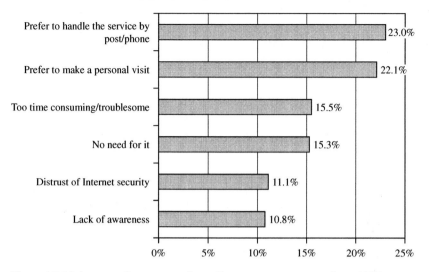

Figure 6.8 Main reason for not accessing online government transactions, 1997
(Source: National Computer Board 2000)

Malaysia

National IT policy: the Multimedia Super Corridor

In 1996, Prime Minister Dr. Mahathir Mohamad officially launched the national
IT plan, the Multimedia Super Corridor (MSC), the main vehicle for achieving
Vision 2020.[12] The overriding objective of the MSC is to build the necessary
environment for the new era and nurture knowledge-based industry in conjunction with the manufacturing sector, by attracting both multinationals and
domestic world-class players. The whole plan is divided into three phases:[13]

> Phase 1: 1996–2003:
> 1 establish Cyberjaya and Putrajaya as world-class intelligent cities
> 2 establish Cyberlaws
> 3 launch seven Flagship Applications
> 4 attract 50 world-class companies
>
> Phase 2: 2004–2010:
> 1 establish more intelligent cities
> 2 link the MSC to other cities and the world
> 3 establish a cluster of 250 world-class companies
>
> Phase 3: 2011–2020:
> 1 establish more intelligent cities
> 2 transform Malaysia into a knowledge-based society
> 3 establish a cluster of 500 world-class companies.

Table 6.3 *Bill of Guarantee*

• Provide a world-class physical and information infrastructure
• Allow unrestricted employment of local and foreign knowledge workers
• Ensure freedom of ownership by exempting companies with MSC status from local ownership requirements
• Give the freedom to source capital globally for MSC infrastructure, and the right to borrow funds globally
• Provide competitive financial incentives
• Become a regional leader in intellectual property protection and cyberlaws
• Ensure no Internet censorship
• Provide globally competitive telecommunications tariffs
• Tender key MSC infrastructure contacts to leading companies willing to use the MSC as their regional hub
• Provide a high-powered implementation agency to act as an effective one-stop super shop

Source: www.mdc.com.my/mdc/index/html.

Malaysia has approximately 22 million people and is 330,000km^2 in size, so it is impossible to build a nationwide information infrastructure as rapidly as Singapore did. A specific feature of the MSC is that the government decided to develop a corridor 15km wide and 50km long from Kuala Lumpur City Center to Kuala Lumpur International Airport as an area of concentrated IT infrastructure and industry. Here, two of the world's first smart cities, Cyberjaya and Putrajaya, are being developed.[14] In addition, the government enacted six necessary cyberlaws.[15] The Multimedia Development Corporation (MDC) was established as a one-stop-shop for companies to ease the process of getting MSC status. In addition, the government set a Bill of Guarantee as new incentives for MNCs (see Table 6.3).

The key projects for the MSC are the Flagship Applications: "Multimedia Development" and "Multimedia Environment" (see Table 6.4 and 6.5). The former is to realise e-government and provide online services for the public. The latter is to provide an optimal environment for companies entering the MSC to facilitate high value added activities.

Flagship Applications aim to increase efficiency and to transform people's lives. Some public services have already reduced their procedure times: passports are received five days after an application has been made rather than the two weeks that it used to take, and the time taken to reissue ID cards has been reduced from six months to two weeks.

The MSC is expected to yield high returns, but it is unclear if it will bring the expected social development. As we see in the case of Singapore, such sophisticated services can only work if there is a solid IT foundation and

Table 6.4 *"Multimedia Development" Flagship Applications*

Flagship Applications	Lead agency
Electronic government	Malaysian Administrative Modernization Unit
Multi-purpose card	Bank Negara
Smart schools	Ministry of Education
Telemedicine	Ministry of Health

Source: http://www.mdc.com.my/msc/flagship/index.html.

Table 6.5 *"Multimedia Environment" Flagship Applications*

Flagship Applications	Lead agency
R&D cluster	Ministry of Science, Technology & Environment
Worldwide manufacturing webs	Ministry of International Trade & Industry
Borderless marketing	MDC

Source: http://www.mdc.com.my/msc/flagship/index.html.

understanding within society. Malaysia still lacks such a basis, especially in rural areas.

Diffusion of PCs and the Internet in Malaysia

In Malaysia today, the penetration of both PCs and the Internet is approximately 7 percent, but there is potential for expansion. International Data Corporations (IDC) predicts that there will be about 4 million Internet users by 2004.[16] There is no doubt that the number is increasing, but the increase tends to be restricted to the metropolitan areas.

Table 6.6 shows the number of telephones per 1,000 people, mean monthly gross household income and the Internet access rate in each state. The scatter-grams in Figures 6.9, 6.10 and 6.11 clearly show that IT penetration is related to income. Higher income states, such as Kuala Lumpur, Selangor, Pulau Pinang, and Johor, have higher rates of both telephone ownership and Internet access. A typical Malaysian household can spend 17 percent of total income on optional goods and services such as PCs and TVs. The higher incomes of the urban population leaves them with about RM580 (about US$150) disposable income, whereas rural residents have about RM285 (about US$70).[17] The cost of PCs and Internet access puts large financial constraints on rural residents.

Table 6.6 *Correlation between household income and Internet penetration, 1997*

State	Telephone sets per 1,000 people	Mean monthly gross household income (RM)	Internet access (%)
Johor	187.6	2,772	11.1
Kedah	140.7[a]	1,590	3.1
Kelantan	76.7	1,249	0.8
Melaka	186.3	2,276	3.2
Negeri Sembilan	180.9	2,378	2.6
Pahang	127.2	1,632	1.7
Parak	185.4	1,940	5.3
Perlis	140.7[a]	1,507	0.5
Pulau Pinang	259.0	3,130	10.5
Sabah	80.8	2,057	2.6
Sarawak	110.3	2,242	7.2
Selangor	309.1	4,006	26.3
Terengganu	102.9	1,497	1.1
Kuala Lumpur	239.8	4,768	23.9
Malaysia	172.7	2,607	99.0

Note:
[a] Figure is combined total for Kedah and Perlis.
Source: NITC 2000.

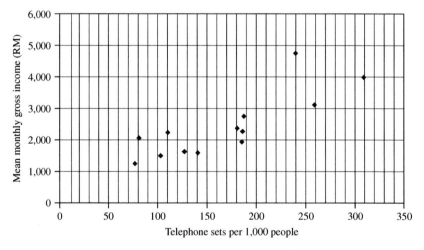

Figure 6.9 Telephone sets per 1,000 people and mean monthly gross household income (Source: NITC 2000)

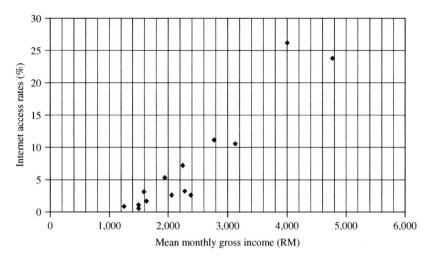

Figure 6.10 Mean monthly gross income and Internet access rates (Source: NITC 2000)

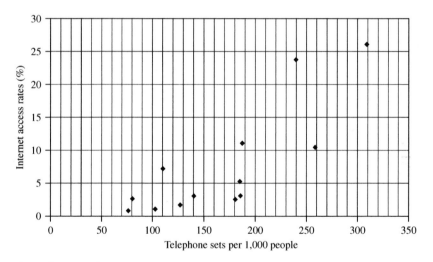

Figure 6.11 Telephone sets per 1,000 people and Internet access rates (Source: NITC 2000)

In addition, not all rural areas are served by even a fixed telephone. As can be seen in Table 6.7, despite increased investment in telecommunications since the 1980s, the gap between the metropolitan area and the rural cities has widened. The diffusion of IT in Malaysian society is still at an early stage, although the government is laying a solid IT foundation. Against this backdrop, the

Table 6.7 *Penetration of telephone lines and investment in the telecommunications sector, 1993 and 1998 (%)*

Country	Year	Largest city	Other cities	National	Investment in telecommunications (% of GDP)
Malaysia	1993	13.6	12.5	12.6	0.73 (1987–1991)
	1998	30.0	18.9	19.5	1.52 (1992–1996)
Thailand	1993	17.2	1.8	3.8	0.41 (1987–1991)
	1998	36.1	4.7	8.4	0.19 (1992–1996)

Source: Ohki 2000; OECD 2000.

Malaysian government is implementing ambitious projects, but the MSC will benefit only the upper level of society as the effect is concentrated in Kuala Lumpur and large cities.

Thailand

National IT policy

In 1992, the National Information Technology Committee (NITC) was established to prepare, implement, and oversee IT development policy, and the National Electronics and Computer Technology Center (NECTEC) was assigned a secretariat role. At present, many NITC projects are implemented through NECTEC.[18]

In May 1995, the NITC announced a national IT plan, IT2000. The overriding object was to support national development and to create equal opportunity of employment, education, and public services for all segments of society through the application of IT. Three agendas were announced as fundamental prerequisites:[19]

1 Build an equitable national information infrastructure:
   • build universally accessible information infrastructure in accordance with the new information age
   • ensure that a reasonable share of the benefits is given to rural regions
   • deregulate and privatize the telecommunications sector
2 Invest in people:
   • develop IT manpower at all levels to eliminate the current shortage
   • fulfil the aspirations of all citizens for continuing education and skills upgrading
   • make full use of IT in education
   • create user friendly and attractive content to meet local demand

3 Enhance government services and forge a strong information
   industry:
   • make full use of IT in all public agencies to provide efficient social
     services to all citizens at reduced costs
   • provide full support, in particular to SMEs, for the local informa-
     tion industry.

The government was not so interested in making Thailand a regional information
hub, but much attention was paid to creating equal opportunity, individual
development, and other social aspects. However, the government launched a
new plan in 2000 before achieving its IT2000 targets, as it feared being left
behind Singapore and Malaysia. This compromised equal social development
in favour of the creation of an information hub city in Phuket.

In May 2000, the government issued a new plan called "Phuket IT City."
Today, the project is called "The Greater Phuket Digital Paradise Project (PhD)."
Four billion baht was required to build the information infrastructure, educational campuses, and other facilities for the project, but the project ran into
funding problems and there were criticisms about the readiness of Phuket's
basic infrastructure.[20]

Diffusion of PCs and the Internet in Thailand

PC and Internet penetration rates in Thailand are approximately 2 percent
and 1.6 percent respectively. Compared to Singapore, the penetration rates in
Thailand are exceedingly low, even lower than those of Malaysia. Thailand is
still at a very early stage but many statistics and IT-related literature anticipate
rapidly rising rates.

According to SG Security Research, PC penetration in Thailand will be 1.7
million people in 2001, 2 million in 2002, and 2.5 million in 2003. IDC predicts
that Internet users in Thailand will grow by 40 percent a year until 2004 and
the government estimates that Internet users will reach 14 million by 2008.[21]
However, Thailand is faced with the same problem as Malaysia.

According to the statistics of the NITC, approximately 70 percent of Internet users are resident in the Bangkok Metropolitan area. While there are 7.66
million available fixed telephone lines, there are 5.22 million connections.[22]
Of them, more than half are concentrated in the Bangkok Metropolitan area.
The *Bangkok Post* said, "Most major provincial towns outside Bangkok now
have a local number that users can call to access the Net, but a more pressing
problem exists in that telephone lines to homes or even businesses outside the
major provincial centres are virtually non-existent."[23] Even so, investment in
the telecommunications sector decreased from the 1980s to 1990s and the gap
has widened (see Table 6.7).

Another aspect is that a PC costs more than two or three times as much as the
monthly income of most people. However, PCs at home may not be necessary

because people can use them at school or in the workplace. In Thailand, 21.1 percent of secondary schools and 100 percent of universities are connected to the Internet. The fact that 69 percent of users are in their teens and twenties reflects the fact that most of them access the Internet at school or in the workplace.[24] However, accessing the Internet at these places puts some limitations on time and contents. A PC at home is key to expanding IT literacy.

One factor that always figured as an obstruction to Internet diffusion in Thailand is the monopolistic structure of the telecommunications sector. Internet service providers (ISPs) must give a 32 percent stake to the Communications Authority of Thailand (CAT) to get a license, whilst CAT does not make any capital investment. Also, ISPs must reserve another 3 percent shareholding for CAT employees on a voluntary basis. In addition, ISPs must use expensive CAT connection lines. These factors combine to make operating costs high. The Cabinet finally decided on the October, 26 2000, to liberalize the telecommunications sector. CAT and the Telephone Organization of Thailand (TOT) will be privatized by 2006.

Conclusion: does it meet people's requirements?

In Southeast Asia, every government has committed to IT policy. All of them are at different stages of development and each country has its own aims and understandings of the information society. However, from the experiences of Singapore, Malaysia, and Thailand, we can envisage some of the common issues that other countries in the region will have to face sooner or later.

First, there is a gap between the government and the public. In the case of Singapore, the government has prepared the information infrastructure with equal access and more than a hundred online public services, yet users do not make much use of newly developed services. PC and Internet penetration rates are one of the highest in the world, and there is IT education in every school, but usage is not sophisticated enough to utilize the new services. More must be done to develop people's consciousness, understanding, and computer literacy to bridge the gap between the government and the people. The issue is more serious for Malaysia and Thailand.

Second, in Malaysia and Thailand, there is a gap between urban and rural areas. For the time being, IT widens the gap between them as IT users are concentrated in metropolitan areas. Even fixed telephone lines are not yet consolidated in rural areas. Even so, their national IT policies do not pay much attention to the social aspects but focus on economic and business aspects. The case of Singapore tells us that the success of IT projects are, to a large degree, dependent on the basic IT foundation in society in terms of infrastructure and IT literacy, awareness, and understanding. Without them, the effect of the project will be much restricted, and only centered on certain cities.

Third, there is a gap between rich and poor. In the case of Malaysia, we see that the higher income states have higher Internet access rates. Even in Singapore, where people can afford to buy PCs and subscribe to the Internet more easily than in the other two countries, we see a similar trend. GDP per capita of Malaysia and Thailand is still about US$4,000 and US$2,000 respectively. Other countries in the region have significantly lower income levels. PCs and other related materials are still expensive for them, so income is always a key factor of diffusion.

Singapore has realized both economic development and an information society. Malaysia and Thailand are trying to leapfrog intermediate stages by benefiting from latecomer's advantage: technological innovations and wireless communications might help them to bridge the gap between urban and rural; liberalization and competition will reduce prices and may bridge the gap between rich and poor. The total impact and results of IT cannot be judged at this stage. We are still in the period of transition. However, as we see in the case of Singapore, there is no guarantee that people will respond to the new technology and apply it skilfully to everyday life. Policy-makers should recognise that ongoing projects may not meet with public demand and that ongoing national IT projects may be restricted to certain people and areas.

For many governments, IT becomes a political and economic goal. But IT is not a goal, it is an instrument for improving quality of life and developing a better society. While many governments commit themselves to IT, much attention is paid to the supply side of government and business activities. We should be more careful about other aspects, especially the needs of the people.

Notes

1. The land mass of Singapore is 618km^2. According to the latest census, the population of the country is 4,017,733 and Singapore residents number 3,263,209.
2. Yip 2000, p. 155.
3. Rodan 1998, p. 70.
4. TradeNet is an EDI system that links all kinds of companies involved in international trade. It reduced the submission time of applications and other related procedures from one to two days to fifteen minutes. SchoolLinks links primary and secondary schools with the Ministry of Education to improve the efficiency of schoolwork. LawNet is the first full text legal database in Southeast Asia.
5. OECF 1996, p. 50.
6. See http://www.s-one.gov.sg/overview/s1def01.html for more details.
7. Singapore ONE incorporates the latest digital technologies in an optimized integrated network. With its huge amounts of bandwidth, Singapore ONE delivers information to subscribers at least at a hundred times faster than the speed of Internet

dial-up through a normal 56.6kbps analog modem. See http://www.s-one.gov.sg/ overview/s1def01.html for more details.

8. Takayasu 2000, p. 142.
9. National Computer Board 2000. This is the fourth survey; the first was conducted in 1990.
10. The figure is as of October 2000 from Statistics for Telecom Service, available at http://www.ida.gov.sg.
11. CICC http://www.cicc.org.sg.
12. Vision 2020 is a national agenda aimed at making Malaysia a fully developed nation by 2020.
13. Multimedia Development Corporation (MDC), www.mdc.com.my/mdc/index/ html.
14. The core of infrastructure is Cyberjaya and Putrajaya. Cyberjaya will be a city of 7,000 hectares (core area is 2890ha) offering a world-class information communication network and facilities. Residential, commercial, public, and entertainment areas are also being developed. As a nucleus of the MSC, there will be about 500 companies and 100,000 residents in the area by the end of 2020. Putrajaya will be a new administrative city of 4580ha with 76,000 working people and 250,000 residents. It will be the center of electronic government by 2005. In July 1999, the Office of the Prime Minister and the residence of Prime Minister Mahathir moved to the city from Kuala Lumpur. For more details, see Kumagai 2000.
15. The six laws are Digital Signature Act, Computer Crime Act, Copyright Act, Telemedicine Act, Electronic Government Act, and Multimedia Communication Act.
16. Malaysian Business, April 1, 2000.
17. National Information Technology Council of Malaysia (NITC) 2000, Discussion Paper on "Access and Equity: Benchmarking for Progress."
18. NECTEC was established in 1987 to provide research and development in electronics, computers, telecommunications, and information. Since 1992, as a secretariat of NITC, NECTEC also plays the role of serving local electronics and computer industries and giving research funds to universities, etc.
19. See National Information Technology Committee (NITC), http://www.nitc.go.th/it-2000/exec.en.html.
20. *Nihon Keizai Shimbun*, June 23, 2000 and *Bangkok Post*, November 8, 2000.
21. *Bangkok Post*, 2000a.
22. The figure is from Koanantakool 2000.
23. *Bangkok Post* 2000b.
24. *Nihon Keizai Shimbun*, November 1, 2000.

References

Arun, M. and Yap, M. T. 2000, Singapore: the development of an intelligent island and social dividends of information technology, *Urban Studies*, 37(10), 1749–1756.
Bangkok Post 2000a, *Bangkok Post Economic Review 2000 Mid-Year Edition*, http://www.bangkokpost.net/MidYear2000/11ecommerce.html.
    2000b, *Database 10 Years*, http://www.bangkokpost.net/data10y/pages/new2.html.

Center for the International Cooperation for Computerization (CICC) 2000, *Report on Information Technology Policy and Industry in Asian Countries* (in Japanese), Tokyo, July 2000.

Corbitt, B. 1999, Exploring the social construction of IT policy – Thailand and Singapore, *Prometheus*, 17(3), 309–321.

Kajiwara, N. and Matsumoto, Y. 2000, IT situation in Asia Part 2 (in Japanese), *Overseas Investment*, September 2000, 4–23.

Khoong, C. M. (ed.) 1999, *IT2000: Beyond The Web Lifestyle*, Singapore: Prentice Hall.

Koanantakool 2000, The struggle towards a knowledge-based society, paper presented at Information Technology and Development Cooperation, July, 2000, Tokyo, Japan.

Kumagai, S. 2000, Sophistication of industrial structure and the policy for information communication industries (in Japanese), in K. Kitamura (ed.), *The Progress of Information and Approach of Asian Countries*, Chiba: IDE-JETRO, 157–195.

Multimedia Development Corporation (MDC), *What is the MSC?*, http://www.mdc.com.my/masc/index.html

National Computer Board (NCB) 2000, *Information Technology Household Survey 1999*, in Infocomm facts and figures, http://www.ida.gov.sg/Website/IDAhome.nsf/Home?OpenForm.

National Information Technology Committee (NITC) 1995, *IT2000*, http://www.nitc.go.th/it-2000/full.en.html

　2000, *Access and Equity: Benchmarking for Progress*, http://www.nitc.org.my/resources/AccessEquity.pdf.

OECD 2000, *Knowledge-based industries in Asia*, Paris.

Ohki, T. 2000, Progress of development of information telecommunication infrastructure in Asia and e-commerce (in Japanese), *RIM 3* (50), 16–29.

The Overseas Economic Cooperation Fund (OECF) 1996, *Information Technology Service Industries in Developing Countries: Cases in India and Singapore*, Tokyo.

Rodan, G. 1998, The Internet and political control in Singapore, *Political Quarterly*, 113(1), 63–89.

Takayasu, K. 2000, Initiative of computerization and economic development in Singapore, in K. Kitamura (ed.), *The Progress of Computerization and Approach of Asian Countries*, Chiba: IDE-JETRO, 121–155.

Tan, B. F., Corbett, P. S., and Wong, Y. Y. 1999, *Information Technology Diffusion in the Asia Pacific: Perspectives on Policy*, Electronic Commerce and Education, Hershey: IDEA Group Publishing.

Yip, S. G. 2000, *Asian Advantage: Key Strategies for Winning in the Asia-Pacific Region*, Cambridge: Perseus Books.

7 The IT revolution, the Internet, and telecommunications: the transition towards a competitive industry in the European Union

Emanuele Giovannetti

Introduction: pricing, penetration and the digital divide

European Union governments agreed on Tuesday to open access to the "last mile" of telephone lines into people's homes by January 1, 2001 . . .

Spokesman Per Haugaard said EU telecommunications ministers meeting in Luxembourg reached a political agreement on the Commission's proposal requiring full unbundling of the local loop by that date "in accordance with the wording of the regulation." The Commission, the EU's executive body, made a proposal in July under which EU countries would have to scrap remaining monopolies on phone lines into people's homes to make Internet access cheaper and faster. Such fast approval of a Commission proposal by EU ministers is virtually unheard of. Industry Commissioner Erkki Liikanen said in July that the plans to open up competition on the so-called "last mile" of copper wires connecting individuals to the telecommunications network would be "an adrenaline shot for industry and the Internet." He said the plans were the key to Europe catching up with the Internet revolution in the USA and Asia.

Source: EU telecommunications ministers open access to "last mile." Adapted from Reuters, October 3, 2000.

The pattern of cross-country Internet penetration and its consequences, for example e-commerce, is largely explained by the cost of Internet access. Persisting differences in penetration growth rates may lead to a growing "international digital divide", that is, diverging prospects for those with and without access to information and communication.

Access to and the development of information and communication resources are increasingly viewed as critical for economic and social development, and the pricing level and structure of Internet access is widely believed to be one of the major factors inhibiting existing users from staying online longer, and potential users from getting connected. Figure 7.1 shows the scatter of Internet hosts[1] per 1000 inhabitants for fifteen countries in the European Union, and the Internet access costs for a basket of twenty hours at peak time, including Internet service providers (ISPs) and public switch telephone networks (PSTN) charges. Figure 7.1 clearly shows that low access prices are at least a necessary condition for high Internet penetration.

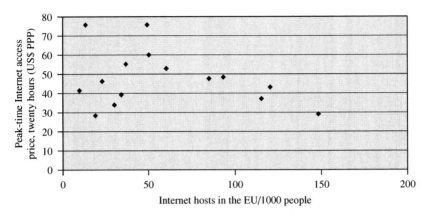

Figure 7.1 Internet hosts and Internet access prices, 2000 (Source: OECD 2000a)

In this chapter, I wish to review the regulatory debate informing ongoing liberalization in the European Union. Compared to the USA, Western Europe has indeed arrived late, despite early experiences in introducing competition into the telecommunications industry, and this shows in the different levels of Internet penetration. At the same time, we argue that there might be an unplanned late-adopter advantage in pushing towards full liberalization now, since technologies, particularly broadband, are just ripe for introducing competition into the "last mile" of the telecommunications network. This, as we will see, might be the most important network element for Internet diffusion and dissemination of the so-called Information Society.

Liberalization in the USA and the EU

The most relevant recent experience of regulatory reform comes from liberalization in the US telecommunications industry. This started with the divestiture of AT&T in 1984 which resulted from a negotiated settlement of an antitrust lawsuit. The twenty-two Bell Operating Companies (BOCs) have been reshaped into seven Regional Bell Operating Companies (RBOCs) and prevented, among other things, from providing almost any long-distance services. This resulted in the need to regulate the, now necessary, interconnection agreements between the newly established local monopolies and the competitive long-distance carriers such as AT&T, MCI, and Sprint. The main problems faced by the Federal Communications Commission (FCC), the federal regulatory authority, were in securing non-discriminatory interconnection conditions and evaluating the contribution they had to make towards the fixed costs of the local networks. In 1996, the Congress passed the Telecommunications Act, removing regulatory barriers to competition, including market segmentation between local and long-distance carriers.

Three sets of orders issued by the FCC (1996) defined the details of the implementation of this liberalization process. Among these are the Interconnect Orders which established the criteria for pricing access to unbundled network elements, usually the last mile or local loop. The philosophy on which the Act is based is captured in the following quotation from the FCC:

> Preventing access to unbundled loops would either discourage a potential competitor from entering the market in that area. . . . denying those consumers the benefits of competition, or cause the competitor to construct unnecessarily duplicative facilities . . . misallocating societal resources.[2]

In Western Europe, the UK also liberalized the telecommunications market early, in 1983. This has led to the construction of a wide cable network which, since the policy review in 1991, has been allowed to broadcast television programs and to provide telephone and Internet services to the residential market. The incumbent operator, British Telecom, was prevented from providing entertainment services. This opening up the telecommunications market based on competition with duplication in infrastructure has led to a cable network now reaching 12 million homes. However relevant, the investment in the new infrastructure has not been sufficient to deliver universal broadband services. This could be achieved with DSL technologies (discussed later in this chapter) or via third-generation mobile networks.

Germany realized early that it was possible to have local access competition without building a new network with its associated huge sunk costs. From October 1, 1996, the Network Access Ordinance (NZV) forced the incumbent, Deutsche Telekom, to provide unbundled access to all network elements including the local loop. Since January 1998, Deutsche Telekom has offered full unbundled services across the entire country. Germany's experience has shown that it is possible to open the local access market to competition within a short time and without geographical discrimination. The main principle of German regulation is that, whilst the line is still owned by Deutsche Telekom, customers belong, after the unbundling of the local loop, to the entrant.

Early competition within the US telecommunications industry is thought to be the source of its success in Internet penetration rates. Penetration in the USA is seven times that of the EU, and just over eight times that of Japan. One key element introduced by competition is the availability of fixed-fee, unmetered local access.

This feature of the Internet pricing structure is thought to be the reason for the different average times spent online in the USA and in countries where the unmetered option is not available (OECD 2000a). In turn, average online time is

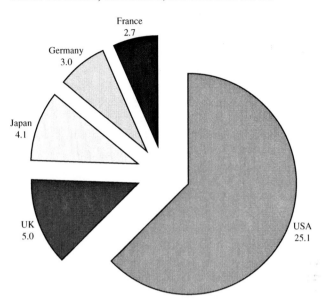

Figure 7.2 Additional Internet hosts per 1,000 inhabitants, September 1999 to March 2000 (Source: OECD 2000a)

a crucial indicator for the development of new contents and services, including multimedia services supporting electronic commerce.

Figure 7.2 shows the US advantage in the increasing number of Internet hosts per 1,000 inhabitants between September 1999 and March 2000.

Regulation and competition policies in the EU

Until recently, the telecommunications industry was dominated by state owned, vertically integrated monopolies, and the primary objectives of regulation were to prevent monopoly abuse and to improve efficiency by making each company responsible for a high fraction of its costs. In the telecommunications industry, the delivery of the final product or service to the final consumer takes place along a complex network architecture between call origination and termination, sometimes crossing continents and separately owned international, national, and local networks. The diffusion of the Internet made network interconnection issues more complex, since its transmission algorithm, the TCP/IP, decomposes an original message into many small information packets which can then follow different routes before being recomposed into a coherent message for the receiver.

Opening the telecommunications industry to competition, therefore, must be a gradual and complex process that is accompanied by delicate interconnection issues. Without some degree of cooperation between competing firms, the telecommunications network would be inoperable. In the present transitional period, when elements of monopoly power coexist with more competitive segments of the industry, there might be a need for an even greater intensity of regulation (see Bergman et al. 1998). Incumbent firms have huge advantages, such as the monopoly of essential facilities and a captured customer base, compared to new entrants which need to interconnect with the incumbents in order to reach end users. The final policy objective is, of course, to reach a phase in which competition has been established and the role of regulation would finally diminish. Transition from an initial, and long lasting, phase with an incumbent monopolist, through the stage of entry and interconnection via the network facilities of a still dominant incumbent, towards a fully competitive industry, will not occur by chance. Whilst the original transmission technologies induced a natural monopoly structure where high fixed and low marginal costs generated decreasing average costs with associated economies of scale, the new technologies of the IT revolution are eroding some of these natural monopoly characteristics. The early evolution of the Internet, as a network of independent networks, has been the most convincing evidence of the potential for digital technologies to eventually decouple the notion of network industries from that of natural monopoly.

In 1993, the European Community and its member states made a commitment to liberalize the telecommunications sector by January 1, 1998. The political objective was "the need to secure growth, employment and competitiveness and protect the interests of consumers, of ensuring a wide choice of providers and services, innovation, competitive prices and quality of service."[3] Following the full liberalization of January 1998 in ten of the EU member states, and the subsequent liberalization of Spain, Ireland, Luxembourg, and Portugal, Greece also decided to liberalize its telecommunications industry from December 31, 2000.[4] This means that all of the 380 million people of the European Union now share a legally liberalized telecommunications market. Nevertheless, whilst the regulatory framework has been rapidly evolving across Europe, the market structures are changing at a slower pace. In all EU member states, the incumbents continue to have a firm bottleneck control on competition in the local loop. To date, Europe has deregulated, but it has done this without divestiture.[5] As a consequence, whilst competition in long-distance and international telephony is developing at a fast pace, the incumbent operators still dominate local markets.

The "adrenaline shot" for implementing competition in the local access market in 2000 was followed by a period of disenchantment over the ability of the EU to effectively liberalize the telecommunications industry. Results from

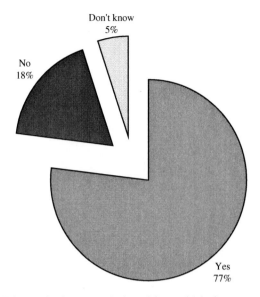

Figure 7.3 Are the former PTOs benefiting unfairly from current regulatory conditions regarding local loop unbundling? (Source: Total Telecom 2000)

a survey of 180 telecommunications professionals, shown in Figures 7.3, 7.4, and 7.5, demonstrate this. An overwhelming majority of respondents believe that:

1   the former public telecommunications operators (PTOs) have been benefiting unfairly from the current regulatory delays in introducing local loop unbundling;
2   the EU has been too slow in implementing the local loop unbundling;
3   this has adversely affected e-commerce development in Europe.

In the next section, we describe the events in the drive to introduce liberalization and unbundling by the end of 2000.

eEurope

In December 1999, the European Commission launched the eEurope initiative, with the objective of speeding up the process of bringing Europe online. As a complement to eEurope, the Commission also presented a communication on "Job strategies in the Information Society", analyzing the linkages between the Information Society and job prospects in Europe. The link between the changing technological environment and the labor markets, which we shall discuss later, is twofold: on the one hand, there will be an increase in the demand for workers

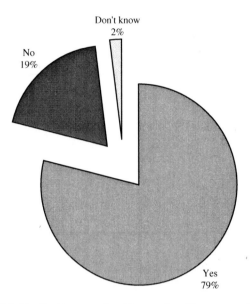

Figure 7.4 Has the European local loop unbundling process been too slow?
(Source: Total Telecom 2000)

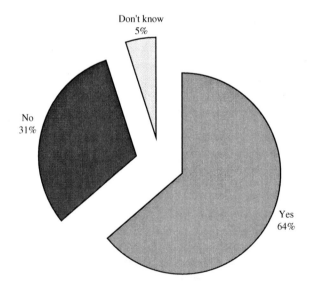

Figure 7.5 Has the development of e-commerce in Europe been adversely affected by
the unbundling timetable? (Source: Total Telecom 2000)

Table 7.1 e*Europe objectives*

1 A cheaper, faster, secure Internet
a   Cheaper and faster Internet access
b   Faster Internet access for researchers and students
c   Secure networks and smart cards
2 Investing in people and skills
a   European youth into the digital age
b   Working in the knowledge-based economy
c   Participation for all in the knowledge-based economy
3 Stimulating the use of the Internet
a   Accelerating e-commerce
b   Government online: electronic access to public services
c   Health online
d   European digital content for global networks
e   Intelligent transport systems

Source: http://europa.eu.int/abc/off/index_en.htm.

with skills appropriate to the technological transformations, whilst on the other, the IT revolution will make many existing products, processes, and business models obsolete, so that firms that are not able to adapt with sufficient rapidity will fail.

The *e*Europe plan identified three main objectives (see Table 7.1) for the EU to achieve as rapidly as possible. During the Lisbon European Council of March 2000, heads of state and governments committed themselves to achieving these *e*Europe targets by accelerating the development of an appropriate legal environment, and by supporting new infrastructures and services across Europe, all without compromising budgetary discipline. Moreover, benchmarking has been introduced as a method for ensuring efficiency in reaching the targets. Following the Lisbon Summit, the Feira European Council endorsed, in June, the *e*Europe action plan identifying unbundled access to the local loop as a short-term priority that would bring about a substantial reduction in the cost of using the Internet. On October 3, the EU telecommunications ministers reached an agreement on the Commission's proposal and finally, on October 26, 2000, the European Parliament passed regulation on unbundled access to the local loop into European law. Articles 3(1), 3(2) and 3(3) of the Regulation state that:

Notified operators shall publish from 31 December 2000, and keep updated, a reference offer for unbundled access to their local loop and related facilities. . . . Notified operators shall from 31 December 2000 meet reasonable requests . . . for unbundled access to their local loops and related facilities, under transparent, fair and non-discriminatory conditions . . . Notified operators shall charge prices for unbundled access of their local loop. . . . . set on the basis of cost orientation.

Article 4(2) states that

National regulatory authorities shall have the power to: impose changes of the reference offers for unbundled access to the local loop. . . . they may intervene. . . . in order to ensure non-discrimination, fair competition, economic efficiency and maximum benefit for users.

The application of the regulatory package in member states is the task of the national regulatory authorities (NRAs). In recent years, they have become fully operational throughout the EU and the main criteria they are required to satisfy are: independence from the operators, decision power, a clear division of competencies between NRAs, ministries, and national competition authorities, and speed and transparency of procedures. Other tasks are the setting of licensing procedures and fees in the different sectors of telephony, the enforcement of fair provision of interconnection, and the physical linking of networks and services to enable users of one network to communicate with those of another and/or to access services provided over another. In this respect, the Commission requires the provision of non-discriminatory tariffs, irrespective of the purpose for which interconnection is required.

The national frameworks for licensing are generally in place. A significant number of interconnection agreements have been signed, and the benchmarking of interconnection rates across Europe, established by the Commission, has given some of the lowest interconnection rates in the world. Local call origination and termination rates are of the order of 1 Eurocent/minute. Finally, each member state has at least two GSM and one DCS 1800 license for spectrum frequencies, and many more in some states, adding up to some eighty licenses across Europe.

Unbundling in practice

By 2001, European Internet penetration could well reach 20 percent, but this potential can only be realized if the EU's 380 million customers can access the Internet with broadband. The technologies delivering broadband access depend on the medium of access. The local fixed-line access markets account for approximately 40 percent of the revenues and 70 percent of the costs of the average incumbent operator, and they are particularly relevant as a source of broadband access to the Internet.

Three alternative strategies for fostering competition at the local market level have been suggested by the US Telecommunications Act. The first, and most obvious, is for entrants to build their own infrastructure and compete against the incumbent. This is the case of cable television networks, providing telephone services and competing against the incumbent. This is not a short-term strategy, since it requires large investment and produces local loop proliferation that might soon become unnecessary. A second option is entrants reselling services bought from the incumbent, so that entrants are both its customers and competitors. The rationale for this option is to let entrants into the market only if they are able to be more efficient than the incumbent. They pay for services at a retail price minus avoided costs, and their profitability is in delivering services at a lower cost than the incumbent. With this option, all the strategic network choices remain in the hands of the incumbent. Finally, the Telecommunications Act enables local loop unbunding (LLU), where the entrant leases the local loop. Unlike the resale option, with LLU the entrant takes over the continuation and termination of the call that would otherwise be left to the incumbent network.

The ability to provide differentiated services, thereby enhancing variety and consumer choice, depends on the exact network elements that have been unbundled. When unbundling reaches the twisted copper pair link that is then linked to its own signalling switches, the entrant can provide digital subscriber line (DSL) broadband access. This alternative is considered extremely important for its potential influence on Internet access prices and, therefore, for penetration. This possibility, of course, does not occur with resale, where the entrant is forced to provide the services chosen by the incumbent. Without any of these three options for local market competitions – infrastructure building, resale, or LLU – entrants are reduced to competing on different grounds, such as long-distance, Internet access through dial-up, or other value added services.

The advantage of LLU over the alternatives is that it allows entry for efficient firms that do not have the financial strength to establish a new local network. Moreover, LLU creates the possibility of local market competition without duplicating facilities. Armstrong (1999) suggests a finer argument in favour of the LLU: participating in local market competition without sunk costs has an option value for the entrant. It reveals the profitability of future infrastructure investment once the entrant has come to know the market. LLU can therefore be seen as a test bed, not as an alternative, to infrastructure competition.

Since fixed telephony now reaches some 190 million subscribers in the EU, whilst mobile reaches some 75 million, and cable some 40 million, the local unbundling of the incumbent's networks is, in the short term, the most important step for Europe's chances in the world's Internet market. It can introduce competition in infrastructure without wasteful network duplication, can provide an appropriate response to the demand for broadband, and gives incentives to reduce prices and expand capacity. Finally, the unbundling of the local loop can be a valuable instrument for competition policy in a scenario where vertical and horizontal mergers are taking place to (re-)create integrated networks able to provide end-to-end products.

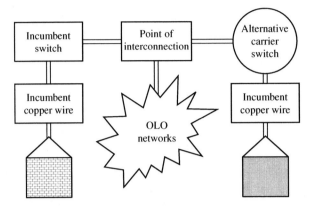

Figure 7.6 Alternative modes of competition

Figure 7.6 provides a simplified description of two alternative ways of competing in the local access market. The shaded house is connected via LLU to an other licensed operator (OLO) switch whilst the brick house is connected with the alternative carrier via an interconnection passing through the incumbent switch.

Technological opportunities

The old telecommunications industry characterized by the monopoly provision of voice telephony is changing rapidly: first, because voice telephony can be provided by alternative methods such as mobile, Internet, cable, and satellite telephony; and, second, because the original copper pair can now be used for entirely new services, such as broadband Internet access with its host of multimedia applications. This is due to the increase in bandwidth made possible by the appearance of new technologies of the xDSL type, such as asymmetric digital subscriber line (ADSL)[6] or very high rate digital subscriber line (VDSL).[7] The impact of these technologies on the diffusion of the Information Society is due to their role in facilitating unmetered, always-on access to broadband Internet.

Technically there are different options for opening competition, i.e., unbundling the local loop. These can be grouped in the following ways:

1   full unbundling of the local loop
2   shared use of the copper line
3   high-speed bit stream access.

In the first case, with *full unbundling of the local loop*, the incumbent which has built the network rents the final link, the copper pair, to an OLO which operates a competitive communication system. With this unbundling option, the entrant has the chance of supplying a full range of services, including high-speed data applications through a DSL technology. With the second option, the *shared use of the copper line*, the incumbent only offers the entrant the possibility of delivering high-speed data services using its own ADSL modems. This requires introducing a *splitter* between the customer premises and the incumbent's switch. Under this option, only the high frequency spectrum of the local loop, the part used by DSL systems, is open to third-party access. Finally, the third option of *high-speed bit stream access* does not imply a real unbundling of the local loop; with this option the incumbent provides a high-speed connection to the customer's premises and then makes this link accessible to competing operators, either to provide high-speed services or to carry traffic to their own point of presence.

Pricing the local loop

The main practical and theoretical problem related to unbundling is the pricing of access to unbundled network components. The FCC devised a methodology called the total element long-run incremental cost (TELRIC) method to price the lease of the local loop. TELRIC is "The forward-looking costs that can be attributed directly to the provision of services using that element, which include a reasonable return on investment, plus a reasonable share of forward-looking joint and common costs" (FCC Interconnection Order 1996).

The incremental part of these costs is the difference between a firm's total costs with and without the provision of a given service, due to individual network elements. The common costs are all the costs that are not incremental and not imputable to the provision of a given service. Both these notions of cost include capital costs, the rate of return that invested capital could otherwise earn with alternative, comparable risk projects.

The presence of common and incremental costs is at the origin of much of the debate on the pricing of unbundled network elements (UNEs) as it is for the LLU. Earning economic profits on a UNE might indeed be required in order to recover the common costs of the joint network infrastructure of which the UNE is an element.

Sidack and Spulber (1997) argue against the pricing rules set by the FCC, maintaining that the presence of common costs and of regulated cross-subsidies mandating the incumbent local exchange carriers (ILEC) to provide services at negative profits, would also make them unable to recover their costs, potentially leading to under-investment in local access networks. The authors claim that "Regulation must allow the incumbent LEC the opportunity to earn a reasonable profit – a zero economic profit – across the full aggregation of regulated services that the local exchange carrier (LEC) is required to offer" (Sidack and Spulber

1997, p. 1089). To this end they propose a pricing formula for the lease of the UNE, based on a combination of what they called market-determined efficient component-pricing rule (M-ECPR) and competitively neutral end-user charges. This way of pricing LLU is based on the sum of direct and opportunity costs incurred in providing the UNE, where the opportunity costs are given by the UNE's value in *its best alternative use*, given the actual market conditions.

Economides (1998) strongly criticises the M-ECPR, on the grounds that it is based on *private* opportunity costs, since these are calculated with respect to the final price of the service provided by the unbundled network element which would typically include supernatural profits of the incumbent as well as past inefficiencies. Economides suggests, instead, that only social opportunity costs should be included.

Regulation during the transition: economic considerations

The previous distinction between private and social opportunity costs, introduced by Economides in debating the pricing formula for the LLU, leads to a very interesting set of issues on the economics of interconnection. We mentioned at the beginning of this chapter that, paradoxically, the transition from a monopolistic network industry toward a competitive one, requires intense regulation because of the presence of highly contentious interconnection issues.

Features of deregulated equilibrium access prices can be best analyzed within a game theoretic framework, since these are prices arising from the economic interaction of a few self-motivated players. The effects of different regulatory strategies can then be evaluated against the unregulated case. Strategic access pricing problems in network industries have been analyzed in detail in the economic literature. Armstrong, Doyle, and Vickers (1996) studied the problem of access pricing arising when a vertically integrated dominant firm controls the supply of a key input for its competitors. In this framework, the upstream monopolist has a strong incentive to adopt anti-competitive behavior by setting high access prices, thus raising the downstream rival's cost. Laffont, Rey, and Tirole (1998) developed a model of competing interconnected networks. In their model, interconnection is bilateral so that each network pays the other an access charge to terminate calls originated on its own network and directed to the other network customers. They found that access charges can be used as a collusive device to raise prices and profits for the two networks. Armstrong (1998) showed that in a two-way unregulated network the equilibrium access price is chosen to maximize joint profits if there is enough product differentiation. Economides and Woroch (1992) analyzed an integrated network where a dominant firm controls an end-to-end route, and a competitor supplying an alternative link for the final part of the route needs to connect to the dominant

Table 7.2 *Local loop pricing (euros)*

Country	One-off charge	Monthly rental	Service availability
Austria	54.50	12.35	Since July 1999 RIO available since June 26, 2000
Belgium	n/a	n/a	Public consultation was carried out between April 1 and July 1, 1999
Denmark	47.08	8.30	Since September 1, 1999
Finland	n/a	n/a	n/a
France	n/a	n/a	n/a
Germany	97.98	12.99	Since February 8, 1999
Greece	n/a	n/a	n/a
Iceland	n/a	n/a	n/a
Ireland	n/a	n/a	n/a
Italy	151.85	13.58	Since May 2000
Liechtenstein	n/a	n/a	n/a
Luxembourg	n/d	n/d	n/d
Netherlands	133.90	12.50	March 1999
Norway	n/a	n/a	n/a
Portugal	n/a	n/a	Public consultation ends September 1, 2000
Spain	90.15	30.05	March 26, 1999
Sweden	94.80	15.00	March 2000
UK	248.84	15.30	January 1, 2001 (previously set for July 1, 2001)

Source: The World Regulatory Colloquium 2000.

firm for the first part. The competitor is, therefore, at the same time complementing and competing with the dominant network. In this framework, they found that the dominant firm, which has monopoly power on a bottleneck, does not benefit from foreclosing the rival network: without interconnection with the rival, the integrated network earns monopoly profits on its end-to-end service but it loses the profits arising from the monopolized supply to the hybrid service.

Giovannetti (2002) analyzed access prices in a stylized Internet network, finding that network interconnection lowers retail and access prices only when the downstream retail services are not very differentiated.

In practice, prices for the lease of the local loop in the EU are either those set out by the incumbent in what is called a Reference Interconnection Offer (RIO) or those defined by the national regulator. Table 7.2 shows the prices for a transferred unbundled local loop copper pair in the EU countries in which LLU has been made available.

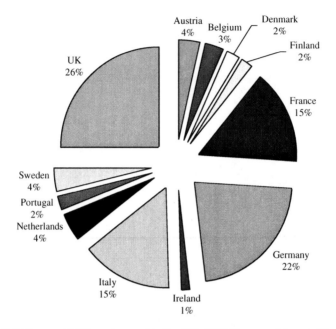

Figure 7.7 Shares of ICT employment in the EU, 1997 (Source: elaborated from OECD 2000b)

Concluding on human capital bottlenecks

Recent, ongoing, and future developments in technological opportunity and regulatory liberalization are rapidly transforming the ICT industry, both world-wide and in the EU. However, whilst the physical bottlenecks of the telephone networks are being opened up, both by regulatory pressure and by new satellite and/or wireless technologies that bypass part of the wired local market access, new constraints in the form of human capital are appearing.

Figure 7.7 shows the distribution of IT employment in the EU (excluding Greece, Luxembourg, and Spain). The total number of IT employees amounted to 4.44 million, roughly equivalent to the number of IT employees in the USA. The European telecommunications industry witnessed an increase of 2 percent in employment in 1998, but the European Information Technology Observatory (EITO) (2000) estimates that there was a shortfall of 510,000 jobs in the IT sector in 1998, out of 9.3 million existing "equivalent IT jobs." This shortage is estimated to be growing at a compound annual rate of 33 percent, reaching a level of 1.6 million over 12.3 million employees by 2002 (see Figure 7.8).

These shortages are a byproduct of the widespread increase in demand for technically skilled employees and a structural weakness of the European

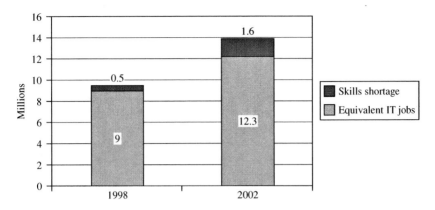

Figure 7.8 IT employment and skills shortage in Western Europe, 1998 and 2002 (Source: EITO 2000)

educational systems in producing an adequate number of graduates in the relevant fields. The entire process is, of course, aggravated by the obsolescence rate of existing technical skills.

As a result of the IT revolution, the digital divide is likely to increase within the EU: the Commission Communication on strategies for jobs in the Information Society, reports that "Internet penetration rates vary widely among member states as well as according to income and gender. The vast majority of European Internet users is still concentrated in the north of Europe. . . . High income individuals are about twice as likely to be Internet users (37 percent) as medium income individuals (19 percent) and nearly three times as likely as low-income ones (13 percent)" (Commission of the European Communities, 2000, p. 7).

To prepare the future European workforce, the Commission has made the following recommendations:[8]

- to link every European school to the Internet, to increase the multimedia capability of their PCs, and to ensure that all teachers are verifiably competent in Information Society skills by the end of 2002
- to provide every worker with the opportunity for achieving Information Society literacy by the end of 2003
- to set up framework conditions and practical arrangements to enable telework to take place on a wide scale by the end of 2000
- to increase capacity and uptake in tertiary level education, maintaining gender balance and matching industry requirements by the end of 2003
- to promote IT courses at secondary level education, including the use of industry-certified training courses from 2000.

The resulting effects of the IT revolution coupled with the progressive globalization of the IT labor market will depend on the balance between different forces. More programming intensive activities might be outsourced to different countries, as the development of the Indian software industry analyzed in this book by Kattuman describes. Western Europe could also act as a brain magnet, both for highly skilled workers educated in the Central and Eastern European countries and from other developing countries. Western Europe is also risking a *brain drain* toward the USA. Likely consequences of the human capital bottlenecks are: rising salaries, worldwide competition to attract the knowledge workers, and, on a wider scale, inability to implement the full range of desired IT projects because of the lack of qualified human resources, potentially leading to a slower pace in fulfilling the promises of the Information Society.

Acknowledgments

The author gratefully acknowledges the generous support of the Institute of Developing Economies (IDE-JETRO) and the British Economic and Social Research Council under the grant reference number R000238563.

Notes

1. *Network Wizards* uses the following definition of hosts: "A host is a domain name that has an IP address record associated with it. This would be any computer system connected to the Internet (via full or part-time, direct or dial-up connections)," see http://www.nw.com.
2. US Federal Communications Commission, First Report and Order in the Matter of the Implementation of the Local Competition Provisions in the Telecommunications Act of 1996.
3. Commission of The European Communities 1999, *Fifth Report on the Implementation of the Telecommunications Regulatory Package Brussels* 10.11.1999. European Commission.
4. The Greek Parliament voted a liberalization bill on November 21, 2000.
5. By doing so, the EU has inverted the temporal pattern of the USA of the liberalization process.
6. "ADSL is a new modem technology, converts existing twisted-pair telephone lines into access paths for multimedia and high-speed data communications. ADSL transmits more than 6Mbps (optionally up to 8Mbps) to a subscriber, and as much as 640kbps (optionally up to 1Mbps) in both directions. ADSL can literally transform the existing public information network from one limited to voice, text, and low resolution graphics to a powerful, ubiquitous system capable of bringing multimedia, including full motion video, to everyone's home this century." (Source: http://www.adsl.com)

7. "In simple terms, VDSL transmits high-speed data over short reaches of twisted-pair copper telephone lines, with a range of speeds depending upon actual line length. The maximum downstream rate under consideration is between 51 and 55Mbps over lines up to 1000ft (300 meters) in length. Downstream speeds as low as 13Mbps over lengths beyond 4000ft (1500 meters) are also in the picture. Upstream rates in early models will be asymmetric, just like ADSL, at speeds from 1.6 to 2.3Mbps. Both data channels will be separated in frequency from bands used for POTS and ISDN, enabling service providers to overlay VDSL on existing services. At present the two high-speed channels will also be separated in frequency. As needs arise for higher speed upstream channels or symmetric rates, VDSL systems may need to use echo cancellation." (Source: http://www.adsl.com)

8. For the full set of recommendations see the Commission of The European Communities. 2000.

References

Armstrong, M. 1998, Network interconnection in telecommunications, *The Economic Journal*, 108, 545–564.

1999, Arguments for local loop unbundling, paper presented at the conference on "Local Loop Unbundling for Whom and at What Price?", London Business School, June 1999.

Armstrong, M., Doyle, C., and Vickers, J. 1996, The access pricing problem: a synthesis, *Journal of Industrial Economics*, 44, 131–150.

Bergman, L., Doyle, C., Gual, J., Hultkrantz, L., Neven, D., Röller, L. H., and Waverman, L. 1998, *Europe's Network Industries: Conflicting Priorities*, London: CEPR.

Commission of The European Communities 1999, *Fifth Report on the Implementation of the Telecommunication Regulatory Package*, Brussels COM (1999) 537 final, http://europa.eu.int/comm/information_society/policy/telecom/5threport/pdf/5threp99_en.pdf.

2000, *Strategies for Jobs in the Information Society*, Brussels, COM (2000) 48 final.

Economides, N. 1998, The Telecommunications Act of 1996 and its Impact, Discussion Paper EC-98-08, Stern School of Business, New York University.

Economides, N. and Woroch, G. 1992, Benefits and Pitfalls of Network Interconnection, Discussion Paper no. EC-92-31, Stern School of Business, New York University.

European Information Technology Observatory (EITO) 2000, *European Information Technology Observatory Millennium Edition*, Mainz.

Federal Communications Commission 1996, *First Report and Order in the Matter of the Implementation of the Local Competition Provisions in the Telecommunications Act of 1996*, Washington DC.

Giovannetti, E. 2002, Interconnection, differentiation and bottlenecks in the Internet, *Information Economics and Policy*, 14(3), 385–404.

Laffont, J.-J., Rey, P., and Tirole, I. 1998, Network competition: 1. Overview and nondiscriminatory pricing, *Rand Journal of Economics*, 29, 1–37.

OECD 2000a, *Local Access Pricing and e-Commerce*, http://www.olis.oecd.org/olis/ 2000doc.nsf/linkto/+dsti-iccp-tisp(2000)1-final.
2000b, *Measuring the ICT Sector*, http://www.oecd.org/dsti/sti/it/prod/ measuring_ict.pdf.
Sidak, J. G. and Spulber, D. F. 1997, The tragedy of the telecommons: government pricing of unbundled network elements under the Telecommunications Act of 1996, *Columbia Law Review*, 97(4), 1080–1161.
Total Telecom 2000, http://www.totaltele.com.
The World Regulatory Colloquium 2000, http://www.regulate.org.

8 Globalizing information? The IT revolution in Central and Eastern Europe

Tanga McDaniel

Introduction

For the Central and Eastern Europe countries (CEECs), the information age has corresponded to an age of transition from centrally planned to market economies. The influence of the move toward a knowledge society on most aspects of their economy therefore becomes muddied by the impact of transition itself. Similarly, the adoption of IT is associated with transition reforms. For example, one motivation for liberalization and economic openness is the anticipation of benefiting from information architecture. Communication infrastructure varies in CEECs, but is outdated or insufficient in some countries. The need for significant upgrading expenditures along with the benefits of being connected to neighboring networks can provide additional incentives for economic reforms. Moreover, the collapse of the Council for Mutual Economic Assistance (CMEA) in 1991 began a new trading era for countries of the former Soviet Union, along with the associated need for trading new partners.

In this chapter, we discuss many of the IT issues confronting CEECs. The state of the world among these countries differs for a number of reasons, location being just one. The magnitude of foreign direct investment, labor force skills, electricity infrastructure, and private sector participation will also influence national access to and use of information.

It is convenient to discuss the Eastern European countries in three groups: Central Europe, the Baltics, and Eastern Europe. Countries within groups have similarities, yet differences across groups are rather striking. Additionally, there are substantial differences in data availability and conformity among these countries, so we provide statistics on important IT indicators, with more detailed information on country-specific experiences where the data allows. Data is more readily available for countries with organizational memberships. The Czech Republic, Hungary, and Poland have recently joined the OECD, for example, and there is better information for these countries with respect to Internet cost and usage.

The remainder of this chapter proceeds as follows: the next section describes the penetration of IT resources in CEECs according to standard indicators and discusses different experiences which have influenced the adoption of IT. Then I focus on factors which inhibit the spread of IT across Central and Eastern Europe, particularly the span of network infrastructures and the cost of using information resources. Finally, I look at issues relating to human capital.

IT adoption and international integration

The speed of change in the information sector is so rapid that data on indicators such as the number of Internet hosts in a country are soon obsolete. Many transition economies are witnessing growth rates in information sectors of 100 percent a year. For some, this still means that their absolute penetration level is low. Others however have surpassed the average of EU members in a number of key areas. It is not surprising that much of the data and information for IT research comes from Internet sites as opposed to hardcopy sources; as data becomes obsolete so quickly one relies heavily on this sector to produce rapid updates about itself and its users.

In CEECs, the fact that IT use is low is not so much a matter of potential, but is rather a consequence of a number of important obstacles. The lack of sufficient infrastructure – both telecommunications and electricity – is one such obstacle, especially for the Eastern European group, and this represents a medium- to long-term problem that most of these countries will require financial assistance or foreign investment to overcome. Conversely, other obstacles to usage in the short run could be overcome by measures that bring down the cost of local phone services. Increased liberalization is one course which should be pursued, but the restructuring of access charges would also benefit those who are already users.

Proximity along with the need for cross-border trading has made it easier for some countries to receive funding from their richer neighbors. Many transition economies are not in a position to fund significant infrastructure enhancements and this fact further distances them from the West as their location makes it difficult to access the European networks.[1]

The remainder of this section describes two aspects of IT adoption: (a) penetration of information resources; and (b) examples of national attributes which have enhanced or hindered utilization. These aspects are in turn related to the scale of integration with the international community, either directly through infrastructure connection and trade relations or indirectly through receipts of foreign investment.

Penetration

Table 8.1 provides data on standard IT indicators in CEECs. While the penetration of telephone mainlines is not vastly different across regions or countries,

Table 8.1 ICT penetration by region and country, 1998

Country	GNP per capita	Telephone mainlines per 1,000 inhabitants	PCs per 1,000 inhabitants	Internet hosts per 10,000 inhabitants	Internet hosts per 10,000 inhabitants, 1999	Mobile phones per 1,000 people	Waiting list (thousands)	Waiting time (years)	Population
Central Europe									
Czech Republic	5,150	364	97	64	72	94	141	0.3	10,294,900
Hungary	4,480	336	59	73	83	105	80.3	0.2	10,114,000
Poland	3,910	228	44	26	28	50	1801	1.8	38,666,200
Slovak Republic	3,700	286	65	26	33	87	174.6	1.2	5,391,000
Slovenia	9,780	375	251	91	90	84	9.2	0.2	1,982,000
Baltics									
Estonia	3,360	343	34	131	152	170	59	2.0	1,449,710
Latvia	2,540	302	–	33	43	68	39.9	3.3	2,449,000
Lithuania	2,380	300	54	24	27	72	74.5	1.3	3,703,000
Eastern Europe									
Albania	820	31	–	0	0	1	167.1	5.5	3,339,000
Bosnia	900	91	–	1	1	7	70	2.9	3,768,000
Bulgaria	1,220	329	27	7	9	15	41.6	7.0	8,257,000
Croatia	4,650	348	112	14	15	41	72	0.8	4,501,000
Macedonia	1,690	199[a]	–	2	3	15	40	1.7	2,009,900
Moldova	380	150	6	–	1	2	70	4.0	4,298,000
Romania	1,430	162	10	6	7	29	966	4.3	22,503,000

Notes:
[a] 1997.

Source: World Bank and ITU World Telecom Development Report, 1999.

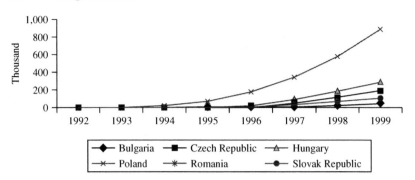

Figure 8.1 Total Internet subscribers, 1992 to 1999 (Source: World Bank, *Information Infrastructure Indicators, 1999–2010*)

the variability in PCs and Internet hosts is much more obvious. Within regions, Slovenia, Estonia, and Croatia are outliers with substantially more computer readiness, either with respect to PCs, Internet hosts, or both. In Croatia, for example, telephone mainlines reached approximately 35 percent of the population in 1998 and over 11 percent had a PC. This figure stands out relative to even Poland and Hungary. It is perhaps unsurprising that these three outlier countries are also the richest with respect to GNP per capita in their region. Slovenia's penetration level is impressive compared to a large number of EU countries. In 1998 Slovenia surpassed France, Greece, Italy, Spain, and Portugal in PCs per capita; both Slovenia and Estonia surpassed Greece, Italy, Spain, and Portugal in numbers of Internet hosts.

Figure 8.1 shows the numbers of Internet subscribers in six countries between 1992 and 1999. The growth pattern among these is very similar, with the four Central European countries doing better than the Eastern European countries (Bulgaria and the Slovak Republic are very close, with Romania having slightly more subscribers). Growth only begins in 1995 and with a much more rapid rate in Poland. Yet, even there, absolute subscription rates are low. That 1995 is an important year is not too surprising in the context of the "Internet timeline."[2] For instance, it was only in 1991 that menus such as Gopher were introduced and, more importantly, the World Wide Web was also released that year. Browsers such as Mosaic and Netscape were introduced in 1993 and 1994, respectively, and major companies such as America Online only began to provide Internet service in 1995. The explosive growth of the Internet around this time also coincides with Intel Corporation's introduction of the Pentium chip in 1994.

The number of mobile phone users continues to rocket in most parts of Europe. The number of users in Estonia already equals half the number of fixed-line users and in Hungary the ratio is nearly one-third. This technology could eventually be an important substitute for countries with poor fixed-line networks. However, mobile usage in Albania, Bosnia, and Moldova remains low.

National characteristics and utilization

The current economic status as well as readiness to participate in the information age can be attributed to a long list of national characteristics and circumstances which are well beyond the scope of this chapter. To question the effect of advances in communication technologies on any aspect of the economies of CEECs involves some discussion of the reforms occurring during transition, along with the implications of those reforms. Even for the most advanced economies there is little data available on the impact to date of information and communication technologies on national productivity. For CEECs, factors which are related to the transition process will either help or hinder the transformation to knowledge societies, and we discuss several of these including: membership in the CMEA, location and organizational memberships, and the cost of using information resources relative to wages. Other factors may slow the rate of growth of the information sector in the future and these are discussed in the following section.

CMEA membership

A significant number of the CEECs were long-time members of the CMEA which was created in 1949 and only dissolved in 1991. Previous members within the former Soviet Union include Estonia, Latvia, Lithuania, and Moldova; previous members within Eastern Europe include Bulgaria, Czechoslovakia, Hungary, Poland, and Romania; Albania was a member only until 1961. Essentially, under the leadership of the Soviet Union, CMEA members had very specialized production roles, and a large share of their output was traded among other member nations. The collapse of the Council forced members to restructure their production activities as well as find new trading partners. This has had a number of consequences that manifest themselves indirectly through national IT usage. For example, Hungary was in a relatively good position post-CMEA because its specialization had been to serve as a link between the EU and other CMEA members for trading technology goods (Sercovich et al. 1999). Partly through this process, Hungary had established a reputation among EU countries which helped it to attract foreign investors as well as new trading partners. As with most CEECs, Hungary's primary trading partners are now EU member states.

The Baltic countries provide an illustration of how the ending of the CMEA and the industrial restructuring that followed has resulted in an urban/rural divide that will be difficult to bridge. As with many countries of the former Soviet Union, the production sector of Estonia, Latvia, and Lithuania was dominated by heavy industry. Parts of the economy, particularly rural areas, were classic "mono-enterprise regions"; that is, regions consisting of large vertically integrated enterprises whose outputs were dictated from Moscow. In addition to employment, the businesses typically supplied health care, housing, and education. The collapse of the Soviet Union along with the accompanying supply of low-cost raw materials and guaranteed output market left these areas economically shattered. Although the capitals and larger cities in the Baltics are now attractive areas for new business, these former mono-enterprise areas continue to have difficulty recovering (OECD 2000a).

The necessity to transform production sectors has led to a shift in the Baltics away from industry and manufacturing toward service-related industries. In 1995, the value added in the transport, storage, and communication sectors from each country surpassed not only that of the other CEECs, but also the USA, Japan, and the UK.

Organizational memberships

The possibility of a fifth European Union enlargement encouraged more rapid reforms in those countries wishing to apply for accession. Of the fifteen CEECs in this study, ten have applied for EU membership: Bulgaria, the Czech Republic, Estonia, Hungary, Latvia, Lithuania, Poland, Romania, the Slovak Republic, and Slovenia. Three of these recently joined the OECD: the Czech Republic (1995), Hungary (1996), and Poland (1996). In meeting the requirements for EU accession these countries have simultaneously made changes which have enhanced their IT capabilities. Five of these – the Czech Republic, Hungary, Poland, Estonia, and Slovenia, denoted TE-5 – are on the 'fast-track' route to accession, and have several things in common. First, apart from Estonia they each share a border with an existing EU member, and, of the Baltic countries, Estonia is "closest" to a member state. Second, using the average of 1995–1999, Slovenia, the Czech Republic, Hungary, and Poland have the highest GNP per capita among the CEECs (with Estonia only just behind the Slovak Republic). Third, within the sample we consider, they are among the seven highest recipients of foreign direct investment per capita.

One criteria of EU membership is that candidate countries prove ready to cope with the competitive pressures within the EU. To the extent that IT capability improves efficiency, the CEECs that fall below the EU average with respect to important indicators will be competitively disadvantaged. On the other hand, one force attracting enterprise to this region is the relatively high skilled, low wage labor force. As foreign enterprises shift their companies or expand their corporate base to include CEECs, they bring with them the technological skills and resources the countries lack on their own. These two forces

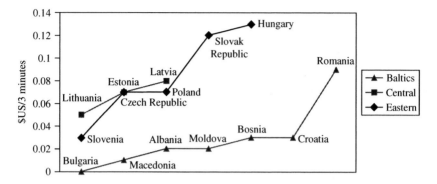

Figure 8.2 Local telephony prices, 1998 (Source: World Bank, *World Development Indicators 2000*, Table 5.10 Power and Communications)

(the attractiveness of the labor force versus the current lack of essential infrastructure) can interact in a number of ways in the future. As the skill base increases so will wages in these sectors, otherwise there is the threat that the newly trained workers will find it more desirable to emigrate. If this happens more quickly than the infrastructure expands, then one of the major benefits which brought those companies to the region will no longer remain. Conversely, if infrastructure growth is rapid, then even if wages are also increasing rapidly, those companies will be no worse off than if they had located elsewhere in Europe and maybe even better off if their initial outlays were lower.

Cost of information

One reason that the USA holds a dominant position in statistics on Internet usage is because of free local telephone access. This luxury is not commonly available in Europe. Although there are a growing number of free ISPs in many European countries, this term is very deceptive. Even if customers receive free connection for unlimited periods, there is still the local phone rate to pay while connected. Figure 8.2 shows the price of local calls in each country in the sample by region. There is a clear ranking of charges among the regions which favors the group of Eastern European countries, yet this in itself is not very informative as it is not necessarily indicative of infrastructure availability. For instance, in Table 8.1 which shows waiting times for new phone lines, the ranking is reversed. Although Bulgarians with phones pay least for local calls, there are 416,000 people on a seven-year waiting list for telephone service; this is approximately 11 percent of the population. James (1999) suggests that mobile phones may act as a substitute in developing countries where waiting lists are high for fixed lines. The same argument might be applied to CEECs, though the evidence here is difficult to judge.

Table 8.2 *Internet access for twenty hours at peak, discounted PSTN rates, including VAT, 2000*

	PSTN fixed charge		PSTN usage charge		ISP charge		Total	
	US$	PPP	US$	PPP	US$	PPP	US$	PPP
Italy	12.43	13.97	12.35	13.88	0.00	0.00	24.78	27.85
USA	14.29	14.29	2.33	2.33	16.45	16.45	33.07	33.07
Japan	18.45	10.61	22.71	13.05	19.87	11.42	61.04	35.08
Norway	19.17	14.52	25.50	19.32	11.82	8.95	56.49	42.79
Spain	11.55	14.08	26.00	31.71	0.00	0.00	37.55	45.79
UK	19.12	16.48	43.00	37.07	0.00	0.00	62.12	53.55
Poland	5.88	10.89	31.77	58.83	0.00	0.00	37.65	69.73
Czech Republic	4.82	11.22	30.10	69.99	12.35	28.73	47.27	109.93
Hungary	9.78	22.23	35.55	80.79	12.57	28.58	57.91	131.60
OECD average	12.62	13.54	21.08	24.04	10.23	12.01	43.93	49.59

Source: OECD 2000c, July (from table A2).

On average, local phone charges for one hour are US$1.68, US$1.33, and US$0.57 in Central Europe, the Baltics, and Eastern Europe, respectively, not including fees to an ISP. One sees here the relative burden for these countries (particularly households) of using the Internet as a source of information compared to Western economies where average local phone fees are lower and GNP per capita is higher. Table 8.2 and Figure 8.3 illustrate this more clearly. Table 8.2 presents total access prices for twenty peak time hours of connection in the three CEECs that are OECD members and a selection of other member countries. Figure 8.3 maps the access fees against the number of Internet hosts for these same members. Among all of the OECD countries, Hungary and the Czech Republic have the highest access cost and have among the lowest number of Internet hosts. Access cost in Poland, the Czech Republic, and Hungary are approximately US$70, US$110, and US$130 (PPP) per month respectively for twenty hours. This can be compared to the OECD average of just under US$50 per month. Most countries with a number of Internet hosts above the OECD average also have lower access fees, the extreme example being the USA with more than 1,600 hosts per 10,000 inhabitants and access costs of approximately US$35 per month. Italy is the second lowest in total charges among all OECD countries for twenty off-peak hours of connection (Korea is first), but this advantage diminishes as the number of connection hours increases. For thirty hours, Italy moves to fourth and at forty hours the USA takes the top spot while Italy moves to sixth.

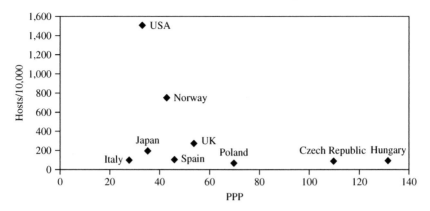

Figure 8.3 Access prices and Internet hosts (Source: OECD 2000c)

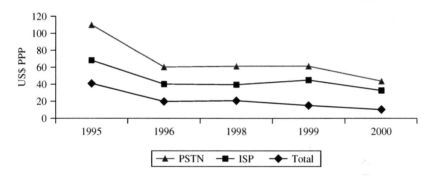

Figure 8.4 Trends in Internet access pricing at peak rates for twenty hours (Source: OECD 2000c, Figure 10)

In the absence of liberalization, there are a number of pricing arrangements that would reduce overall access fees. Arrangements differ very little across Europe, and all European OECD country charges for local phone calls are metered. Only Hungary and the UK offer a choice of either metered or un-metered charges for Internet access (OECD 2000c).[3] Because of competition and new entry in the ISP market, prices for that portion of the market have declined and this has brought down total access prices since 1995. Yet PSTN charges have moved very little over the period. Figure 8.4 shows the movement of PSTN, ISP, and total access charges on average for the OECD. The CEE members of the OECD have among the highest access prices in the group, so the price trend for them will be above this average.

Table 8.3 *Foreign direct investment per capita,*
1995–1999 (net inflows in current US$)

	Average 1995–1999	Total 1995–1999
Hungary	258	1,032
Estonia	205	821
Czech Republic	190	761
Latvia	145	582
Poland	126	502
Croatia	110	442
Slovenia	107	426
Lithuania	102	406
Slovak Republic	62	247
Romania	44	174
Bulgaria	33	133
Macedonia	20	79
Albania	19	77
Moldova	12	48
Bosnia	0	0

Source: World Bank Country Studies.

Foreign direct investment

The privatization, liberalization and regulation that has accompanied the transition phase for most CEECs has enhanced the opportunities for receiving foreign direct investment (FDI). For countries such as Hungary, the relationships formed throughout the duration of the CMEA, as well as its attempts at early reform, increased its desirability as a location for foreign investors (Sercovich et al. 1999). This investment matured from the initial phase consisting of purchases of former state-owned enterprises in the early 1990s to later development of greenfield industries. To outside investors, the location of Hungary relative to Western Europe is a factor in its favor. Table 8.3 shows the average and total of per capita foreign direct investment in each country between 1995 and 1999. The top five recipients with respect to both total and average investment during this period were Hungary, Estonia, the Czech Republic, Latvia, and Poland. Of the Eastern European group only Croatia has received substantial FDI.

Two factors which attract foreign investors are advanced liberalization and transparency. The former is essentially a matter of opportunity – not only opportunity to enter, but to enter a market with substantial profit potential. Regarding the latter, investors are wary of environments in which the rules of the game are not clear or are rapidly changing. For this reason, the existence of independent regulatory bodies is a positive signal, particularly regulatory bodies which are independent of the political powers. As shown in Table 8.4, seven of the CEECs have a regulatory authority in the telecommunications sector – Albania, Bulgaria, Estonia, the Czech Republic, Hungary, Latvia, and the Slovak Republic – but only the first three have regulators that are independent of political bodies. Importantly all of the regulatory agencies are independent from the incumbent firm. This point is essential for countries seeking EU membership as it is a stipulation of the EU telecommunications directive.

This is not a sector that is liberalizing rapidly, as only the Czech Republic has competition at the local level and all still have monopolies at the long-distance and international levels. Liberalization has been swifter at the data and mobile levels, and all of the CEECs have potentially competitive ISP markets.[4]

Increased IT capability creates potential for increased transparency as it becomes easier for government and other bureaucratic institutions to publicize information quickly.[5] This can be extremely valuable to countries seeking investors. For Bulgaria, lack of transparency has played a substantial part in its inability to attract foreign investment – even in the high-tech areas in which it specialized as a member of the CMEA.

Clumsy administration and bureaucracy, political uncertainties related to frequent changes of government, the lack of transparency in business-state relationships, 'incessant' changes of legal and regulatory framework, the customs regime, and unfair competition from contraband, are often cited as impediments to foreign investment.

OECD 1999, p. 91

The need for foreign investment in the transition economies seems clear, particularly for expanding network infrastructures. Moreover, foreign investors often bring new technologies and training opportunities for employees. On the other hand, a downside of a substantial foreign presence in the production sector (as discussed by Sercovich et al. [1999] in the context of Hungary) is the impact on domestic small and medium-sized enterprises (SMEs). For them, the influx of FDI has led to losses due to their relative inefficiencies as well as their inability to compete with foreign enterprise for capital loans. If a major result of FDI is that foreign companies crowd out domestic enterprises, then its positive role of introducing new technologies and labor force training will diminish if there are not equivalent opportunities available to the former employees of domestic businesses.

Domestic SMEs are disadvantaged by further costs not faced by newcomers, namely, the cost of changing corporate culture to accommodate new technologies. On the one hand, one might expect this cost to be especially high in Eastern European countries, many of which spent half a century under a regime of highly centralized planning. Yet on the other hand, a comment often made of the transition economies is their remarkable ability to adapt. It must be admired that a large subset of the CEECs have taken less than a decade to transform their entire economies to a degree which qualifies them for EU membership.

Table 8.4 *Regulation in the telecommunications sector*

	Name of authority, year created	Independent from incumbent	Independent from political power	Reports to:	Financing of the authority	Is it a collegial body?
Czech Republic	Telecommunications Regulatory Entity, 1998	Yes	Yes	Head of state	License fees	Yes: 5 members
Hungary	Communication Authority, 1990	Yes	No	Ministry		No: President
Slovak Republic	Telecommunications Office, 1998	Yes	No	Ministry	Government appropriation	No: director general
Estonia	National Communications Board, 1998	Yes	Yes	Ministry	Other: state budget	No: director general
Latvia	Ministry of Transport Department of Communications, 1992	Yes	No	Ministry	Government appropriation	Yes: members, department of communications: 12, tariff council: 7
Albania	Telecommunications Regulatory Entity, 1998	Yes	Yes	Head of state	License fees	Yes: 5 members
Bulgaria	State Telecommunications Commission, 1998	Yes	Yes	Ministry	License fees	Yes: 5 members

Source: ITU *World Telecommunications Regulatory Database.*

Commercial activity and infrastructure

e-commerce

The dangers of lagging behind in e-commerce for CEECs are more likely to been seen in business-to-business transactions (BtoB) as opposed to business-to-consumer (BtoC) in the short term. However, the potential for e-consumerism increases along with increased penetration of PCs and Internet users, as does the threat to competitiveness for countries not ready to take advantage of online opportunities. Yet, there are a number of obstacles for potential dotcomers in Central and Eastern Europe. Among these are several psychological barriers which are not particular to this region of the world, though they may be exaggerated due to national experiences with corruption, for example. Others are more tangible and include the lack of transaction security. Successful e-commerce requires the use of sophisticated encryption technologies to transmit personal and payment data between buyers and sellers. The number of secure sites is one indication of a country's potential to take advantage of online commercial activity.

Table 8.5 shows the number of secure Internet sites for CEECs as well as a selection of comparator countries. What is most striking about these numbers is not so much their magnitude, but the rate of growth in this area; growth rates in the Czech Republic, Poland, Slovenia, and Hungary match those of the USA and the UK.

Two surveys by Deloitte and Touche (2000a, 2000b) on electronic business in the Czech Republic illustrate how rapidly change is occurring in e-commerce.[6] Two features which stand out in their results are the changes in the commodity mix sold and in the revenues over the period. In 1999, sales of service-related items made up less than 0.01% of Czech turnover whereas airline tickets alone made up 11.4% of turnover in the USA and Canada and held the number one sales position. Appliances (24.39%), books (21.85%), music (14.27%), and consumer electronics (12.79%) made up the majority of online sales in the Czech Republic according to their survey. By the first quarter of 2000, the sale of airline tickets had taken over the top spot of sales turnover, and while the total revenues of Czech companies is still fairly low in absolute terms (approximately US$1.2 million in 1999), the growth rate is impressive: 611 percent between the first quarters of 1999 and 2000.

In the Deloitte and Touche studies, less than 5 percent of the turnover was from international sales for eleven of the twelve firms surveyed. The need for security technologies increases as cross-border trading increases. Once a company steps outside the national domain it becomes subject to the regulations of international or region specific legislation. Governments which restrict access to encryption technology for national security reasons will at the same time inhibit the growth and future competitiveness of businesses that face electronic rivals.

Table 8.5 *Number of secure websites, 1999*

	March 1999	December 1999	
Czech Republic	55	108	
Poland	55	92	
Slovenia	36	64	
Hungary	23	44	
Estonia	18	29	
Croatia	16	25	
Latvia	14	23	
Slovakia	16	22	
Romania	12	21	
Lithuania	10	17	
Bulgaria	6	10	
Moldova	1	3	
	February 1999	July 1999	March 2000
USA	24,300	31,355	45,951
UK	1,259	1,743	3,251
Japan	961	1,163	1,896
Sweden	299	407	632

Source: Choi 2000.

Finally, a number of practical problems apart from resource availability and security limit the online potential of many firms in Europe. Unlike the US experience, it is sometimes common for credit companies to prohibit the use of Internet purchases with their cards. The lack of alternative payment options, including options for individuals who have trouble obtaining credit, is an additional issue which requires attention.

Electricity networks

Low penetration rates of IT resources in CEECs arise from poor electricity infrastructure in addition to inadequate telecommunications networks. Increased IT use requires increased energy use and many CEECs are still in a state of restructuring their energy sectors. Moreover, due to a history of electricity prices that are significantly below costs, increased liberalization will be accompanied by higher electricity prices for some of these (in Bulgaria average prices were less than 4 US¢ a kWh in 1998).[7] Thus, while liberalization of the telecommunications sector should bring telephony prices down and thereby lessen the burden of use charges for existing users, this benefit could be offset in the short run by rising energy prices. As energy prices represent a higher proportion of household expenditures than corporate expenditures, increased

Table 8.6 *Average pre-tax wages, 1998*

	Average wage (US$ per month)[a]
Estonia	293
Latvia	226
Lithuania	239
Bulgaria	107
Romania	153
Slovak Republic	284
Slovenia	952

Note:
[a] US$ at current exchange rates.
Source: OECD 2000a (from Table 28).

Table 8.7 *Educational attainment of the labor force, second quarter 1998 (% of the total)*

	Up to secondary	Upper secondary	Tertiary
Estonia	12	58	30
Latvia	14	68	18
Lithuania	17	64	19
Czech Republic	12	75	13
Hungary	22	60	18
Poland	20	65	15
OECD	34	40	26

Source: OECD 2000a.

electricity prices resulting from the rationalization of that sector may serve to preserve the low household usage of Internet services, both in absolute terms and relative to corporate and academic communities.

IT and the labor force

For investors, an attractive feature of most CEECs is their stock of relatively high-skilled, low-waged labor. The average monthly earnings of an individual in the Hungarian industrial sector was approximately US$300 (gross) in September 2000.[8] Table 8.6 shows average wages for several CEECs and Table 8.7 compares the education composition of the labor force in several CEECs to the OECD average.

Even though wages in CEECs are low by Western standards, relative wage differences within countries can be a stumbling block for domestic firms faced with the growing need to hire and train skilled workers. In most countries, the financial intermediation sector receives the highest wages on average. In Estonia, for example, average gross salaries for the third quarter of 2000 were approximately US$607 and US$336, in the financial and the transport/storage/communication (TSC) sectors, respectively. Gross wages there are significantly higher for men than women by over 20 percent and the gap is larger now than in 1992.[9] Wages in Slovenia are significantly higher; gross earnings in the TSC sector were just under US$1,000 per month in 1999. Slovenia is interesting in that, while the financial sector is the highest paid (US$1,360 in 1999), the TSC sector was about average, with educators, social and health service providers, and public administrators all earning more.[10] Using education levels as a measure of human capital, the CEECs in Table 8.6 do very well. In all cases, the combined proportion of upper secondary and tertiary achievement of the labor force is higher than in the average OECD member country.

Using other measures, such as the indicators in Table 8.8, the story is broadly consistent with what one might expect from a legacy of socialism that placed high emphasis on education but very little on national R&D. Within the Central European and Baltic groups there is a strong relationship between expenditure on R&D and the level of intellectual infrastructure. As in other respects, Slovenia and Croatia stand out within their regions, with Slovenia having more scientists and engineers than the European average. Moldova surpasses the UK, Japan, and the European average with respect to technicians and has the largest percentage of science and engineering students.

Conclusions

The countries in this study have undergone an amazing transformation over the past decade. Many of them have had the experience not only of making a transition from a highly centralized, planned economy to a market-based economy, but have had to make this adjustment during a period of global technological revolution. The effect of the information revolution on these countries is linked to their individual transition process as well as their proximity to Western neighbors. Standard IT indicators show most CEECs keeping up with more developed economies in terms of growth, and several are remarkably in step with many EU members.

Becoming a part of the knowledge society for CEECs is more a matter of overcoming obstacles than a matter of potential. Firstly, the human capital element is enormous and high level resources are available, though currently to very limited numbers. Changing access pricing structures for Internet usage

Table 8.8 *Human capital indicators for the IT sector, 1987–1997*

	Scientists/ engineers in R&D (per 1 million people)	Technicians in R&D (per 1 million people)	Science/engineering students (% of total tertiary students)	Expenditure in R&D (% GNP)
Slovenia	2,251	1,027	26	1.46
Czech Republic	1,222	693	28	1.20
Slovak Republic	1,866	792	40	1.05
Poland	1,358	1,377	28	0.77
Hungary	1,099	510	32	0.68
Lithuania	2,028	631	31	0.70
Estonia	2,017	391	27	0.57
Latvia	1,049	51	23	0.43
Albania	–	–	19	–
Bosnia	–	–	–	–
Macedonia	1,335	546	47	–
Croatia	1,916	714	30	1.03
Moldova	330	1,641	52	0.90
Bulgaria	1,747	967	27	0.57
Romania	1,387	581	21	0.07
Sweden	3,826	3,166	38	3.76
Japan	4,909	827	21	2.80
USA	3,676	–	19	2.63
France	2,659	2,873	37	2.25
UK	2,448	1,017	34	1.95
Europe EMU	2,126	1,510	38	2.16

Note: Data for latest year available.
Source: World Bank, *World Development Indicators 2000* (1987–1997).

and increasing liberalization in telecommunications will contribute positively in altering usage patterns, but to reap fuller benefits substantial infrastructure investments are required. One factor leading to high usage fees throughout most of Europe is the cost of local phone services. This is especially true in CEECs where local access is still monopolized.

Secondly, employee training remains a high priority especially in areas where domestic SMEs have found it difficult to compete with an increasing number of foreign enterprises. Institutions have arisen to educate small business about the opportunities afforded by new technologies as well as the experience required to keep up in a rapidly changing economy. The Hungarian Foundation for Enterprise Promotion is one example. Others, such as the Association for Information Technology and Communication of Romania, are engaged in promoting IT by stimulating both the supply and demand of software and related products and by monitoring their quality.

Thirdly, increasing the availability of encryption technology as well as increasing producers' and consumers' awareness of the international codes of online commercial activity will improve the competitiveness of e-businesses in CEECs. Finally, efforts to increase transparency and resolve confusing laws and regulations will improve a country's ability to attract foreign investments.

When writing about CEECs, one is tempted to highlight the success stories, but this should not draw our attention away from the areas that are in most need of infrastructure development and technological investment, particularly Albania, Bosnia, Moldova, and Macedonia. For them, the journey along the information highway is just beginning.

Notes

1. The importance of location for the CEECs is recognizable and favors Central Europe and the Baltics over Eastern Europe. Central Europe has benefited from EU contributions to its telecommunications networks while the Baltic group has received substantial contributions from Scandinavia.
2. A number of Internet timelines can be found on the Internet. Two examples include: Hobbes' Internet Timeline v5.2, by Robert Zakon (http://info.isoc.org/guest/zakon/Internet/History/HIT.html#1990 s), and Brief Timeline of the Internet (http://www.webopedia.com/quick_ref/timeline.html).
3. "Unmetered" implies the user is not charged according to the amount of time connected. With these plans, users typically pay a flat monthly fee to the ISP. However, this does not necessarily imply that their local PSTN charges are also unmetered.
4. ITU World Telecommunication Regulatory Database.
5. One informal heuristic for comparing levels of IT sophistication is to browse national websites. Doing so, one finds a surprising variation in data (statistics, for example) and use of language.
6. These surveys were conducted on "pure-play" e-businesses; that is, they do not include hybrid companies that also have other sales avenues (retail shops or catalogs). Also excluded is global e-business generated in the Czech Republic.
7. Bulgaria entered an agreement with the IMF in 1998 for a program to raise prices in four tranches between January 1, 1999 and April 1, 2001. Successive planned increases were: 3.57%, 7.9%, 1.7% and 7.8% (OECD 1999).
8. Hungarian Central Statistical Office.
9. Statistical Office of Estonia.
10. Statistical Office of the Republic of Slovenia.

References

Choi, D. 2000, Internet infrastructure development in transition economies, in *World Market Series: Global Electronic Commerce, CD-ROM*, http://www.wmrc.com.

Deloitte and Touche 2000a, *Survey of E-commerce Revenues in the Czech Republic, First Quarter 2000*, Czech Republic.

2000b, *Survey of E-shop Revenues in the Czech Republic, 1999–2000*, Czech Republic.

Hungarian Central Statistical Office, http://www.ksh.hu.

James, J. 1999, *Globalization, Information Technology and Development*, London: Macmillan.

OECD 1999, *Economic Surveys: Bulgaria*, Paris.

OECD 2000a, *Economic Surveys: Baltics*, Paris.

OECD 2000b, *Internet Infrastructure Indicators*, Paris.

OECD 2000c, *Local Access Pricing and E-commerce*, Working party on telecommunications and information services, Paris, July 2000.

Romanian Statistical Office, http://www.cns.ro/indexe.htm.

Sercovich, F., Ahn, C., Frischtak, C., Mrak, M., Muegge, H., Peres, W., and Wangwe, S. 1999, *Competition and the World Economy: Comparing Industrial Development Policies in the Developing and Transition Economies*, United Nations Industrial Development Organization, London: Edward Elgar.

Statistical Office of Estonia, http://www.stat.ee/wwwstat/eng_stat/index.html.

Statistical Office of the Republic of Slovenia, http://www.sigov.si/zrs/eng/index.html.

World Bank, The Information for Development Program, Information Infrastructure Indicators, 1990–2010, project number 375-990628, Cambridge, MA: Pyramid Research, http://www.infodev.org/projects/internet/375pyramid/fin375.htm.

World Bank Development Data, http://devdata.worldbank.org.

9 Human capital in the move up the value chain: the case of the Indian software and services industry

Paul Kattuman and Kumar Iyer

Introduction

Revolutions beget openings of one kind or the other. The IT revolution would appear to have opened a beneficial window of opportunity for the Indian economy. Against moderate growth performance in other sectors of the economy, the Indian software and services industry is estimated to have grown at nearly 50 percent annually over the last five years.[1] While the rest of Indian industry averaged 7.6 percent growth, domestic sales of software grew at nearly 40 percent per year while exports grew at 52 percent per year on average (see Figure 9.1). Estimates are that over the next five years, software and services might come to account for 25 percent of total Indian exports, up from 5 percent currently.[2] In 1999–2000, the Indian software industry, comprising nearly 1,000 firms, earned US$5.7 billion in revenues, of which US$4 billion came through exports. While this is a minuscule fraction of the world market, estimates are that Indian firms hold 18.5 percent of the global market in customized software (though only 1 percent of the packaged software market), and attracted close to 40 percent of Fortune 500 companies as clients in 2000. The ambitious aims of the National Association for Software and Services Companies (NASSCOM) are 23 percent of the global customized software market and 5 percent of the global software products market by 2003. These numbers are to be appreciated against the estimated size of the global market in software and services of US$500 billion in 2000, growing at over 20 percent annually.

The story of how this enclave of international competitiveness came to be is an interesting one. It goes beyond the commonly maintained plot line, the fortuitous match between the country's human capital and the skilled labor requirements of the industry. Ever since the 1950s, optimistic about demand from a modernizing economy, the publicly financed higher education system has increased the output of science and engineering graduates at an impressive rate. But the growing stock of human capital did not find optimal use or rewards

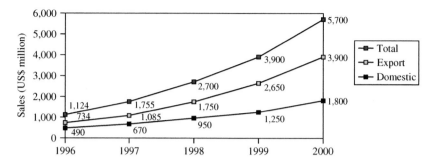

Figure 9.1 Size of the Indian software industry (sales), 1996–2000
(Source: NASSCOM 2000b)

within the country in those early years, as heavy-handed planning undermined the basis for the growth of private enterprise for four decades. The economic liberalization process started slowly in the 1970s with the software sector, and gathered pace in the late 1980s with gradual easing of the system of regulation.

Freedom of enterprise coincided with the explosive growth of the IT market in the developed world. The combined effect drew both entrepreneurship and human capital into the software and services sector, which had the advantage of requiring relatively low financial resources. The cost advantage and size of the trained and trainable pool of human resources in India matched the occupational requirements of the software industry for programmers and analysts, computer scientists, and engineers.[3] In the meantime, the stream of Indian students who had been emigrating since the 1950s, attracted by the prospect of graduate studies and employment in the West, primarily the USA, had grown into a sizable stream, and by the late 1980s a good number of non-resident Indians (NRIs) had worked their way up the executive structures of IT intensive multinationals.[4] As the industry took off, these NRI executives played key roles in the growth of the industry by facilitating the matching of buyers of software services from the West with sellers from India. From the point of view of government policy, the growth of the industry must be attributed to early liberalization and benign neglect rather than active strategic support.

The boom in the IT sector is now India's main opportunity to endogenously escape onto a trajectory of higher growth. The potential for learning-by-doing in the IT industry makes it a natural candidate for self-reinforcing growth. To date, the competitive strength of the Indian IT industry has rested largely on the wage cost advantage in supplying offshore services. But rising out of the cumulative scale of activity oriented toward exports, a few firms at least have built up sufficient knowledge and organizational capital to move up the value chain. That lead has demonstrated the potential of the sector as a whole for endogenous growth. Will that potential be realized, with a significant proportion of firms in the sector moving up the value chain on sustainable growth paths?[5] This will be of interest to other developing countries. The evidence will also have a bearing on the emerging trends in the international division of labor.

This chapter assesses the development of the Indian software and services industry with the focus on the factors driving the development of the industry and the growth of firms in it. The next section outlines the main features of the current structure of the industry. Against that background, the following section provides an assessment of key factors in the growth of software firms. The labor market holds the key to the future, and the final section concludes with a discussion of the direction open for the industry's evolution, given constraints and opportunities.

The development of the Indian software sector

Origins of the Indian software and services industry go back three decades to the founding of Tata Consultancy Services (TCS), a spin-off within the TATA business group, the oldest Indian conglomerate. The initial market was domestic, mainly software development for a few public sector firms and fewer large private sector firms. At this stage, government policy toward the sector was ambivalent, though the Department of Electronics held watch over the sector, following recognition of the export potential of software by the Electronics Committee Group (1968). The planning approach to development, which included wholesale regulation of private enterprise, and import restrictions (for example, on hardware) frustrated the development of the industry. The first entrants were enticed when policy reforms made import entitlements (for hardware) conditional on exports. Demonstrated export success by early firms boosted entry into the industry. Encouraged by this, by the early 1980s, the government put together an export policy that liberalized the import of hardware and software as well as the establishment of wholly owned foreign firms (Heeks 1996). In the mid-1980s, the government developed software technology parks as export processing zones. Economic reforms gathered pace through the late 1980s and 1991 marked a watershed year, when the rupee was devalued, non-tariff barriers slashed (on telecommunications equipment, for example), and tariffs and taxes reduced. Through the 1990s, it is the export-oriented software sector more than any other that has been galvanized most by the new freedom of enterprise.

Population dynamics of Indian software firms

The early entrants into the industry were cross-entrants. A few large firms in other sectors, including computer hardware firms, diversified into software, notably TATA, Hindustan Computers Limited (HCL) and Wipro. Many of these cross entrants spun off in-house computing service divisions into independent business units, to serve the limited domestic market in a regime of import substitution. This process of cross-entry has continued over the years.

The liberalized policy toward foreign direct investment was seized upon by NRIs as well as multinational corporations. A group of NRI executives in Texas Instruments promoted the setting up of a subsidiary in 1984 in Bangalore. Other MNCs followed. By the 1990s, many foreign firms had set up offices and subsidiaries in India, often with domestic partners. While their initial objective was to sell software and hardware products in the Indian market, as the advantages of locating software development in India became evident, many firms moved to establish development centers in India: firms such as Oracle, Texas Instruments, Motorola, Siemens, and Microsoft. A number of firms have followed this lead and have established significant operations to take advantage of the pool of relatively cheap skilled workforce to sell software services in the international market.[6]

As is typical of young industries with technology embodied in human rather than physical capital, and comprising many market niches, established firms served as incubators for entrepreneurs. In the late 1980s, *de novo* entrants began to spring up in large numbers in the industry, the best known of which is Infosys. Many of these firms were started by breakaway groups of professionals from established software firms.[7]

In this self-reinforcing process, the growing population of firms served as the growing set of incubators of future firms. A small but potentially significant variant within this set was the class of the firms set up by NRIs, some (not all) relocating in India having gained experience abroad. In a short period, the class of *de novo* entrants has come to dominate the industry in terms of numbers.

The market structure

Starting with thirty-eight members in 1988, NASSCOM has grown to have nearly 700 members by 2000. The industry is now estimated to employ about 280,000 people, while the number of firms has grown at over 12 percent annually in recent years (see Figure 9.2).

The size distribution of the software and services firms – by employment, by sales revenue, by exports – is highly skewed (see Figure 9.3).

By end of 1999, about fifty Indian software and services firms were listed on the Indian stock exchanges; two were listed on the NASDAQ and one was listed on the London Stock Exchange. The market capitalization of software firms on Indian stock exchanges stood at US$42 billion, accounting for well over a fifth of the total market capitalization of the Bombay Stock Exchange, the largest stock exchange in the country.

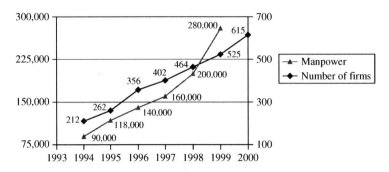

Figure 9.2 Number of firms and manpower, 1993–2000 (Source: NASSCOM 2000b)

Location along the value chain in domestic and export markets

Where do Indian firms, small and large, stand in the value chain? Which market segments do they occupy? A popular model of software development, the waterfall model (Royce 1970), provides a benchmark for this assessment. The waterfall model sets out software development in terms of a hierarchy of sequential steps (see Figure 9.4). The first stages (conceptualization, requirements analysis and high level design) are the high value added stages, while the later stages (low level analysis, coding, etc.) are low value added segments.

The Indian software industry has been driven by exports; indeed, it has been claimed that limited interaction with the rest of the domestic economy, and its inherent inefficiencies, explains a large part of the success of the sector (Ghemawat and Patibandla 1997). In the international market, Indian firms are dominant in low level design, coding and maintenance. Figure 9.5 gives the composition of software development and services by types of software developed for the export and the domestic markets. The larger proportion of low level work is reflected in the slow growth and relatively low level of gross labor productivity: revenue per employee was only US$16,000 in 1999 in India; comparable figures were US$150,000 for Israel and US$70,000 for Ireland, in 1997. (Arora et al. 1999).

Most of the export earnings of Indian firms have come from developing small application solutions, enhancing existing systems, migration to client-server systems, porting, re-engineering and maintenance, and, until the end of 1999, Y2K solutions. Much of this work is on site, and there is also a significant segment supplying skilled workers at relatively low wages to work for clients at their sites, in other words body shopping. The USA accounts for over half of all exports (see Figure 9.6). Typically export projects are small,[8] and the bulk of the low value end type of work cannot be characterized as critical from the buyer's point of view. Yet, even at the low end, price margins in export are substantially higher than those in the domestic market.

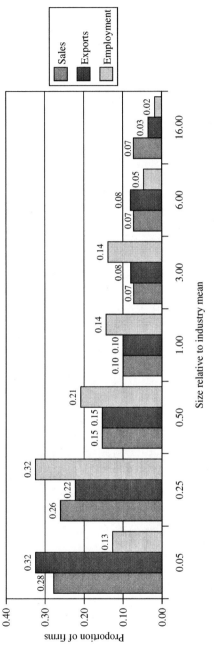

Figure 9.3 Size distribution of Indian software firms, 1999 (Source: compiled from NASSCOM 2000a)

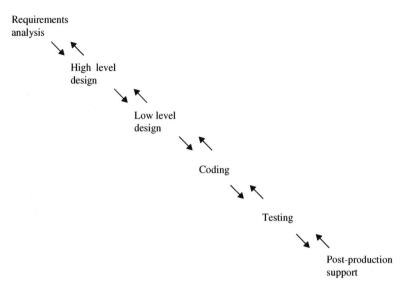

Figure 9.4 The waterfall model of software development (Source: adapted from Royce 1970)

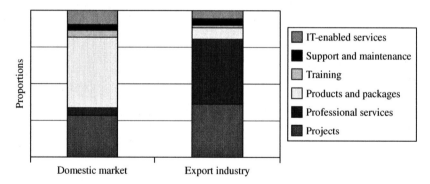

Figure 9.5 Composition of Indian software development services, 1999 (Source: computed from NASSCOM 2000b)

It is not surprising that many firms do not see the domestic market as the primary market, but use it as a training ground for new programmers or as a market to absorb excess labor. Despite this, the domestic market has grown at 40 percent annually over the past five years. Countering the problems of price sensitivity and smaller margins, the domestic market offers the full range of software development and project management activity. Some domestic software projects have been very complex, for example the nationwide interlinked

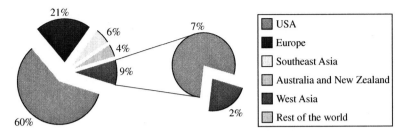

Figure 9.6 Destination of Indian software exports, 1999 (Source: computed from NASSCOM 2000b)

reservation systems for Indian Railways. There has also been a gradual picking up of the domestic market for software packages, for example word processing packages for Indian regional languages. The domestic business services market for customized software has been boosted by a change in the Indian business mind-set, fueled by the take-off of software exports. There is an enhanced perception among Indian businesses that software is useful and important. Interviews suggest that there is increasing spillover into the domestic business market of business practices embodied in software developed on export projects by Indian firms. On the other hand, there is not much evidence of spillover of the wider range of project management abilities developed by software firms in the domestic market into their export activities. The management and technical skills required are in different leagues and indeed vary from one client to the next.

Where is the industry headed in terms of the value chain? There has been movement toward higher value added activities. Until the early 1990s, almost all Indian software exports were on-site professional services (90 percent in 1988), now this figure is under 60 percent, showing a trend toward more work done within India under direct Indian supervision and management. Some of the larger firms, such as TCS, are well-regarded international first-tier contractors for software projects. However, it is not clear that there is widespread thirst across most firms to move into the big league. The larger proportion of older firms does not appear to be involved in serious R&D work to move up toward the high value end. Some of the CEOs we interviewed said that they faced little competition since the demand was growing rapidly both domestically and internationally; competition is not yet a zero-sum game and there is profit to be found in the low value end and copycat products markets. But demand cannot be expected to continue growing at the present rate indefinitely.

The exception is a growing segment of ambitious smaller firms that have been liberated by the Internet, and have strategic business plans that involve significant expenditures on R&D and new technologies. While new small firms have to build credibility before moving into the high value end, these firms have an established presence in the newest market segments, including the market for IT-enabled services. Among CEOs of these firms, we found the strong view that the structure of the industry will have to change. In a pincer movement, against the background of a deceleration of international demand, competition is rising, even as the labor market for computer professionals tightens.

Research on productivity dynamics across many countries has established that the basis of aggregate productivity increase is the entry and expansion of efficient firms which occupy the market shares of inefficient firms which contract and exit. In real industries, unlike the case in representative agent models, firms have heterogeneous fortunes that vary widely from the average for the industry. When an industry is expanding, the tide of growth will be shared by most firms, while when competition gets tougher, only a few productive firms will expand, countering the general pattern of contraction and exit of firms. The key route for Indian software firms to move up the value chain will be through the recruitment and retention of talent and experience in the technical domain as well as business practice domain. This will require firms to grow larger. It is likely that there will be a wave of consolidating acquisitions and mergers involving the focused newer and smaller companies that have committed themselves to a path up the value chain. The market structure may get more concentrated yet. In the next section, we explore the factors important to the growth of firms into the high value end of the market.

Determinants of growth

More than in most industries, growth of firms in this sector is based on human capital, the competence of employees, the knowledge base, the organizational capital, and the reputation of the firm, all built up cumulatively. Strategies that firms can follow for growth, the choice between the high value road toward first-tier project contracts and eventually, software products, and the low value road of body shopping services depends on the supply and cost of the programming talent pool, as well as the caliber and knowledge of business managers.

Human capital and the labor market

The key driver for the Indian software and services industry has been the availability of relatively inexpensive skilled computing professionals fluent in the English language.

Over the last fifty years, annual growth rate in science education in India has been 11 percent in terms of number of graduates and 9 percent in terms of institutions (see Figures 9.7 and 9.8). The number graduating annually in science and engineering (including computing) from Indian universities currently stands

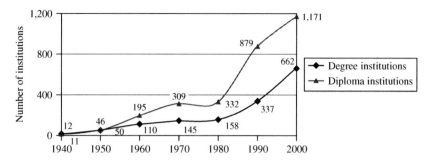

Figure 9.7 Growth in technical education in India: institutions, 1940–2000
(Source: AICTE 2000)

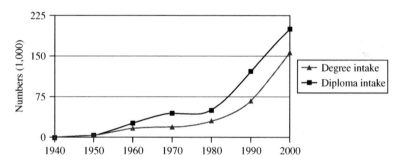

Figure 9.8 Growth in technical education in India: student intake, 1940–2000
(Source: AICTE 2000)

at about 150,000 (only a few more than 16,000 would have done a four-year engineering bachelors degree) while the more vocation-oriented polytechnics produce about 200,000 diploma graduates with technical training. There are also well over 2,000 recognized private training institutes offering a mix of short and long conversion courses in programming and software engineering to the large number of aspirant converts from other disciplines, including experienced technicians and engineers from other sectors of industry. About 75,000 persons are estimated to have joined the IT sector in 2000, well short of the demand projected at nearly double that number.

The rapid growth of the sector in India has tightened the labor market for IT professionals. Wages are projected to increase by about 20 to 25 percent each year, and the quit rate in the industry runs at about 20 percent. The supply gap is, of course, larger in countries with smaller pools of raw human capital potential. In the USA, 350,000 vacancies are estimated among programmers, systems analysts, computer scientists, and engineers. The International Labour

Organisation (ILO) estimated that by 2002 there would be 1.6 million vacant IT jobs in Europe. Estimates place the wages costs of Indian programmers at one-fourteenth of US programmers, but at the higher end, the differentials are less: Indian systems analysts cost one-fifth, and network administrators one-third of their US counterparts. Firms report difficulty in retaining professionals with more than two years experience. One reason is of course that a large number of trained professionals emigrate, generally to the USA.[9] Even among software specialists posted abroad to work at clients' sites, a significant proportion are said to quit within two years, lured away by more rewarding packages. The other side of this particular coin is the reverse flow of software professionals from secondments in the West, returning to work for Indian firms or to set up on their own. Returnees from short secondments tend to be narrowly specialized and lacking in project management skills.

The high rate of attrition in this tightening labor market poses a serious difficulty for firms that seek to progress beyond low end activities of coding, analysis, and maintenance. The main avenue for reducing employee attrition is to provide employees with career paths into management, and financial incentives to stay. At the same time, firms need to try to make the organization independent of individuals and to stress documented procedures. To deploy these strategies, firms need to grow in size.

While the rewards offered by the sector attract aspiring students and trainees, the supply response of the market for professionals will depend on the dynamism of educational institutions, both public and private, in filling the gap with quality education.

Alive to the seriousness of the human capital constraint, the government supported the setting up of a number of Indian Institutes of Information Technology (IIITs) and an International School of Business (ISB).[10] These institutes will be private universities, offering high quality education in software engineering, communications, and IT-based applications, and established jointly by leading international and Indian IT firms. The first IIIT started in Hyderabad in 1998.[11]

To conclude the discussion on human capital, it is worth noting the continuing role of NRIs. In the early days, NRIs, particularly in the USA, played a key role in guaranteeing the quality of deliverables entrusted to Indian software firms. In recent years, there has been a continuous trickle of NRI professionals returning to work for firms in India or to set up on their own. Among these NRIs, some are outstandingly experienced. In the move to the high value end of the international market, this pool of human capital constitutes a resource for transcending barriers in management and business culture.

Specialization versus diversification

An analysis of the portfolios of Indian firms show great breadth of involvement in lines of IT technologies (see Table 9.1) and industry applications

Table 9.1 *Technical domains of activity of Indian software firms, 1999*

Technical domain area	% of firms reporting activity
Web content development	92
Web technologies	67
Software product development	59
Dataprocessing, medical transcription	57
E-commerce	51
Software maintenance and migration	49
RDBMS / datawarehousing / datamining	45
ERP / MRP solutions	43
System integration / networking	40
Business process consultancy / Re-engineering	35
Y2K	34
Euro currency solution	28
Telecommunications solutions / communication	28
software	28
Product distribution / support / implementation	26
IT education and training	22
Facility management	14
CAD / CAM / CAE	13
Localization of software	12
GIS / imaging	11
CD-ROM publishing / multimedia	10
Chip design / microprocessor / ASIC	6
Computer games / computer graphics	4

Source: Estimate from NASSCOM (2000a).

(see Table 9.2). Firms are active in a number of technical sub-markets (Web technologies, ERP, etc.) and in a variety of sectoral sub-markets (finance, telecommunications, etc.). A close look reveals that firms are highly cross-diversified. Figure 9.9 is a classification of NASSCOM member firms by the number of industries they serve against the number of technical segments they engage. The pattern of the cluster shows how large firms serve more industries as well as engage in larger technical portfolios. But smaller firms appear more diversified in terms of technical domains relative to the number of industries they serve; the scatter spills out relatively more above the diagonal. This supports the view that in their choice of growth strategy, smaller firms have generally opted to grow by diversification, through generic technical competencies, for example in networking, systems software, and conversion and porting, competing in cost and delivery time. This has been a profitable strategy in a growing market.

Table 9.2 *Industries served by Indian software firms, 1999*

Industries	% of firms reporting activity
Online information services	62
Manufacturing	60
Finance	52
Telecommunications	37
Engineering	34
Health	34
Office automation	28
Education / libraries	24
Public services administration	18
Travel, hotel and leisure	18
Transport	17
Library management systems	17
Airlines / railways	16
Oil / petroleum	14
Printing and publishing / advertising	13
Defence	13
Electronics / design automation / robotics	13
Textiles	9

Source: NASSCOM 2000a.

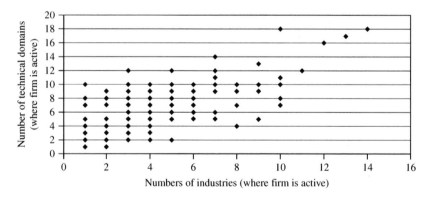

Figure 9.9 Specialization versus proliferation: activities of Indian software firms, 1999 (Source: computed from NASSCOM 2000a)

Figure 9.9 also shows that at the larger end, firms are, on average, active in fewer technical domains relative to the number of industries they serve. But few firms have developed domain-specific high level competencies to specialize in particular industries. The route to successful specialization in a dynamic technology intensive field lies in R&D and continuous and reciprocal learning from clients in the market for complex projects. Some of the newer and smaller firms have been more agile in targeting the latest technical developments[12] and the newer markets in professional services. However young firms find it difficult to signal credibility (Banerjee and Duflo 1998). And growth in size is important to provide employees with career path incentives.[13]

In summary, the software industry can be characterized as an endogenous sunk cost industry due to its R&D intensity. Characteristics of the industry are such that competition will increasingly take the form of escalation of R&D. Firms straddle many sub-markets and many technological trajectories. If the effectiveness of R&D is high, in the sense that R&D spending along a technological trajectory will increase the quality and thereby the demand for a product and pay-off in terms of market share, and if R&D spillover effects are also high in the sense that R&D into one product group has positive spillover effects on other product groups,[14] then the relative advantage of the specialized escalation strategy will be high (Sutton 1998).[15] The route to growth lies in specialization (which may lead in course of time to diversification at the high value end). A more concentrated market structure arrived at through a period of restructuring and consolidation is likely.

Quality

One critical determinant of the growth of firms is a guarantee of quality. In each component of the waterfall model of software development, there are established software engineering practices and clear methods of measuring process improvement. Adhering to these is the essence of the quality program. International certification has been the route available to developing country firms in establishing credibility in product and process quality. The most popular quality certification of the software development process among Indian firms has been the set of standards defined by the International Standards Organization under ISO9000.[16] This developed out of European Union guidelines for two-party contractual situations, which requires firms to have well-defined processes documented and followed in an externally verifiable way. The focus is on minimizing variations in quality, and not necessarily increasing quality. The competing standard in certification is the Capability Maturity Model (CMM)[17] which, in contrast to ISO9000, is specific to software, and prescribes up to five levels of increasing maturity of software development process and organization. These levels guarantee that process discipline is in place to repeat success, and that firms have established basic project management processes to track costs, schedule, and functionality. The firm will have well-defined and documented processes for software development that will allow it to better manage software development.

While many firms see certification as a marketing tool, it turns out to be more than just a signaling mechanism. The advantage of the certification is that it requires firms to expend effort to define and formalize their software development processes and methodologies. This is a first step in commitment to quality. Arora and Asundi (1999) find that ISO certification is an important determinant of growth of both revenues and revenue per employee.

Indian firms have clearly not been lacking in this type of commitment to quality. This is evidenced by the fact that more than a quarter of NASSCOM membership have ISO9000 certification. By the end of 1999, there were nineteen companies worldwide with CMM Level 5 certification, of which twelve were Indian. The first such company to attain this level was Motorola's unit in India, generally seen as a beginning of the quality branding of the India label. Recognizing the importance of quality standards, the government encourages ISO certification through subsidies, and the ambitious objective of NASSCOM is 100 percent ISO certification for firms with more than ten employees.

In the technologically dynamic segment, we also found the view among CEOs that while quality certification can help to build up credibility, it is not always practical. With the dynamism of Internet development, the pace of change of the market, and the constant changes in the specification, adhering to certified standards is less valuable. In very dynamic markets, there is no lead-time to document standards and adhere to them. For example, standards are unwieldy for Web design. In these areas, some companies have started to use price guarantees instead of certification as a signal. Overall, the evidence is that Indian firms take quality very seriously.

Conclusion: the future of the Indian software industry

In the immediate future, the growing international market may yet accommodate firms following the less demanding proliferation strategy. But that route will not be sustainable a few years from now, as human resource constraints begin to bite in earnest. In programming, competition from other countries (China, for example) will grow much fiercer. At the higher end, the cost advantage in terms of professionals such as software developers and network administrators is eroding rapidly. Firms report difficulty in attracting and retaining experienced talent. Pinned down by higher wage costs on the one side and static revenue per unit effort on the other, firms will decelerate in growth and become less attractive to talented professionals. To grow, they will have to move on to higher value added segments based on domain expertise and proprietary software tools, marketing their consulting practices worldwide. This will require proven competence in conceptualization, high level design, and marketing. A few first-tier firms have demonstrated this ability to combine management ability with technical ability. These firms are the potential incubators for business talent to be nurtured among the graduates of institutions such as the IIITs and the ISB and spun off into the entrepreneurial market. There clearly is potential that a satisfactory human capital supply response will be forthcoming from India.

As innovation continues apace in the IT sector, the parable of the internationally mobile professional offers some guidance on an emerging trend in international division of labor in the IT sector. The success of at least some NRIs in harnessing their experience-based knowledge of technology and management with the cost advantage of software development in India holds a lesson for ambitious Indian firms. They may be expected to move toward multinational organizational structures so that their future leaders can learn by engaging in all aspects of project management in the international market. In a continuously innovating technology industry, firms will need to set the stage for their growth by building in this aspect of multinationality.

What we have not addressed here is the difficult question: can the growth of this internationally competitive enclave spill over beneficially upon the illiterate half of the 1 billion Indians and that third who subsist below the poverty line?

Acknowledgments

We are pleased to acknowledge the support of the Institute of Developing Economies (IDE-JETRO) for the preparation of this paper, and thank participants at the IDE workshop on "International Division of Labor" for comments. Kumar Iyer would like to thank the Rajiv-Gandhi Foundation for financing his field work in India.

Notes

1. The source of most of the data analyzed in this chapter is the National Association for Software and Services Companies (NASSCOM), based in New Delhi (see http://www.nasscom.org/). The member firms of this trade association account for 95 percent of the software revenues of India.
2. The market for software and services comprises a set of sub-markets, primarily custom-developed software and software packages. The above figures from NASSCOM do not include embedded software or software developed by users.
3. A recent estimate (*Economist*, February 20, 1999) placed the number of engineers and technicians per 10,000 population at 40 in India, well above the 18 in the USA (and well below the 135 in Israel).
4. By far the majority of graduates of the internationally recognized Indian Institutes of Technology (IITs) and Regional Engineering Colleges (RECs) emigrated to study and work abroad. It is reported that over one-fifth of Silicon Valley startups in recent years were by NRIs (*Newsweek*, September 27, 1999).

5. The broader and more critical question is whether the performance of this sector will spill over into other sectors of the economy.

6. With the advent of high quality communications, one advantage of India that has come to the fore is the time zone, making the location a prime site for 24-hour continuity in the development process. This is one reason why many MNCs are currently considering more development in India. The same advantage is enjoyed, as far as the US market is concerned, by Indian firms that develop in India and test software among clients in the USA.

7. For example, Infosys was started by a group of managers who left another early entrant, Patni Computer Systems, sustained initially by a maintenance contract from a client of their previous company.

8. Arora et al. (1999) report that their survey of US firms placed the median duration of the most important projects of 95 US firms sourced to Indian firms at 150 man-months. So typical export projects are much smaller and, in many cases, Indian firms serve as subcontractors to larger foreign firms. There are few cases where Indian firms get projects directly from the end user.

9. For example, it is reported that 30,000 H1-B visas were granted to Indians in 1999. In 2000, Germany and the UK liberalized work permits for software specialists from the Indian subcontinent.

10. The International School of Business is a partnership between Wharton and Kellog Schools of Business, along with a number of Indian businesses.

11. A sense of both the extent of interest and the caliber of the entrants is revealed by the fact that 28,000 candidates took the entrance examination for the fifty places.

12. For example, in Java-based applications and the development in object-oriented languages.

13. Among other reasons for growth, specialization at the high end does require firms to shift platforms as needed, for example from mainframes to open systems. Larger firms are easier able to span platforms, for example across mainframes, UNIX workstations, and Windows NT.

14. Spillover effects have two dimensions, one on the supply side whereby they create scale economies in R&D, and the other on the demand side where they allow the development of different product lines in different sub-markets; this is particularly appropriate for software, where cross-applied innovations constantly lead to the development of completely new trajectories within the industry.

15. Where R&D intensity is high we know its effectiveness is high, but the resulting effect on market concentration depends on the spillover effects of R&D. The higher the spillover effects, the greater the advantage of escalation vis-à-vis proliferation.

16. International Standards Organization 9000 series is a European standard consisting of five documents: 9001 – models of quality assurance in design, development, production, installation, and servicing; 9002 – production and installation; 9003 – quality assurance in final inspection and testing; and 9004 – supporting guidelines. The general aim is to fulfil the buyer's need of guarantees of consistent process standards followed by sellers of goods and services.

17. The Software Engineering Institute (SEI), which developed the CMM, was established in 1984 by the US government in Carnegie Mellon University, Pittsburgh.

The CMM classifies levels of maturity, rigor, and best practice attained in the development of software, categorizing competence into five levels. Movement from level 1 to 5 indicates a shift away from ad hoc development, organization, and testing to the adoption of comprehensive practices for planning, engineering, development, maintenance, and design, providing gains to companies in terms of cost, schedule, functionality and product quality.

References

All India Council for Technical Education (AICTE), http://www.aicte.com.

Arora, A. and Asundi, J. 1999, Quality certification and the economics of contract software development: a study of Indian software and services industry, NBER Working Paper 7260, Cambridge, MA.

Arora, A., Arunachalam, V. S., Asundi, J., and Fernandes, R. 1999, *The Indian Software Industry*, mimeo, Carnegie Mellon University, Pittsburgh.

Banerjee, A. and Duflo, E. 1998, Reputation effects and the limits of contracting: a study of Indian software industry, unpublished paper, MIT, Cambridge, MA.

Ghemawat, P. and Patibandla, M. 1997, India's exports since the reforms, in J. Sachs, A. Varshney, and N. Bajpai (eds.), *India in the Era of Economic Reforms*, New Delhi: Oxford University Press.

Heeks, R. 1996, *India's Software Industry: State Policy, Liberalization and Industrial Development*, New Delhi/Thousand Oaks/London: Sage Publications.

NASSCOM 2000a, *A Directory of Indian Software and Service Companies*, New Delhi. 2000b, *The IT Software and Services Industry in India: Strategic Review*, New Delhi.

Royce, W. W. 1970, Managing the development of large software systems: concepts and techniques, WESCON technical papers, Vol. 14, p. 723.

Sutton, J. 1998, *Technology and Market Structure*, Cambridge, MA: MIT Press.

10 Internet access and regulatory reform: the experience of South Africa

Emanuele Giovannetti

Introduction

Nelson Mandela pledged support for a telecommunications development fund that aims to extend communications "to every village in Africa." On the opening day of Africa Telecommunications '98, Mandela described the "daunting" task ahead in closing the gap between the world's information haves and have-nots: "We have to say our collective vision is in danger of failing where it counts most, namely the goal of universal access to basic telecommunications services." Mandela said telecommunications development would best be achieved through partnerships between the public and private sectors, rather than relying on public funding alone.

Source: Mandela voices support for African telecom development, Sheridan Nye and Vineeta Shetty, *Communications Week International* (June 5, 1998).

The telecommunications industry, broadly defined, has been completely transformed by technological development in fiber optic cables, wireless technology, miniaturization of digital switching components, etc. However, these changes have had even deeper implications for the process of regulatory reform under liberalization and privatization. Moving on from the definition of pricing guidelines for the old state-owned telecommunications monopolies, regulatory policies have now shifted toward new issues such as opening up the industry to competition at each layer of the network infrastructure, from backbone interconnection to the local loop. A milestone in this process has been the WTO's *Generalized Agreement on Trade and Services* of 1997, when sixty-nine governments committed to the liberalization of their basic telecommunications services.

One of the major trade-offs in implementing regulatory reform, particularly of the telecommunications sector in developing economies, is the need to foster competition at the same time as extending universal service.[1] Both these objectives are important steps in enabling societies to compete successfully in global markets. The need to maintain these two goals independently arises from possible market failures associated with the liberalization process. A typical cause of market failure in a network industry is the presence of network externalities: "while for a firm it might not be profitable to provide services for a remote community, the social value of using the network for each consumer increases with the number of other users connected." This makes the provision of universal service socially desirable. Of course, services to be included in the definition of universal service differs widely between developed and developing countries. However, the challenges and opportunities posed by the emergence of the global information society make the goal of extending access to the Internet a common priority. One interesting experience, aimed at improving shared access to information technologies in developing countries, is provided by South Africa's Multipurpose Community Telecenters. These are public, multifunctional loci of shared access where demand for connectivity can be pooled so that, after an assisted start-up period, supply becomes commercially feasible and self-sustaining.

Community Telecenters are a good example of the use that can be made of new IT technology in a geographically diverse and socially segmented society. They encourage access to the Internet through high quality connectivity, and idiosyncratic Web content. The current digital divide can be explained with a few socio-economic statistics: access to electricity is limited to 58 percent of the population and running water to 45 percent; the literacy rate is only 64.5 percent; life expectancy is estimated to fall from the current 68 to 48 years due to the HIV/AIDS epidemic. As a legacy of the apartheid era, the socio-economic divide has a clear ethnic base. Figure 10.1 and Table 10.1 give a snapshot of the divide in access to telecommunications in 1995.

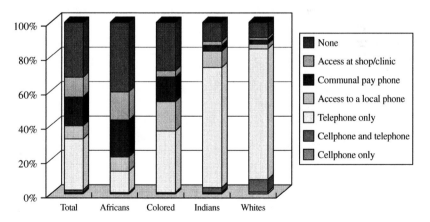

Figure 10.1 Access to telecommunications according to ethnicity, 1995
(Source: Statistics SA 1995)

Table 10.1 *Access to telecommunications according to ethnicity, 1995*

	Total	Africans	Coloreds	Indians	Whites
Cellphone only	0.4%	0.2%	0.2%	0.4%	1.3%
Cellphone and telephone	1.7%	0.2%	0.5%	3.4%	7.0%
Telephone only	30.1%	13.2%	36.5%	70.4%	76.6%
Access to a local phone	7.7%	8.1%	17.3%	9.2%	2.6%
Communal pay phone	16.4%	21.6%	13.7%	3.4%	2.4%
Access at shop/clinic	11.7%	16.2%	4.3%	2.2%	1.6%
None	31.9%	40.6%	27.6%	10.9%	8.5%

Source: Statistics S.A. 1995.

Telecommunications policy in South Africa

Two main pieces of legislation are of particular relevance for the telecommunications industry and the development of a South African information society: the Telecommunications Act of 1996 and the Competition Act of 1998. The Competition Act establishes a Competition Commission and a Commission Tribunal with substantial political independence and power to investigate and adjudicate possible offences against the Act, focusing both on vertical and horizontal practices and on the abuse of market power.

The Telecommunications Act, which followed a widespread national debate initiated by the Green Paper on Telecommunications, has granted the incumbent monopoly, Telkom, an exclusivity period from 1997 until 2002, making it the dominant player in the telecommunications services industry. In 1997, an equity stake of 30 percent was sold to an international consortium, Thintana Communications, 60% owned by the US company SBC Communications International and 40% by Telekom Malaysia Berhard. A further 10 percent is planned to be sold to national black empowerment groups.[2] The license awarded to Telkom for providing the public switched telephone network (PSTN) services lasts twenty-five years but is open to competition after the first exclusivity period. The government had to make a number of major concessions to make the deal attractive, including a five-year monopoly on mainstream services and strong management control for the equity partners who committed to doubling the telephone network over five years.

The first three years of Telkom's transformation resulted in extended digitalization of the network and in a net increase of 1.6 million access lines, of which just over 1 million were installed in underserved areas (see Figure 10.2). In addition, residents in 2,091 villages received a phone service for the very first time (see Figure 10.3). 13,890 priority customers (hospitals, schools, and

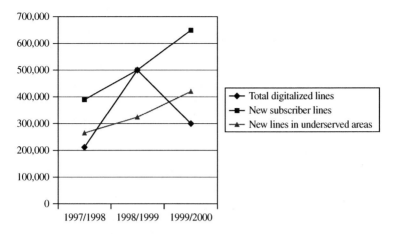

Figure 10.2 Network expansion, 1997–2000 (Source: Telkom 2000)

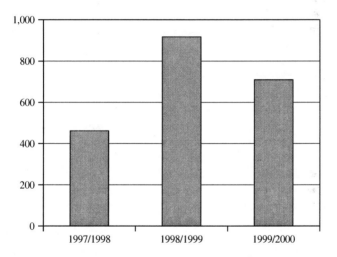

Figure 10.3 Number of villages connected for the first time to a telephone, 1997–2000 (Source: Telkom 2000)

libraries) were provided with a service, of which 8,911 received it for the first time, and 86,107 new public pay phones were installed (see Figure 10.4).

In addition to a period of exclusivity for the incumbent, the Act also mandated:

- the creation of a regulatory body, the South African Telecommunications Regulatory Authority (SATRA)[3] separate from the national operator and from the Ministry of Post Telecommunications and Broadcasting

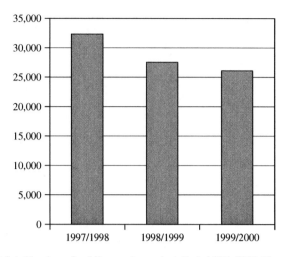

Figure 10.4 Number of public payphones installed, 1997–2000 (Source: Telkom 2000)

- the provision of licenses for existing operators
- funds for the establishment of universal service and for human resource development, as well as for the relevant control agencies.

One of the motivating factors behind the founding of the regulatory authority (SATRA-ICASA) was to enforce a clear separation of the functions and responsibilities of the three main players in the telecommunications environment: the government, responsible for telecommunications policy; the operator(s), responsible for providing telecommunications services; and the regulator, responsible for the administration of government policy, issuing licenses, managing the frequency spectrum, and implementing a wide range of tasks mandated by the Telecommunications Act. The regulatory authority is also required by the Act to promote the growth and development of the telecommunications sector and to correct the racial imbalances in information access inherited from the apartheid era. To this aim ICASA is administering the *Joint Economic Development Plan* (JEDP), a ZAR2.5 billion (US$315 million) economic development plan spanning ten years and based on public–private partnerships.[4]

Since the beginning of regulatory reform, South African telecommunications policies have had two ambitious, and seemingly contradictory, objectives: to redress imbalances in the provision of services with a deliberate bias toward severely under-served areas, whilst stimulating the industry to deliver internationally competitive and high quality products for the business sector. The country is coping well with the second task, it is showing one of the world's highest growth rates for the take-up of mobile telephony and a relatively high

Internet user density. However, the aims of bringing distance learning to people nationwide, letting schools benefit from Internet access, and the use of telemedicine to link rural clinics to urban centres remain a challenge. A realistic goal is to provide telecommunications where everyone in the country can have reasonable access to it through joint efforts from business, government, and communities. To this aim the Telecommunications Act also mandated a Universal Service Agency, responsible for making recommendations to expand access, monitor progress toward universal access, and manage the universal service fund.

Since 1997, the Universal Service Agency has launched numerous telecenters, providing the means and location for people residing in underserved villages, to learn about and use telecommunications products and services. These telecenters are managed by a partnership between the Universal Service Agency and community-based organisations.

Telephone infrastructure

South Africa is the telecommunications leader of the African continent with approximately 6 million installed telephones. The average number of phone lines per 100 of the population is 15: in some rich suburbs, this figure rises to 50, whereas in parts of the Eastern Cape it is around 0.1.

South Africa has a large transmission infrastructure, necessitated by the country's vast geographical area of 1.2 million square kilometers. Covering approximately 120 million circuit-kilometers, the transmission network constitutes the backbone of all telecommunications services with some 98 percent of the network already digital.

There are two cellular telephone networks, Vodacom and MTN (Mobile Telephone Network), which were officially connected on April 1, 1994. Telkom owns 50 percent of Vodacom. MTN's shares are divided between Cable and Wireless (25 percent), M-Cell (29.5 percent), SBC (15.5 percent), Transtel (20 percent), and Naftel (10 percent). The mobile phone industry itself is continuing to grow, with approximately 4 million active mobile phone subscribers, and mobile penetration is approaching fixed-lines levels (see Figure 10.5).

Three other important players are active in the telecommunications sector: Transtel, for satellite communications; Sentech, which provides all broadcasters with their terrestrial and satellite broadcasting facilities; and Eskom, the electricity supplier.[5] These three companies are expected to jointly operate the second fixed-line operator license which will be issued at the end of Telkom's exclusivity period, and the privatization of these parastatal agencies is also expected shortly. Table 10.2 summarises the key players in the telecommunications sector.

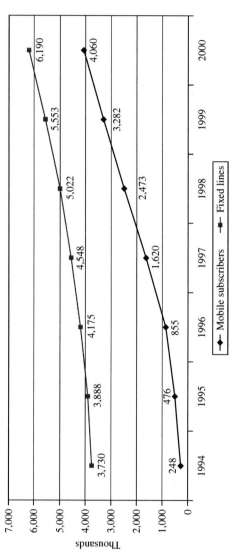

Figure 10.5 The growth in mobile subscribers compared to fixed lines, South Africa, 1994–2000 (Source: World Bank 2000c)

Table 10.2 *Key players in the South African telecommunications sector*

Sectors	Operators	Key players
Fixed wire telephony	1	Telkom
Cellular	2	MTN, Vodacom
Paging	23	Audiopage, Paging Plus, Radiospoor
Value added network services (VANs)	25	EDS Africa, FirstNet, Trafex
Radio trunking	3	Fleetcall, Qtrunk, One-to-One
Satellite	4–5	Iridium, Orbicom, Sentech, Telkom, Transtel
Public enterprise	2	Eskom, Transtel
Wireless data	2	Swiftnet, WBS

Source: SAITIS Baseline Studies 2000.

The Internet in Africa and South Africa

Measurements of Internet diffusion are based on indicators such as connectivity, number of hosts, number of websites, languages used, number of users, and other compound indices. Despite its rapid growth, from eleven connected states at the end of 1996, to the full fifty-four by September 2000, Internet access in Africa has been largely confined to the capital cities, although a growing number of countries do have points of presence (POPs) in some of the secondary towns (Jensen 2000). Moreover, connectivity speed in Africa is very low – many nations have international connectivity speeds roughly equivalent to a single analog modem (Press 2000). Future prospects (see World Bank 2000a) are particularly worrying, since OECD countries' per capita spending on information infrastructure (US$129.11) is eleven times that in Sub-Saharan Africa (US$11.56). This has obvious implications for the future divergence for quality, speed, and density of connectivity between developed countries and Sub-Saharan Africa. Another worrying aspect is related to the asymmetries in contents creation: Network Wizards[6] conducted a host survey showing that Sub-Saharan Africa generates only 0.4 percent of the global Web content (without South Africa this quantity reduces to 0.02 percent). Slow creation of Web content goes with slow diffusion, weak demand, and low usage of Internet technologies, even after the connectivity problem has been addressed.

The total number of African hosts' computers (excluding South Africa) permanently connected to the Internet reached almost 12,000 by January 2000.[7] A recent study by the UN Economic Commission for Africa puts current estimates of Africa's users at about 1 million outside South Africa, by assuming that each computer with an Internet or e-mail connection supports an average of three users. This works out at about one Internet user for every 250 people, compared to a world average of about one user for every 35 people, and a North American and European average of about one in three. This raw data expresses better than any other the extent of the existing digital divide and the possible implications on future development for many African countries.

A powerful description of the shortcomings of Africa's (outside South Africa) international Internet connectivity is provided by an experiment carried out by Semret (1998) at Columbia University in New York. He constructed a map of Africa showing the routes taken by traffic from Columbia University to each African Internet node, on August 3, 1998, and measured the time delay on each link. The nodes and the routes followed, traced with the software traceroute, showed that although almost all countries had at least one node with full (TCP/IP) connectivity, intraregional connectivity was almost non-existent. The "typical" country has a handful of local nodes, connected to a gateway linked via satellite or cable, directly to a major international carrier's network in Europe or North America. Thus, all Internet traffic between Ethiopia and Kenya, for example, goes through the USA. Given the substantial delay on long-distance lines (typically 500–1000ms) this means that, even if traffic is very low, the round-trip time (RTT) between neighbouring countries is typically more than one or two seconds, that is, 10 or 20 times slower than the RTT between Europe and North America. African countries have parallel slow links with the rest of the world whereas a small number of shared high capacity ones would provide much better connectivity, as the box below shows.

Increasing returns from connectivity

The most common mathematical model of a data communications link is the M/M/1 queue. In it, the average delay, T, is given by

$$T = 1/(C - r),$$

where C is the capacity of the link (bits per second) and r is the average traffic arrival rate (bits per second). Suppose two similar neighboring countries each have a long-distance link with capacity C and traffic r. They will both experience the same average delay T. Now if they share a single link with capacity $2C$, and send all their traffic $2r$ on it, they will both experience a delay of

$$1/(2C - 2r) = T/2,$$

i.e. half the delay they had when they both used their own link. This is called multiplexing gain, and it comes from the fact that, statistically, they will not be sending data packets at exactly the same times, so there will be times when one is not sending, and the other will get sole use of the full high-speed link.

Now since the cost of capacity $2C$ is generally less than double the cost of C (most of the cost of a link is independent of the capacity), it means that each provider spends less money, and gets double the performance! Of course, reliability is a good reason for having multiple links. But it is still clear that there is ample room for multiplexing gain in Africa. For content, commerce, etc., to flourish on the Internet in Africa, there must be intraregional traffic. Otherwise, Africans will be pure consumers and not producers in the information economy.

Source: Semret 1998

Internet penetration in South Africa

South Africa differs substantially from the rest of the continent: Web-based global electronic commerce was in the region of US$200 billion by 2000 and corporate use of the Internet is rapidly growing. The revenues of Internet service providers (ISPs) are estimated at ZAR700 millions (US$90 million) for 2000. Local access to the Internet is provided by having POPs in about a hundred cities and towns and local call tariff Internet access across the whole country.[8]

Internet penetration in South Africa continues to rise with half a million new Internet users in 1999, bringing the total to 1.82 million users. Based on current trends, the number of users is estimated to have grown to about 2.4 million by the end 2000. Figure 10.6 provides the evolution of three different indicators describing Internet penetration in South Africa. The first reports the number of Internet subscribers, which is less than the number of users because of multiple usage of accounts. The second indicator, Internet hosts, reflects the number of computers having a domain name. These are updated regularly at the Network Wizard website. The third is the number of Web pages. This last indicator is meant to capture relevant aspects of local content generation and of e-commerce potential.

According to the Media Africa.com (2000), in 1999 560,000 South Africans accessed the Internet through dial-up modems via ISPs, up from 366,000 at the end of 1998 – an increase of 194,000 and a growth rate of 53 percent per annum.[9] Corporate users also increased, with 980,000 users accessing the Internet from corporate networks in 1999, compared to 700,000 in 1998. Academic use of the Internet has also soared: the minimum number of academic users who actually use their accounts is 280,000, of which about 250,000 are catered for by Uninet, whilst privately funded schools have another 30,000 active account users (see Figure 10.7).

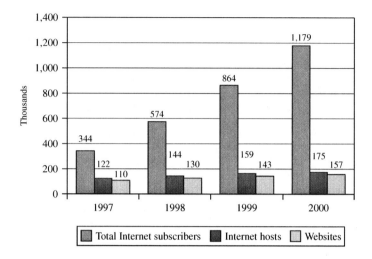

Figure 10.6 Internet indicators in South Africa, 1997–2000 (Source: World Bank 2000c)

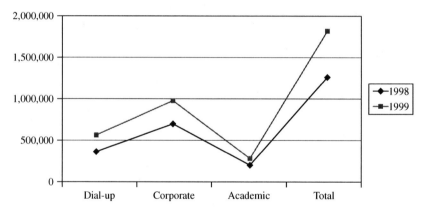

Figure 10.7 Internet users in South Africa by source of access, 1998 and 1999 (Source: Media Africa.com 2000)

Internet connectivity in South Africa

The Internet access sector in South Africa is extremely dynamic and has already proved to be a challenge for the regulatory authority. When, for example, Telkom moved into value added services with its rapid roll-out of POPs, the association of commercial ISPs (ISPA)[10] brought Telkom before the regulator and the Competition Board for allegedly exploiting its monopoly position on the supply of basic telecommunications infrastructure. Two years later the case is still unresolved, as Telkom still disputes SATRA's ruling that Internet access is a value added service and not a basic service.

South Africa's first Internet exchange point, UniForum, was set up in 1996. The basic principle was to provide free access to anyone wishing to connect to it. This peering point initially received support from a number of second- and third-tier Internet access providers, but none from first-tier providers (those with their own international link). ISPA has since established two peering points for its members, one in Johannesburg and the other in Cape Town (JINX and CINX), which are used by most of the ISPs, resulting in extensive savings in international bandwidth costs.

The bulk of South Africa's international Internet traffic is carried on the SAT-2 fiber optic cable which links Cape Town to the cross-Atlantic fiber backbone in the Azores, but there is also a growing number of satellite links operated by Telkom on behalf of some of its first-tier ISP customers. With Telkom's relatively low-cost international leased line tariffs to neighboring countries, access providers in Swaziland, Namibia, and Lesotho obtain their connectivity in the region rather than directly from the USA or Europe. South Africa is likely to expand its supply of cheap international bandwidth into the continent with its fiber optic cables which will soon link directly to Asia, Europe, and countries on the west coast of Africa, as well as with two very small aperture terminal (VSAT) ground stations.

Satellite technology is particularly relevant for connectivity in a sparsely populated country like South Africa. Telkom uses, and is an investing partner in, Intelsat, a commercial satellite communications service provider with seventeen geostationary satellites. Intelsat's global satellite system brings video, Internet, and voice/data service to users in more than 200 countries and provides the space segment for VSAT. The increased use of VSATs reflects the trend toward smaller, more intelligent, and less expensive earth stations, especially attractive in meeting remote location communications requirements. Figure 10.8 shows the takeover of the South African international Internet connectivity over the traditional circuit switch international telephone capacity.

Internet pricing

Pricing of a commodity such as Internet access is the result of the interplay between industry structure (number of firms, relevant technologies, and market power), its degree of competitiveness, and the relevant regulatory policies. At the same time, the industry structure itself is endogenously determined by profitability considerations affected by the prevailing prices. Prices are also essential in determining demand for Internet access, once the required infrastructure is in place, and in sending profitability signals to potential investors. The average total cost of using a local dial-up Internet account for five hours a month in Africa is about US$50 per month (usage fees and telephone time included, but

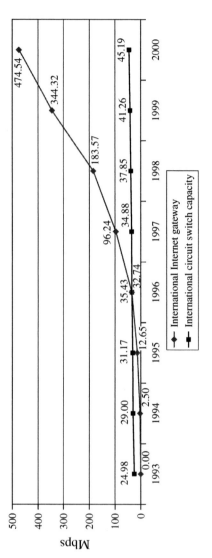

Figure 10.8 Internet international connectivity takes over: South Africa, 1993–2000 (Source: World Bank 2000c)

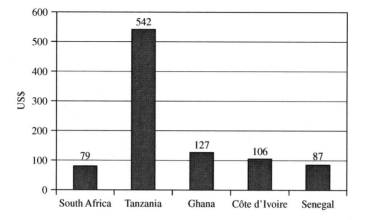

Figure 10.9 Annualized Internet access costs, 1998 (Source: World Bank 2000b)

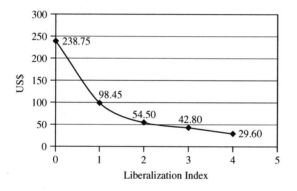

Figure 10.10 Monthly cost of accessing fifty pages per day, 1997 (Source: World Bank 2000b)

not telephone line rental). Nevertheless, ISP charges vary greatly – between US$10 and US$100 a month, largely reflecting the different levels of maturity of the markets, the varying tariff policies of the telecommunications operators, and the different national policies on wireless data services and on access to international telecommunications bandwidth (Jensen 2000). Internet access costs are relatively higher in Africa than elsewhere and they vary between countries, reflecting the degree of market liberalization. Figure 10.9 shows the annualized Internet costs for five different African countries in 1998.

Figure 10.10 shows the relation between the degree of market liberalization and Internet access prices as calculated by the World Bank (2000b).[11] Figure 10.11 shows the composition of the price for access in selected African

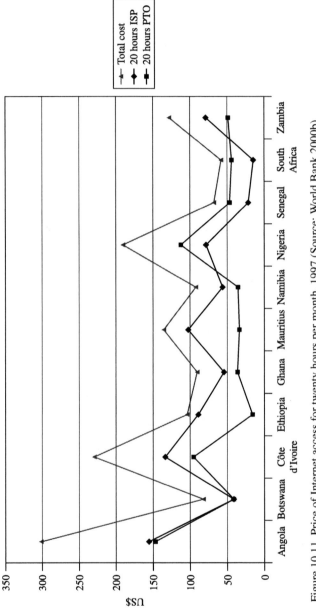

Figure 10.11 Price of Internet access for twenty hours per month, 1997 (Source: World Bank 2000b)

countries and the effect of the public telephone operator (PTO) on the total costs of Internet access. Figure 10.12 shows the relation between price of access and number of Internet hosts in selected African countries.

The shared access alternative

As demonstrated by the number of Internet users, costs for Internet access can be met by a significant number of South Africans but they remain prohibitive for the majority. Nevertheless, Internet access can be an important source of saving through substitution, for example between telephone and e-mail, and for internal and international migrant workers. It is also an important coordinating device for local communities, helping them to organize sporting, educational, religious, and business activities. It can be used to advertize and extend the market horizon of small businesses and to facilitate active participation in all levels of political life, from local non-governmental organizations (NGOs) to international global issues. This explains the growing success of shared access facilities such as kiosks, cybercafes, or PCs in community phone-shops, schools, police stations, and clinics, which can share the cost of equipment and access between a large number of users.

Internet centers are being set up by the government in former township areas. Known as "Dot ZA" centres, they are being established in informal settlements throughout the country, with the first project launched in the Pretoria township of Tembisa. The initiative is based on the Department of Communications donating computers, a place to house them, and Internet connectivity to the community of the area. Each community then runs the Dot ZA centre based on business principles. In addition to Internet connectivity, the centers are also used to conduct computer literacy programs to alleviate infrastructure and human capital constraints and to facilitate Internet access.

Many other similar projects are taking place in South Africa: the Government Communication and Information Service (GCIS) has set up three Multi-Purpose Community Centers, and intended to set up another twenty in 2000; the Post Office has committed ZAR 2 million (US$253,000) to the development of a smart-card-based "Public Internet Terminal" (PIT) which will be deployed at every post office in the country. There is a growing literature on the viability of the Telecenters model[12] and the emerging consensus is for a bottom-up approach, through community participation in the design phase complemented by a feasible commercial model, to provide the incentives required for the continuation of the projects.

The box below describes a revealing case study where radio–satellite links were used to connect two very remote schools to the Internet.

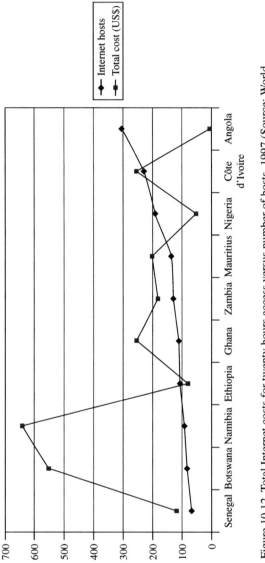

Figure 10.12 Total Internet costs for twenty hours access versus number of hosts, 1997 (Source: World Bank 2000b)

*Connecting two rural community schools in a remote area of
South Africa*

The Information and Communications Unit of the Council for Scientific
and Industrial Research (CSIR) (Mikomtek) supplied Internet access in a
project in Manguzi, a rural community in South Africa's KwaZulu Natal
province near the Mozambican border. The initial part of the project
consisted of the establishment of a Telecenter in the town. At a community
workshop, two headmasters requested connection for their schools, which
had no telephone connection and were 5km away, to the Telecenter. The
challenge lay in devising a cheap, robust, and legal solution.

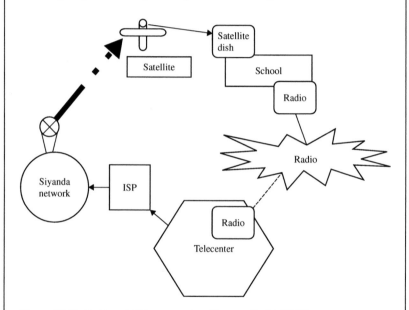

Figure 10.13 Radio-satellite connection (Source: Smith 2000)

The eventual solution combined satellite Internet broadcasting with
the radio network. The radio link via the Telecenter is used for the uplink
path (in place of a telephone line) and the satellite is used to download
Web content directly to the PC at the school. Figure 10.13 provides a dia-
grammatic representation of the network combining the two technologies.
Satellite receivers are usually capable of receiving data at much higher
rates than would be possible via normal telephone lines. The Satellite
ISP chosen, Siyanda, makes use of the PAS-7 satellite. The ordinary
90cm digital satellite broadcasting (DSB) satellite dishes are used for

reception. Requests from clients are sent to Siyanda via virtual private networks (VPNs) over Mweb's (a local ISP) terrestrial infrastructure.

The equipment required at each site is as follows:

- Schools: radio, yagi antenna, satellite receiver card and DSB dish
- Telecenter: radio, omni-directional antenna, connection to Telecenter local area network (LAN).

The total cost, including PCs, is estimated at US$2,300 for the Telecenter and US$3,000 per rural site. The advantage of this solution is that the bulk of the costs are one-off. The recurring monthly cost is minimal (US$40). In the case of Manguzi, an arrangement was made between the schools and the Telecenter that the costs will be funded from the profit made by the Telecenter.

Source: Smith 2000.

Conclusion: the challenge posed by the shortage of human resources

Successful diffusion of the Internet, unlike the adoption processes of earlier, less interactive technologies, requires a minimum level of computer literacy and, at least, basic reading and writing skills. The development of a successful information society capable of remaining competitive in the progressively more global marketplace and succeeding in an e-commerce environment requires large investment in human capital. Two main channels will shape the impact of the IT revolution on the labor market: the first is related to the redefinition of skills and competencies required to perform tasks in an IT intensive work space, whilst the second operates through the opening of a worldwide labor market, created by the mobility of capital rather than workers, once the basic infrastructure and human capital requirements are met. At present, IT skills are in short supply in South Africa and, as with many other developing countries, the country experiences a brain drain. In addition, there is the constraint imposed by the special need of rebalancing the ethnic division of labor within the country as envisaged by the Employment Equity Act of 1998.[13]

Table 10.3 provides official estimates of the net migration flows among professional categories, although there is a wide consensus that these official data are underestimating the real extent of this phenomenon. The country also faces a mismatch in the labor market, with a high unemployment rate and a shortage of an IT skilled labor force. Estimates of this shortage are very severe as shown by Table 10.4.

As a result of increased competition for the services of IT professionals, basic salaries in the sector have increased by 19 percent in real terms in the last four years.

Table 10.3 *Net migration flows, 1989–1997*

Occupation	Net migration
Engineers	−329
Medical practitioners	−28
Medical professionals	−22
Education and related	−228
Accountant and related	−250
Managerial	−528
Total	−1,385

Source: Statistics SA 1997.

Table 10.4 *Skills shortages, 1998 and 2002*

IT job category	Shortage of permanent staff, 1998	permanent staff, Shortage of 2002
Project leaders	15%	38%
Analysts	26%	58%
Programmers	37%	48%

Source: 1998 CPL Salary Survey, from SAITIS Baseline studies 2000.

IT skilled human capital is becoming costlier and more in demand. This combination of factors could introduce a bottleneck in the ability of the most dynamic sectors of the economy to grow at the rate required to fulfil the potential of the transformations taking place. A strong investment in human capital and R&D is essential to cope with these emerging constraints. Strategies to rectify these imbalances between the demand and supply of skilled workers are probably harder to implement than the ongoing sector liberalization and extension of the IT physical infrastructure.

The diffusion of IT skills through the traditional educational system presents, indeed, formidable challenges, since only 7.5 percent of South African schools have adequate telephone lines and electricity and, in 1996, out of 27,066 schools only 2,241 had computers, and these were predominantly white schools located in urban areas. Apart from the focus on post-secondary education, where it is easier to intervene in the short term and which produces highly sought after science graduates, an enormous effort is required to develop new strategies to overcome the human capital constraints. On the other hand, South Africa can act as a brain magnet within its region, competing on the international labor market for highly skilled workers from abroad. However, this strategy, which is already taking place, is not yet sufficient to overcome shortages and will generate further problems among its neighboring countries, whose stability and strength South Africa desperately needs.

Acknowledgments

The author gratefully acknowledges the generous support of the Institute of Developing Economies (IDE-JETRO) and the British Economic and Social Research Council under the grant reference number: R000238563. He also wishes to thank Mr. Yacoob Abba Omar Deputy Chief Executive Officer, Government Communication and Information System (GCIS), South Africa, for his help during the part of the research done in South Africa.

Notes

1. For an overview see Panzar, 2000.
2. The South African government has recently announced a plan to float between 20 and 30 percent of Telkom during the first half of 2001 as part of a privatization drive expected to raise at least ZAR40 billion (US$5.47 billion) over the next three years.
3. It has now become the Independent Communications Authority of South Africa (ICASA) responsible to the SA Department of Communications (DOC) for regulating the telecommunications and broadcasting sectors. The name changed from SATRA after it was merged with the broadcasting authority (IBA) in early 2000. The new body is the result of the South African Communications Authority Bill, amended to the Independent Communication Authority of South Africa (ICASA) Act, signed by South African President Thabo Mbeki recently.
4. When, for example, Vodacom and MTN received their cellular telecommunications licenses in 1994, a condition was the signing of a JEDP agreement.
5. Sentech has some 500 television transmitter towers as well as various FM, medium-wave and short-wave transmitters and satellite services. Eskom has over 250,000km of high-voltage lines, which it is already starting to string with fiber optic cable for future telecommunications links.
6. See the homepage www.nw.com for updated domain surveys.
7. The figure may actually be closer to 25,000 due to the measurement technique, which cannot count hosts that are not referenced in domain name servers and those that are registered under the generic top-layer domains (TLDs).
8. For example, the newly established Telkom SAIX national single POP access number: 086000 7249.
9. ISPs retain a strong customer base, with seventeen having over 1,000 dial-up sub-scribers. There were 112 ISPs in business at the end of 1999.

10. The Internet Service Providers' Association (ISPA) was formed in 1996 with nine member companies, three years after the first commercial ISP opened its door in South Africa. ISPA now represents forty-five Internet access providers in South Africa, and its members provide access to the majority of the country's Internet population. (Adapted from The Star 2000.)

11. Liberalisation is measured through a special Index: each country receives one point for each one of the following: new telecommunications law and regulations; introduction of private investment into non-basic services excluding cellular; introduction of private investment into basic services; introduction of private investment into services.

12. For a review, see Benjamin 2000.

13. The Act requires designated employers to submit yearly plans to the Department of Labor on how they are addressing racial and gender imbalances within their organizations.

References

Benjamin, P. 2000, *Telecentre 2000 Literature Review*, Wits University, http://www.sn.apc.org/community/T2000LitRev.htm, April 2000.

Jensen, M. 2000, *African Internet Status*, http://www3.sn.apc.org/afstat.htm.

Media Africa.com 2000, *4th South African Internet Services Industry Survey 2000*, summary available at http://www.mediaafrica.co.za/3.html.

Panzar, J. C. 2000, A methodology for measuring the costs of universal service obligations, *Information Economics and Policy*, 12(3), 211–220.

Press, L. 2000, From the state of the Internet: growth and gaps, paper presented at the Conference INET 2000, Yokohama, Japan, http://www.isoc.org/inet2000/cdproceedings/8e/8e_4.htm.

SAITIS Baseline studies 2000, *A Survey of the IT Industry and Related Job Skills in South Africa*, IDRC, Pretoria http://www.saitis.co.za/studies/jobs_skills.

Semret, N. 2000, *African Internet Topology and Traffic Report*, http://www.comet.columbia.edu/~nemo/netmap.

Nye, S. and Shetty, V. 1998, Mandela voices support for African telecom development, *Communications Week International*, June 5, 1998.

Smith, R. 2000, Overcoming Regulatory and Technological Challenges to Bring Internet Access to a Sparsely Populated, Remote Area: A Case Study, paper presented at the Conference INET 2000, Yokohama, Japan, http://www.isoc.org/inet2000/cdproceedings/8d/8d_4.htm.

The Star 2000, *Business Report Survey on the Internet Service Providers*, Association, June 6, 2000.

Statistics SA 1995, *October Household Survey*, Pretoria, http://www.statssa.gov.za/default3.asp.

1997, Pretoria, http://www.statssa.gov.za/default3.asp.

Telkom 2000, http://www.telkom.co.za.

World Bank 2000a, The networking revolution opportunities and challenges for developing countries, infoDev Working Paper, http://www.infodev.org/library/NetworkingRevolution.doc.

2000b, *Economic Internet Toolkit for African Policy Makers*, infoDev Report, http://www.infodev.org/projects/finafcon.htm.

2000c, *Information Infrastructure Indicators, 1990–2010*, infoDev, http://www.infodev.org/projects/375/fin375.htm.

11 The IT revolution in the USA: the current situation and problems

Soon-Yong Choi and Andrew B. Whinston

Introduction

The recent economic changes that have occurred against the backdrop of rapid growth of production and use of computers, the Internet, and networked business processes are often referred to as the "Digital Revolution," bestowing on it an importance comparable to that of the Industrial Revolution. Certainly, the IT sector – broadly defined to include computer hardware, software and services, communications equipment, and communications services industries (see Table 11.1) – is at the forefront of these changes, and although computers and business applications have been around since the 1970s, the Internet and e-business uses of related IT are catalysts for change.

In order to evaluate the size of the IT industry sector it is necessary to choose an appropriate definition. The US government uses the IT producing industries shown in Table 11.1 as their barometer of the emerging digital economy, and on this basis, *The Emerging Digital Economy* II (US Department of Commerce 1999) reported that the IT sector grew by 17 percent during the second half of the 1990s and accounted for 8.2 percent (US$729 billion) of the US economy in 1999.

As the Internet becomes the means by which computers and other IT products are used as economic tools, the IT sector becomes synonymous with the so-called Internet economy. This view of the sector concentrates on IT as well as digital goods and thus is defined as that part of the economy that deals with information goods (such as software), online material, knowledge-based goods, the new media, and the supporting technology industries that provide computer and network devices.

An alternative view focuses on the fact that the new economy exists on networks, so the IT sector is expanded to include what is often referred to as the e-business sector. This Internet-native sector may coexist with traditional "bricks and mortar" operations within a single company so, to gauge the scale of the Internet economy under this definition, government bureaux now collect

Table 11.1 *Information technology industries*

Sector	Industries
Hardware	Computers and equipment
	Wholesale trade of computers and equipment
	Retail trade of computers and equipment
	Calculating and office machines
	Magnetic and optical recording media
	Electron tubes
	Printed circuit boards
	Semiconductors
	Passive electronic components
	Industrial instruments for measurement
	Instruments for measuring electricity
	Laboratory analytical instruments
Software	Computer programming services
	Prepackaged software
	Wholesale trade of software
	Retail trade of software
	Computer integrated systems design
	Computer processing, data preparation
	Information retrieval services
	Computer services management
	Computer rental and leasing
	Computer maintenance and repair
	Computer-related services
Communications equipment	Household audio and video equipment
	Telephone and telegraph equipment
	Radio, TV and communications equipment
Communications services	Telephone and telegraph communications
	Radio and TV broadcasting
	Cable and other pay TV services

Source: US Department of Commerce 2000.

online retail sales data as a separate category. The US Census Bureau reports that e-commerce retail sales amounted to US$6.4 billion (out of a total of US$800) in the third quarter of 2000 (US Census Bureau 2000). This is less than 1 percent of total retail sales, but e-commerce continues to grow. Whilst total retail sales figures fluctuate around US$800 billion, e-commerce sales have risen continuously from US$5.2 billion in the fourth quarter of 1999.

Although most Internet businesses operate in both physical and digital realms, many have opted to separate out their online business units. Barnes and Noble, for example, operates both physical bookstores and an online venture, barne-sandnoble.com; *The Wall Street Journal* will deliver hard copy to your home or charge a subscription for the online interactive edition.

The narrowly defined IT sector is certainly just the tip of the emerging iceberg. As the effect of the Internet becomes all pervasive, the size and scale of the Internet economy cannot be gauged simply by an amalgamation of various IT sectors, nor by recording the share of the economy represented by online, digital versions of physical products and services. The Internet economy encompasses the whole economic sphere, physical as well as online, which is affected by digital technologies and applications. This definition does, however, render it impossible to measure. Within the context of our discussion, we will use the conventional definition of the IT sector as the computer-related industries.

Economic status of the US IT sector

The IT sector in the USA grew vigorously during the 1990s. Although computers and related industries have steadily increased their output and employment since the late 1960s, desktop computers introduced in the 1980s and Internet networking in the 1990s have been the major sources of growth and economic strength. In the following sections, we review the IT sector under four major headings: output, employment, investment, and productivity.

Output growth in the IT sector

A major aspect of the IT sector is its continuing strong growth during the late 1990s. From 1995 to 2000, according to government reports, gross domestic output grew at an average annual rate of 17 percent, its share of the total economy in 2000 rising to over 8 percent compared to less than 6 percent ten years earlier. More importantly, IT industries accounted for an average 30 percent of total real economic growth.

The GDP growth clearly shows the importance of the IT sector. Such a strong performance is also evident in revenue growths among IT-utilizing firms. The Internet Economy Indicators, developed by the Center for Research in Electronic Commerce at the University of Texas at Austin and Cisco Systems, have produced a more reasonable estimation of the size of the Internet economy as US$300 billion in 1998 (against the estimate of US$729 billion from the US Department of Commerce). Certainly, there is a lack of quality statistics for measuring the size of the Internet economy. The Standard Industrial Classification (SIC) system was developed sixty years ago. A proposed new system, the North American Industry Classification System (NAICS), adds new categories such as the information sector but, nevertheless, the problem remains as IT and the Internet affect almost all sectors of the economy.

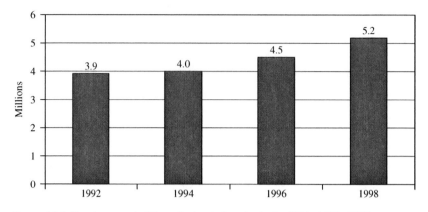

Figure 11.1 Employment in IT-producing industries in the USA, 1992–1998
(Source: Bureau of Labor Statistics)

Employment in the IT sector

Rapidly growing IT output implies strong growth in overall employment. In 1998, the IT sector accounted for 6.1 percent of the US workforce, about 7.4 million workers. This figure includes workers in the IT-producing industries listed in Table 11.1 as well as IT occupations in other industries, such as system analysts, computer engineers, and other personnel operating and maintaining IT infrastructure. From 1994 to 1998, IT industry employment grew by 29 percent, to 5.2 million, whilst IT occupations in other industries increased by 22 percent (see Figure 11.1).

A similar trend is shown in the e-commerce focused Internet Economy Indicators study (Center for Research in Electronic Commerce [CREC] 2000). This study dissects the economy into four layers: network and computer infrastructure layer, application layer, intermediary layer, and Internet commerce layer. Together, these four layers include IT-producing industries as well as the e-commerce sector. According to the report, the Internet economy now employs almost 2.5 million workers in the USA. This number is comparable to the number of employees in such traditionally defined industries as governments, telecommunications and public utility, or insurance sectors.

In addition, the Internet sector is growing rapidly. From 1998 to 1999, employment grew at a rate of 36 percent (650,000 new jobs) (see Table 11.2), but the share of the sector within the overall US economy grew at an even faster rate, rising from US$323 billion to US$524 billion, a growth of 62 percent. This suggests that more and more companies are becoming e-business firms. Individually, Internet economy firms saw a higher revenue growth than physical firms (11 percent versus 4.2 percent).

Table 11.2 *Employment in the Internet economy sector, 1998 and 1999*

	1998	1999	Growth
Infrastructure layer	527,037	778,602	48%
Application layer	513,125	681,568	33%
Intermediary layer	290,856	340,673	17%
E-commerce layer	577,937	726,735	26%
Total	1,819,716	2,476,122	36%

Source: CREC 2000.

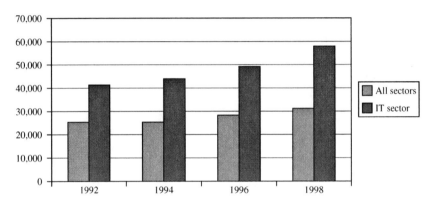

Figure 11.2 Annual wages per private sector worker, 1992–1998 (Source: Economics and Statistics Administration)

The growth in IT workers had a significant effect on the labor market in terms of wage level and market imbalances. IT industry wages are consistently higher than average. For example, the average wage for IT industry was 85 percent higher than that for all private workers in 1998 (US$58,000 versus US$32,400), and the gap is growing (see Figure 11.2).

As demand grows with the rapid deployment of IT and e-commerce, the labor market is failing to supply enough high-skilled workers. Serious shortages in the USA have been met by an increasing number of foreign workers admitted under H-1B visas, some 115,000 in 1998. Currently, 60 percent of H-1B visa applicants are in the IT sector. Federal efforts are targeted at training domestic IT workers, but shortages persist. In this context, the practice of farming out software and other computer-related projects to foreign countries will create a significant change in labor market equilibrium and result in a new phase of the international division of labor.

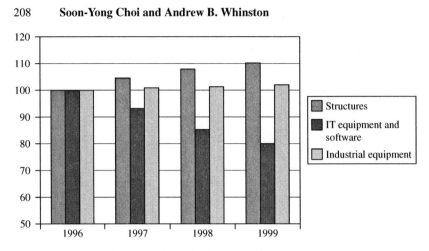

Figure 11.3 Private fixed investment, Price Index, (1996 = 100), 1996–1999
(Source: US Department of Commerce, *Survey of Current Business*, various issues)

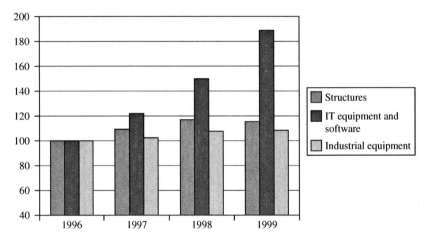

Figure 11.4 Private fixed investment, Quantity Index (1996 = 100), 1996–1999
(Source: US Department of Commerce, *Survey of Fixed Business*, various issues)

Investment in IT capital stock

Industry spending on IT capital equipment, including software, is a dominant factor in capital stock accumulation by private firms. In 1998, 46 percent of all investment was in IT equipment and software. On the other hand, the share of investment in "other capital equipment" such as machinery, has been shrinking.

The primary factor is the declining price for IT equipment and software (see Figure 11.3). Figure 11.4 clearly demonstrates the relative growth in IT investment in comparison to other types of capital investment. The most recent

Table 11.3 *Private investment in IT, 1999/2000*

	Amount in second quarter 2000[a]	% change from preceding quarter			
		III-99	IV-99	I-00	II-00
Structures	277.2	−6.2	9.7	22.3	4.8
IT equipment and software	671.6	28.7	20.5	31.4	29.6
Industrial equipment	164.2	9.3	10.8	16.9	14.0
Residential	371.4	−3.1	0.5	3.2	0.0
Total	1776.4	30.7	7.2	16.4	10.9

Note:
[a] In billions of chained 1996 dollars; all others are in %.
Source: US Department of Commerce, Bureau of Economic Analysis 2000.

figures show a growth of 10.9 percent in total private fixed investment (see Table 11.3). IT equipment and software accounted for 38% of the total, growing strongly quarter on quarter.

Labor and multifactor productivity and IT

Whilst the IT sector shows continued, strong growth and an increasing share of the overall US economy, there is a lingering question about the effect of computers and IT on firm-level productivity. Studies on IT productivity have not provided a clear answer.

Average labor productivity (ALP) measures the amount of output from a unit of labor input or, simply, output per hour. For example, if a worker who used to produce one car in forty work hours now produces two cars in fifty hours, labor productivity has grown by 60 percent, from 0.025 to 0.04. The sources of this productivity growth may be more efficient tools, better working conditions, better work organization, new assembly technology, favorable management, or any other factor. Therefore, growing labor productivity indicates more efficient uses of inputs that conventionally include capital inputs, materials, and energy.

An interesting productivity measure, especially in evaluating the effects of increasing IT equipment, software, and other capital investment, is one that controls not only total labor hours but also other major capital stock. In this measure, we evaluate efficiency gains that are not directly attributable to increasing work hours or more machinery. Such a measure is called multifactor productivity (MFP). The US Bureau of Labor Statistics uses a combined unit of labor and capital inputs in defining MFP. MFP explains the effects of other, residual input factors and measures the growth in output that is not explained by all inputs under consideration. If is often called total factor productivity (TFP).

More formally, consider a simple production function

$$Q = A^* f(K, L)$$

or, taking account of growth,

$$\Delta lnQ = \Delta lnA + r^* \Delta lnK + (1 - r)\Delta lnL$$

where Q is output, K is capital input, L is labor input, and A represents an augmentation factor, a factor by which output grows given a set of capital and labor inputs. (r) and $(1 - r)$ represent the share of labor and capital in the total input, here showing constant return to scale. The change in A represents total factor productivity. To calculate the average labor productivity that relates to output per labor hour (H), we can represent the above equation in terms of $q = Q/H$, and $k = K/H$. The logarithmic expression of this per hour becomes

$$\Delta lnq = \Delta lnA + r^* \Delta lnk + (1 - r)(\Delta lnL - \Delta lnH)$$

or, in other words,

$$\text{ALP} = \text{MFP} + \text{capital deepening} + \text{labor quality}$$

Capital deepening measures the growth in capital services per hour. It makes workers more productive by providing more capital for each hour. Labor quality is defined as the difference between growth rates of labor input and hours worked. The above relationship indicates that average labor productivity is the sum of multifactor productivity, capital deepening, and labor quality. In other words, MFP explains productivity gains that are not explained by capital deepening and increases in labor quality.

A series of previous studies on labor productivity showed IT's minimal impact on productivity. Roach (1987) found that the labor productivity of "information workers" had failed to keep up with that of "production workers." Baily and Chakrabarti (1988) found similar results and suggested several possible reasons, including incorrect resource allocation, output measurement problems, and redistribution of output within industries. Similar results are found in others studies including Morrison and Berndt (1990), Berndt and Morrison (1991), and Roach (1991).

The early phase of IT investment in firms was even more disappointing. Loveman (1994), who analysed the impact of IT and non-IT capital, as well as labor and inventory on the productivity of large firms primarily in the manufacturing sector during 1978 to 1984, found that the output elasticity of IT capital was negative. This suggests that investment dollars in IT could have been spent more efficiently elsewhere.

This inability to discern a positive relationship between IT investment and productivity measurements underlies the "IT productivity paradox": ubiquitous computers do not generate noticeable productivity gains.

Table 11.4 *Average annual percentage contributions of IT to labor productivity, 1991–1995 and 1996–1999*

	1991–1995	1996–1999
IT contribution through capital deepening	0.51	0.96
IT contribution through MFP growth	0.23	0.49
All other contributions	0.79	1.12
Total	1.53	2.57

Source: US Department of Labor, Bureau of Labor Statistics.

But new studies indicating IT's positive contribution to productivity are beginning to emerge: Bresnahan's (1986) study found a sizable consumer surplus due to investments in computing technologies in the unregulated parts of the financial services sector; Brynjolfsson and Hitt (1993, 1996) and Lichtenberg (1995) found significant productivity gains from investments in computer capital. With the same data used by Loveman but with different input deflators and modeling techniques, Barua and Lee (1997) and Lee and Barua (1999) also found that IT contributed significantly more to firm performance than either labor or non-IT capital.

A significant break in productivity growth occurred in the mid-1990s. Although growth in the early 1990s was greater than in the previous decade, it picked up remarkably from 1996. Table 11.4 shows this trend with its three major components. First, "capital deepening" means that firms accumulate more capital relative to labor inputs, for example more computers per employee. A significant source of capital deepening in the 1990s was the continuously falling prices for computer hardware and software. In comparable terms, firms in the 1990s increased investment in IT capital – computer hardware and software – at a rate of double-digit annual percentage points whilst other capital stock averaged less than one percent.

Significant growth is seen in the multifactor productivity measures. MFP refers to productivity gains that are attributed to inputs other than labor and capital stock – for example technical and organisational changes, improvements in services, and economies of scale. Improvements in business services, process innovations, and similar qualitative changes are all reflected in MFP growth. In this sense, the productivity gains from the use of IT and the Internet in manufacturing and service sectors may be represented by strong MFP growth in the 1990s.

The sudden acceleration since 1995 in overall labor productivity as well as MFP, strongly suggests the maturing of the Internet and networked IT applications. In earlier years, IT often consisted of expensive proprietary applications such as forecasting sales, managing inventory, controlling quality, accounting, etc., that were used to improve firms' efficiency. Since the mid-1990s, we have witnessed a rapid increase in the power of PCs and the proliferation of network technologies characterized by the Internet and the World Wide Web. As a result, there has been a dramatic change from centralized mainframe-based computing to a Web-based distributed computing environment. Today Internet-based IT is not just used to make internal improvements, but also to interact with customers, manage the supply chain, and to coordinate and collaborate with trading partners. The Internet economy provides the opportunity to do business in completely new ways through the innovative use of IT. These gains may be reflected in the strong MFP growth in the late 1990s.

IT in e-business implementation

As firms and markets make greater use of computers and software, an over-riding feature of IT-intensive firms doing business in the networked environment is a closer, real-time interaction between suppliers, producers, distributors, and consumers. Interactive processes alone place new demands on firms and open up new opportunities for those that can respond to the need for increased flexibility.

An e-business firm gets its demand information directly from its customers which is passed on immediately to its suppliers, who will be expected to react promptly. A failure to do so will provide market opportunities for its competitors. Such rapid response requires a very flexible organisation.

The use of IT technology helps e-business firms to respond more interactively and dynamically to customers' demands. Online retailers can carry a far greater number of products than physical stores that must optimize their limited shelf space. Even a Barnes and Noble superstore cannot stock all popular titles as well as those that are infrequently requested. Customers who want out-of-stock books must search other stores or request a special order. In addition, revenue-generating or promotional activities, coffee shops, and reading lounges take up space which could otherwise be used to display books. As a result, many customers find themselves better off searching for specific titles in online bookstores. With limited space, a physical store must make a choice that satisfies some customers while neglecting the needs of others.

Characteristics of e-business firms

The digital revolution certainly changes the way in which firms are organized and the economy operates. But we need to define the digital revolution. This is best accomplished by comparing the modus operandi of industrial and digital economies.

In traditional industries, mass production techniques have been chosen as a way of reducing costs and prices but, as a result, the goods lack diversity. In addition, these production techniques are unable to respond rapidly to changing levels of demand: lower demand results in excess capacity, and higher demand could require the building of a new factory. Small, flexible firms can respond to changes in demand and heterogeneous consumer tastes more rapidly than the large, specialized firms that minimize costs through economies of scale. Cost minimization requires a specific production level and at this level the flexible firm will be at a cost disadvantage, but when demand falls, or there is a need for customized goods, the costs of the flexible firm will be lower.

This can be characterized as a trade-off between flexibility and efficiency (Mills 1984). But it is possible to argue that digital technologies will lower costs at all levels of production and, in that case, there is no trade-off to consider: e-business firms will be superior to physical firms in all aspects.

An IT-intensive e-business firm optimizes its production while maximizing customer choices. E-business firms must recognise the flexibility embodied in digital technologies and apply them to meet diverse and changing market demands. When customers' priority is low prices with little regard for choice, mass production is the answer. When customers look for quality products that match their tastes and requirements, a flexible manufacturing regime – even though it may not be the lowest cost solution – is called for. In the Internet-driven economy, the goal of economic operation shifts toward giving more satisfaction to real-time demand.

Organizational effects on e-businesses

The IT revolution is also challenging firms to organize in a way that more closely resembles the natural marketplace where buyers and sellers interact directly. This differs dramatically from the traditional vertical organisational structure. A traditional corporation has many divisions covering purchasing, manufacturing, marketing, sales, financing and accounting, human resources, and customer service. In this unitary (U) form, divisions are organised by function, with each function handling all the firm's products. Since the nineteenth century, many industrial companies have used the U-form to exploit its inherent economies of scale, minimize internal costs, and maximize production and operating efficiencies.

As firms grew in size during the industrial age, larger firms were often organized into multiple divisions, each with their own product lines, and independent functional divisions operating within each unit. This multidivisional form, the M-form, is epitomized by General Motors which includes Chevrolet, Buick, Cadillac, and other divisions, each in turn organised in a U-form. In both of these traditional organisational forms, the firm's internal structure for control and monitoring is hierarchical. At the highest level, the CEO makes planning and strategic decisions, while the functions are progressively narrowed as we move down the hierarchy through upper, middle, and lower management levels and down to the shop floors. This hierarchical, or vertical, structure of control relies on coordinated decision-making at each level, which covers larger and larger divisions as we go up the hierarchy.

In comparison, marketplaces have a horizontal structure since there is no hierarchical decision-making. Instead, sellers and buyers make purchasing decisions individually, whilst coordination is carried out by the market (for example, through haggling). The advent of the networked economy signals a growing trend toward horizontal coordination within a firm. A "virtual" firm is best understood as a structural form that resembles a market rather than a hierarchical organisation. An e-business firm is primarily a networked business that emphasizes communications and collaboration amongst its employees, as well as with its suppliers and customers.

As the Internet technologies enable a firm to be organized into loosely fitted divisions, or several firms acting as one, association, alliance, and close coordination amongst businesses become important. Like traditional companies, networked associations and alliances come in many shapes and sizes.

An online association may be as simple as having hypertext links between members' websites, the very essence of the World Wide Web. Amazon.com may have only one store but it has built over 100,000 brokers on the Internet who channel their visitors to Amazon's site. These brokers are called Amazon Associates, who feature hypertext links on their Web pages that take the visitor directly to Amazon's product page. Literary review sites including *The New York Times Book Review*, other online publications, and those run by individuals receive referral fees based on actual purchases. Yahoo and other major players redirect their visitors to associated retail sites but they may also take it a step further and own these sites outright. Alliances and cross-ownership amongst Web portals, content producers such as Disney, television networks and magazines, and telecommunications companies are increasingly consolidating Internet businesses into a few large e-businesses.

Information technology and the new economy

The decade-long expansion of the US economy accompanied by strong IT growth and low inflation and unemployment has been characterized as "the new economy." Its characteristics are in a large part related to advances of IT, digital technologies and the Internet in almost all aspects of economic life.

However, defining the new economy becomes more challenging as the seemingly strong economy shows signs of slowdown or even recession. Optimism for a brand new economic reality may succumb to a growing view that IT has

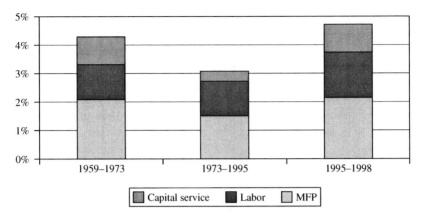

Figure 11.5 Sources of US economic growth, 1959–1998 (Source: Jorgenson and Stiroh 2000)

not been a critical factor in current economic growth. Increasing capital and IT stock as well as software and services account for the largest part of economic growth (see Figure 11.5). Nevertheless, there is a continuing debate on how to interpret the economic effects of IT-related investment.

The new economy cannot be defined by simple measurements of specific sectoral growth or performance. Rather, the widespread applications of IT and the Internet are changing the very nature of production, distribution, and provision of goods and services. As a result, the new economic reality should be investigated in terms of fundamental shifts in the mode of production rather than a shift in sectoral composition within the economy.

The hallmark of our modern economy has been industrial goods and production technologies that can churn out millions of goods at the lowest unit cost. From ordinary household goods such as silverware and dishes, to mass-produced industrial goods like automobiles and consumer appliances, increasing availability and decreasing prices have brought about an unimaginable level of mass consumption. Nevertheless, mass-produced industrial goods are standardized and, as a result, cannot fit specialized needs.

The economics of industrial goods demands the least cost solution and the pervasive focus on costs has become the limiting factor in both product choice for customers and manufacturing options open to producers. Value is created, not from maximizing user satisfaction, but from minimizing costs, not from flexibility in production, but from a production efficiency that often disregards customers' wants and needs. Value creation in the industrial age flows in a linear, rigid, inflexible, and predetermined stage of pre-production research, manufacturing, marketing, and sales. The need to minimize costs is so overwhelming

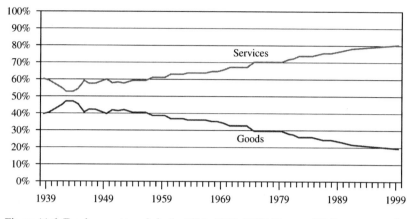

Figure 11.6 Employment trends in the USA, 1939–2000 (Source: US Department of Labor, Bureau of Labor Statistics)

that firms apply the same cost economics to the non-manufacturing stages of their business such as distribution, inventory management, and retailing.

The new service economy

Partly because of the economic efficiency achieved during the Industrial Revolution, manufacturing now rarely accounts for more than half of a firm's total operating costs. Product research, marketing and advertising, sales, customer support, and other non-production activities have become major aspects of a business organization. This trend toward a non-manufacturing profile is reflected in today's focus on business strategies revolving around quality management, IT, customer focus, brand loyalty, and process re-engineering.

In terms of overall employment, four out of five US workers are engaged in service production rather than goods production in 2000 (see Figure 11.6). In terms of gross domestic product by major type of product, the services sector amounted to US$4,563 billion compared to US$3,544 billion for the goods sector in 1999.

In developed countries, the service sector, which includes conventional as well as government services, now accounts for the majority of gross value added, ranging from 72.2 percent (the USA) to 50.2 percent (Korea). Table 11.5 summarizes sectoral contributions. Likewise, the service sector is the engine behind employment growth in the USA and other developed countries. During the period 1970 to 1994, employment in the service sector grew by 70 percent. In contrast, manufacturing employment has not seen any significant growth or has even decreased.

Table 11.5 *Sectoral contributions for*
selected OECD countries, 1998 (percent)

	Agriculture	Industry	Services
Australia	3.3	26.4	70.4
Austria	2.4	33.1	64.5
France	3.2	26.1	70.8
Germany	1.3	32.1	66.6
Italy	3.1	30.4	66.5
Japan	1.7	37.2	61.1
Korea	5.1	44.8	50.2
Mexico	5.3	29.2	65.6
Poland	4.8	36.5	58.7
UK	1.3	28.8	69.9
USA	1.7	26.1	72.2

Source: OECD 2000.

The new economics of choice maximization instead of cost minimization is best applied to the service sector, where meeting customer demands becomes more important than optimizing production costs. However, industrial production techniques have been applied to service production without considering the differences between the two sectors. Knowledge and digital technology are as much an essential part of industrial manufacturing as they are of the Internet-driven economy. The use of knowledge in the digital economy, however, focuses on providing customers with more choice. Instead of standardizing products, the digital revolution drives firms to focus on maximizing value by customizing products and meeting consumption needs.

To offer more choice and satisfaction, business processes must be flexible and responsive. Web-based supply chain management, trading through online auctions, targeted marketing and sales, and interactive customer service create value not simply by reducing costs, but by allowing firms to be responsive to customers' needs.

The new service economy departs from the cost minimization economics of the industrial economy, but this transformation does not come automatically simply because we are endowed with IT and digital goods. For example, typical information goods, such as news and databases, are subject to the same economics as industrial goods as long as they are traded as manufactured goods. Cost minimization is still a necessary concern in the newspaper business. Limitations of the industrial age will translate into the Internet economy even when newspapers and magazines are put on the Web if these online products are nothing more than digitized versions of their physical counterparts. Many content producers and knowledge vendors may be selling digital goods, but they are far from participating in the digital economy if their products still conform to the cost-minimization economics of the industrial age.

The global prevalence of the Internet has brought integration and versatility to the existing computer and network technologies, and has opened up possibilities for widespread applications of these technologies to conduct commerce, to provide entertainment and communication, to file and pay taxes, to manage personal finances, to conduct research and education, etc. In essence, the Internet fits its characterization as "the information infrastructure" necessary to carry out all types of market processes and transactions. The number of tasks based upon network computing is growing rapidly – for example teleconference, remote services, online transactions, chat lines, Internet broadcasting, electronic commerce, etc. Even driving an automobile involves the Internet as it downloads maps and addresses from a satellite. For many, ordinary grocery shopping occurs on the Internet. In short, the economic significance of the Internet and its associated technologies is their ability to affect a wide range of human activities, integrating existing practices and enabling new business and market processes.

However, large scale networks have existed for several decades; investment in IT was rapidly increasing even before the age of the Internet; electronic data interchange, online banking and automatic teller machines, and digital technologies all preceded the Internet. Was the commercial Internet an accident in the larger scheme of technological transformations or was it the driving force behind the digital revolution? Was the World Wide Web responsible for the explosive growth of the Internet?

The strength of Internet-related IT technology lies not in its technological superiority but in its nature as an open networking paradigm. While computers and networking technologies have advanced steadily over the past decades, they have lacked the characteristics of a true infrastructure. The term "infrastructure" was first introduced in France to denote railroad tracks that were laid down by the French government in the nineteenth century. Railroad cars – the superstructure – were owned by private firms and operated on the public infrastructure. An infrastructure needs to be open so as to allow various private enterprises with differing products and goals to compete on an equal footing. An infrastructure must also provide connectivity and uniformity such as a constant track width in its entire system or an open standard such as the TCP/IP protocol of the Internet. Rail cars can only go where tracks are already laid; likewise, the Internet infrastructure delineates the boundaries of products and applications that follow. The Internet is no accident but the first technological medium of its kind that supports a persistent development of universal applications and practices.

There are many advantages of the Internet over proprietary networks. For example, the costs necessary to establish an Internet presence are relatively small. Lower costs in turn allow smaller firms and individuals to be connected, unlike the costly private value added networks that limited EDI applications to large corporations. Open TCP/IP protocols of the Internet also ensure that communicating parties can exchange messages and products across different computing platforms and geographic regional boundaries. In physical markets, geographical distance and political boundaries hinder the free movement of goods and people. Similarly, closed proprietary networks separate virtual markets artificially by establishing barriers to interoperability. This is equivalent to having different track widths so that several sets of identical rail cars must be maintained and passengers must be transferred at all exchange points.

Limitations and problems

As the PC industry is maturing, industry leaders in computer hardware and software are finding it hard to keep up with the extraordinary growth they experienced during the past two decades. The long-term outlook for the IT industry is clouded. Similarly, e-commerce and the Internet-native businesses are no longer forgiven for no, or negative, revenues or sales, while skepticism about the very nature of the digital revolution or the new economy is rising.

Despite some evidence of accelerating productivity gains driven by IT (for example, Jorgenson and Stiroh 2000), skeptics argue that there is nothing new in the so-called "new economy." For example, Gordon (2000) discounts the significance of the Internet and IT as a revolutionary force, compared to some great inventions during the period 1860 to 1900 when electricity, motor, chemical, and other technologies changed the economy fundamentally. The basic issue is how to interpret the sudden and rapid growth in US productivity during the years 1995 to 1999. Despite various alternative explanations of this growth spurt, however, the period under review may be too short to derive any conclusive remarks as to whether the IT revolution is of any long-lasting importance.

Nevertheless, the point is whether we can expect this high growth to continue in the long run. An optimistic view considers the staying power of IT investment that has been growing steadily in the 1990s, and the expectation is that labor productivity will continue to grow strongly. However, the source of rapid labor productivity growth, being coincidental with the introduction of the Internet, may stem from innovative uses of IT capital, not simply from capital deepening. Thus, innovations in business processes and models will play an important role in maintaining the current level of growth.

This also implies that e-business applications have played a significant role in productivity growth. However, there are more immediate problems associated with the IT-driven Internet economy in promoting e-business practices. Foremost of these problems are the privacy issue, digital copyright, taxation related to sales taxes, and online frauds and crimes. Several of these issues require international cooperation to resolve outstanding concerns, for example how to tax foreign sales of digital products that are delivered via the Internet, how to prevent piracy when the Internet offers an opportunity not only to reproduce but also to operate outside legal authorities, and so on.

The phase of technological innovation has not slowed down, but that is a double-edged sword. New technologies and applications come into the market, increasing uncertainty about a particular product or a business model. The majority of workers are ill-equipped to be employed in the IT sector when new technologies and skills appear at an almost dizzying pace. Two years in Internet time is an eternity that makes worker's skills obsolete.

Finally, all this uncertainty may simply stem from inadequate measurements and census data. Government statistics are largely oriented toward measuring the manufacturing industries. Labor productivity also measures the performance of simple labor and capital inputs. Other inputs such as business services, managerial inputs, organisational changes, and technology are seldom measured correctly. We may not know exactly how the US economy is progressing, because IT and the Internet mainly affect factors other than labor and capital. Better measurement models and definitions are clearly needed for precise evaluation of the current situation.

Conclusions

The growing importance of the IT sector in the US economy is clearly demonstrated in the rapid growth in labor productivity since 1995. Its share of the overall economy, employment, and contribution to economic growth have been phenomenal. But besides those measurable indicators, the true impact of IT is felt in the way firms are organized and operate in the new world of e-business. IT-utilizing firms differ significantly from physical firms, the so-called "bricks and mortar" companies. The USA excels in the degree to which it has promoted e-business drivers that are dependent on IT, the focus of Chapter 12. In this chapter, we reviewed economic measurements indicating the so-called IT revolution, and discussed salient features of firms in the new economy, namely flexible organization as a virtual firm. The reorganization under way in US firms toward virtual e-businesses is the fundamental force that is revising many aspects of the international division of labor.

References

Baily, M. N. and Chakrabarti, A. K. 1988, *Innovation and the productivity crisis*, Washington DC: The Brookings Institution.

Barua, A. and Lee, B. 1997, The information technology productivity paradox revisited: a theoretical and empirical investigation in the manufacturing sector, *International Journal of Flexible Manufacturing Systems*, 9, 145–166.

Berndt, E. R. and Morrsion, C. J. 1991, High-tech capital, economic performance and labor composition in the US manufacturing industries: an exploratory analysis, working paper, Boston, MA.

Bresnahan, T. F. 1986, Measuring the spillovers from technical advance: mainframe computers in financial services, *American Economic Review*, 76(4), 742–755.

Brynjolfsson, E. and Hitt, L. 1993, Is information systems spending productive? New evidence and new results, *Proceedings of the Fourteenth International Conference on Information Systems*, Orlando, FL, December 1993.

  1996, Paradox lost? Firm-level evidence of the returns to information systems spending, *Management Science*, 42, 541–558.

Choi, S. Y. and Whinston, A. B. 2000, *The Internet Economy: Technology and Practice*, Austin, TX: SmartEcon Publishing.

Choi, S. Y., Stahl, D. O., and Whinston, A. B. 1997, *The Economics of Electronic Commerce*, Indianapolis: Macmillan Technical Publishing.

Center for Research in Electronic Commerce (CREC) 2000, Internet Economy Indicators, http://internetindicators.com.

Gordon, R. J. 2000, 'Does the New Economy measure up to the great inventions of the past?' *Journal of Economic Perspectives* (forthcoming).

International Labour Organization 2000, *Labour Market Trends and Globalization's Impact on Them*, http://www.itcilo.it/english/actrav/telearn/global/ilo/seura/mains.htm.

Jorgenson, D. W. and Stiroh, K. J. 2000, Raising the speed limit: US economic growth in the information age, *Brookings Papers on Economic Activity 1*, 2000, 125–211.

Kraft, K. 1989, Market structure, firm characteristics and innovative activity, *Journal of Industrial Economics*, 37(3), 329–336.

Lee, B. and Barua, A. 1999, Assessing productivity and efficiency impacts of information technologies: old data, new analysis and evidence, *Journal of Productivity Analysis* 12(1), 21–43.

Lichtenberg, F. R. 1995, The output contributions of computer equipment and personnel: a firm-level analysis, *Economics of Innovation and New Technology*, 3, 201–217.

Loveman, G. W. 1994, An assessment of the productivity impact of information technologies, in T. J. Allen and M. S. Scott Morton (eds.), *Information Technology and the Corporation of the 1990s: Research Studies*, Cambridge, MA: MIT Press.

Mills, D. E. 1984, Demand fluctuations and endogenous firm flexibility, *Journal of Industrial Economics*, 33(1), 55–71.

Morrison, C. J. and Berndt, E. R. 1990, Assessing the productivity of information technology equipment in US manufacturing industries, paper presented at the 1990 "Annual Meetings of the American Economic Association", Washington DC, December 1990.

OECD 2000, *National Accounts of OECD Countries*, Paris.

Roach, S. S. 1987, *America's Technology Dilemma: A Profile of the Information Economy*, Special Economy Study, Morgan Stanley and Co.

  1988, Stop rolling the dice on technology spending, interview with G. Harrar (ed.), *Computerworld Extra*, June 20, 1988.

1989, The case of the missing technology payback, paper presented at the tenth "International Conference on Information Systems," Boston, MA, December 1989.

1991, Services under siege: the restructuring imperative, *Harvard Business Review*, 69(5), 82–91.

Scherer, F. M. 1984, *Innovation and Growth: Schumpeterian Perspective*, Cambridge, MA: MIT Press.

US Census Bureau 2000, *Monthly Retail Trade Survey*, Washington, DC, http://www.census.gov/mrts/www/mrts.html.

US Department of Commerce 1999, *The Emerging Digital Economy II*, Washington DC, http://www.ecommerce.gov/ede.

2000, *Digital Economy 2000*, Washington DC, http://www.esa.doc.gov/de2000.pdf.

US Department of Commerce, Bureau of Economic Analysis 2000, *Survey of Current Business*, Washington DC, September 2000.

12 The effects of the IT revolution on firms and the global economy

Soon-Yong Choi and Andrew B. Whinston

Introduction

The defining characteristic of a digital economy firm is its extensive use of computers, IT, and the Internet. All firms make some use of these techniques, in production, distribution, marketing, and customer service processes, so the true economic effects of IT can be ascertained only after we have determined the ways in which it has effected significant changes in normal business processes, relationships with other firms and customers, and internal organization.

A firm that employs IT, especially real-time networking, is designated as an e-business firm. These firms include not only those that sell products online, but also those that use computer and network technologies in their manufacturing operations, supply chain management, marketing, sales automation, and customer support. In short, any firm that applies digital technologies and networking to organizing and managing its business operations and relationships is an e-business firm.

In defining an e-business firm in this way, the real challenge is to identify the characteristics that distinguish them from conventional businesses. IT-intensive firms have networked, or virtual, components. The internal organization and structure of a firm in the virtual marketplace is primarily a theoretical question – for example, how should a virtual firm be organized without offices, divisions, or regular employees? Some extremists may argue that "virtual firms" existing on a network are the only true e-businesses; at the other extreme is the view that all firms with an IT department may qualify.

Most firms lie somewhere in the middle. Regardless of the degree of "virtualization," e-business firms are organised to take advantage of the capabilities and opportunities presented by internal use of technology, as well as the electronic marketplace. This may involve horizontal, rather than vertical, organization. It may also involve an increased reliance on outsourced manufacturing and distribution, so that contractual relationships and alliances replace internal corporate units. Eventually, e-business firms may also take advantage of a

Table 12.1 *IT-producing industries' contribution to economic growth,*
1994–1997 (percent)

	1994	1995	1996	1997
Changes in real gross domestic income (GDI)	4.2	3.3	3.5	4.7
IT contribution	0.8	1.0	1.2	1.3
All other industries	3.4	2.3	2.3	3.4
IT contribution	19	30	34	28

Source: US *Department of Commerce 2000,* based on Bureau of Economics Analysis
estimates.

market that is a loose network of individual producers transacting in auction
markets.

IT also affects external relationships with suppliers, marketers, and customers, resulting in close interaction in a real-time network. Substantial competitive advantage can result from the optimization of technological benefits
in business relationships. The media are full of reports of successful implementations of Internet technologies in business-to-business trades – for example, supply chain management, customer asset management, automated selling
chains, etc. But anecdotal examples often fail to describe the broader context
that explains just why firms should implement these practices, or how and when
they should employ them.

Factors raising firm-level productivity

The extraordinary performance of e-business firms such as Amazon.com is
attributed to the use of computers and such network technologies as the Internet.
The growth of investment in computer hardware and software since 1973 has
played a significant role in the overall growth of the US economy, especially
during the 1990s. As Table 12.1 shows, IT-producing industries accounted
for an average 30 percent of real economic growth in the latter part of the
1990s.

These performance gains stem from two factors: the relative growth of IT
industries' share of the economy, and productivity gains across industry from
increased IT capital investment. IT industries experienced an average annual
output growth rate of 17% in the second half of the 1990s, increasing its share of
the economy from 6.3% in 1994 to 8.3% in 2000. Significant productivity gain
came from falling IT prices, which fell substantially during the same period.
In comparison, prices in all other industries showed a consistent increase at an
average annual rate of over 2% (see Table 12.2).

Table 12.2 *Changes in price levels, 1994–1997 (percent)*

	1994	1995	1996	1997
GDP excluding IT	2.3	2.5	2.5	2.3
IT sector	−1.4	−4.5	−8.1	−7.1

Source: US *Department of Commerce 2000*, based on Bureau of Economics Analysis estimates.

These statistics describe aggregate performance and, although significant, a microanalysis is needed to distinguish how the use of IT technology affects firms and industries. Productivity gains and performance levels vary across firms and industries.

A major difficulty in discussing firm-level productivity lies in the fact that productivity measurements themselves pose serious problems for quantitative analysis. For example, they include conventional labor productivity and multi-factor productivity. Labor productivity measures the gross product or output per worker hour and indicates the efficiency with which labor is used. In general, labor productivity grew strongly for manufacturing whilst service industries showed varying growth – high in the capital intensive sectors of communications, utilities, and financial services, but low in retail trade.

Differences in productivity gains warrant a closer look at individual industries or firms. There are three factors that affect labor productivity: absolute increase in worker hours, capital investment and deepening, and multifactor productivity (MFP) resulting from the use of information processing, managerial inputs, and other business services. The rapid growth in total output during the 1990s is partially due to absolute growth in working hours (US Bureau of Labor Statistics 2000). However, differences in capital deepening and MFP among industries indicate a more coherent relationship between IT inputs and performance.

Increasing investment in IT equipment and software

Within the manufacturing and service sectors, high levels of labor productivity growth go hand in hand with high investment in IT equipment and software. For example, IT capital stock makes up 84% and 79% of total capital equipment in telecommunications and broadcasting, respectively, and between 1987 and 1997 growth in communications industries was 2.9% per annum. This compares with a total private sector annual growth rate of 1.1% over the same period. The wholesale trade, where IT capital stock accounted for 39% of total equipment, showed the strongest growth at 4.0% during the same period.

Table 12.3 *Labor productivity growth rates in the USA,*
1949–1996 (percent)

	Non-farm	Manufacturing	Non-manufacturing
1949–1973	2.8	2.6	3.0
1973–1996	1.5	2.7	1.0

Source: Triplett and Bosworth 2001.

Overall, the finance service sector grew at an annual rate of 1.6% during this period. However, a close examination shows significant disparity among subsectors. For example, security and commodity brokers, where 56% of capital stock is in IT equipment, grew at 8.8% per annum.

There exists some relationship between IT investment and performance, although industry and firm-level analysis are more difficult due to the lack of industry-specific data. At the firm level, the amount of IT equipment does not translate directly into efficiency and better performance. Computers, for instance, have been applied to production and services since the early 1970s without resulting in noticeable changes in aggregate productivity. In fact, labor productivity decreased at an annual rate of 1.3% during the period 1973 to 1996 compared to 2.8% between 1949 and 1973. Only the manufacturing sector maintained high growth (see Table 12.3).

Whilst macroeconomic data present a confusing picture of the effects of IT on productivity, it is clear that computers and related technological inputs were a major factor in sustaining high productivity gains in manufacturing. The evidence in the service sector is unclear. However, a look at the sub-industry level shows that the use of IT equipment in certain industries did indicate higher performance. Conventional output measures may fail to represent productivity gains in these industries. Productivity growth from factors other than capital deepening – that is, growth in absolute amount in capital stock – is measured by multifactor productivity.

Multifactor productivity

MFP measures output per unit of all inputs, including labor and capital. Thus a change in MFP indicates a change in output that cannot be attributed to changes in either labor or capital alone. As a result, MFP is used to investigate effects on productivity by other factors that may include new technologies, economics of scale, managerial skill, and changes in the organization of production. According to the US Bureau of Labor Statistics (BLS), long-term labor productivity growth can be viewed as the sum of three components: multifactor productivity growth, increased capital intensity, and shifts in labor composition. Table 12.4 reproduces BLS summary data for MFP.

Between 1948 and 1998, MFP accounted for the largest share of the total productivity growth: 1.4% of the total 2.5% growth rate in total productivity.

This gain in MFP stems from increasing uses, especially since the late 1970s, of IT equipment and software as well as managerial and operational improvements. BLS estimates that almost half of the capital effects were accounted for by IT capital. But this says nothing about its utilization. E-business firms, characterized by intensive uses of IT technology, are clearly leading these changes. In the following sections, we investigate how e-business firms implement IT technology and its effect on performance.

Implementation of BtoC and BtoB e-business drivers

The economic performance of an e-business firm depends critically on how technologies are used; a firm in the Internet age leverages IT and networking tools to become a virtual organization, carrying out its manufacturing, marketing, and sales operations within a network of employees, offices, suppliers, and customers. IT utilization at this level focuses on two relationships that are key to operational and financial successes – with customers, and with suppliers. Business-to-consumer (BtoC) e-commerce refers to companies which invest in IT for dealing with customers, and Business-to-business (BtoB) e-commerce addresses various uses of IT in links with suppliers and other business partners.

Although procedural and organizational changes and e-business implementations of IT appear to be the critical components in productivity growth, firms with varying degrees of e-business implementation show a wide range of success or failure in achieving financial and operational goals. Operational excellence in the IT and e-business arenas can be measured by the extent to which its business functions depend on the online and Internet environment, using such indicators as online revenue, online procurement, and online customer service.

Financial performance of IT-based firms

Firms expect that investments in e-business drivers will result in enhanced operational and financial success in terms of increased revenues, profit, return on assets, and capital. Nevertheless, it is not at all clear whether such investment efforts over the past five years have yielded the expected results. Despite some uncertainty, anecdotal evidence suggests that firms which excel in e-business operation, for example Amazon.com, tend to generate higher revenues and, ultimately, profit. An empirical study of 1,100 US e-business firms also suggests there is a strong relationship between financial success and e-business operational excellence (Barua, Whinston, and Yin 2000). The firms in this Center for

Table 12.4 *Compound average annual rates of growth in output per hour of all persons and the contributions of capital intensity, labor composition, and multifactor productivity, by major sector, 1948–1998 (percent per year)*

	1948–1998	1948–1973	1973–1979	1979–1990	1990–1995	1995–1998
Private business[a]						
Output per hour of all persons	2.5	3.3	1.3	1.6	1.5	2.5
Contribution of capital intensity[b]	0.8	1.0	0.7	0.7	0.5	0.8
Contribution of information processing equipment and software[c]	0.3	0.1	0.3	0.5	0.4	0.8
Contribution of all other capital services	0.6	0.9	0.5	0.3	0.1	0.0
Contribution of labor composition[d]	0.2	0.2	0.0	0.3	0.4	0.3
Multifactor productivity[e]	1.4	2.1	0.6	0.5	0.6	1.4
Private non-farm business[a]						
Output per hour of all persons	2.2	2.9	1.1	1.4	1.6	2.3
Contribution of capital intensity[b]	0.8	0.9	0.7	0.8	0.5	0.8
Contribution of information processing equipment and software[c]	0.3	0.1	0.3	0.5	0.4	0.8
Contribution of all other capital services[c]	0.5	0.7	0.5	0.3	0.1	0.0
Contribution of labor composition[d]	0.2	0.2	0.0	0.3	0.4	0.3
Multifactor productivity[e]	1.2	1.9	0.4	0.3	0.6	1.3
Contribution of R&D to multifactor productivity	0.2	0.2	0.1	0.2	0.2	0.2

Notes:

[a] Excludes government enterprises.

[b] Growth rate in capital services per hour times capital's share of current dollar costs.

[c] Growth rate of information processing equipment and software times its share of total costs.

[d] Growth rate of labor composition (the growth rate of labor input less the growth rate of the hours of all persons) times labor's share of current dollar costs.

[e] Output per unit of combined labor and capital inputs.

Source: US Bureau of Labor Statistics 2000.

Table 12.5 *Customer orientation of IT applications, 2000*

	%Agree (somewhat to strongly agree)		
	"No" to increase revenue/employe	"Yes" to increase revenue/employe	Overall
All product-related information available online (e.g. price, description, catalog, etc.)	56%	81%	69%
A comprehensive FAQ section available online	45%	58%	52%
Customers can conveniently contact service representatives or seek service online	61%	83%	74%
Customers can interact using forums and/or communities (e.g. chat rooms, bulletin boards)	23%	33%	28%
Customers see personalized content (e.g. products, prices, order history, order status, etc.) when they log onto the website	27%	40%	34%
Customers can submit orders	54%	82%	69%
Customers can modify orders	30%	57%	45%
Customers can pay online	36%	68%	55%
Customers are notified of their order status automatically	30%	53%	42%

Source: Barua, Konana, Whinston, and Yin 2000.

Research in Electronic Commerce (CREC) study comprise 45% wholesalers, 11% distributors, 35% manufacturers and 9% retailers. Personal and business service providers are not represented in the sample.

Implementation issues in BtoC processes

The e-business tools and drivers that affect a firm's relationship with its customers can be classified by their informational and transactional functions. Informational tools have the primary task of informing customers about products and the firm, whilst transactional tools provide customers with online ordering and payment functions and related services.

The Internet is widely used to disseminate information about products and the company's business. The sample shows that two out of three firms currently offer product information online (see Table 12.5). Overall, firms that have enjoyed

Table 12.6 *Amazon versus Barnes and Noble*

	Amazon	Barnes and Noble
Number of stores	1	1,011
Titles per superstore	3.1 million	175,000
Book returns	2%	30%
Sales growth	306%	10%
Sales per employee	US$375,000	US$100,000
Inventory turnovers per year	24	3

Source: Business Week, December 14, 1998, p. 110.

improved financial performance, such as increasing revenue per employee, have higher customer orientation levels than firms that do not.

Most firms now offer static content and product information, but interactive features and customization lag behind. The trend in the use of transactional feature implementation is similar, shown in the last four rows of Table 12.5; two out of three firms offer online ordering functions, while less than half allow customers to modify their orders. And those firms that are successful in the e-business arena show a higher level of customer orientation in implementing such features.

Online retailing

The importance of IT is highlighted by the example of online retailing and in the continuing high investment in IT. Amazon.com, a typical e-commerce enterprise, demonstrates some of the obvious advantages of an online store: no physical retail outlets and almost unlimited shelf space (see Table 12.6), low return rates, higher sales growth and per-employee sales, and a higher stock turnover rate than Barnes and Noble. Some of these factors can be attributed to the nature of online sales and the intensive use of IT in tracking sales and managing the inventory. Musical CDs and videos are poised to reap similar benefits from going online.

Customer's online readiness

To conduct business online, all parties must be prepared to use the necessary technology. Firms find that their customers are more open than their suppliers to the idea of e-business and e-commerce.

There is a significant gap between attitudes, perception and adoption of e-business/e-commerce by customers and suppliers. A majority of the firms in the CREC survey believe that their customers are comfortable with the security and privacy of e-commerce. However, suppliers and vendors are less confident about security matters, although the larger firms are more open to Internet-based trade, perhaps due to their exposure to EDI and other electronic transactions.

The rationale for expanding e-business practice is to expand market share or to gain more customers. A majority of the firms have acquired some new customers through their e-business initiatives: whilst about 15% of the firms say that they find no new customers through their online operations, one in four has acquired over 50% of their new customers online. Similar numbers of firms also report that over half of their existing customers do business online with them. The majority of the firms find between 20% and 50% of their existing customers transact business online.

Implementation in BtoB e-business drivers

Despite the common assumption that business-to-business processes are more suitable for IT-oriented processes, given EDI and other similar practices employed during the last two decades, firms are more inclined to rely on e-business practices in their customer relations than in their supply chains. For instance, while two-thirds of all firms are engaged in BtoC e-business, only a third have electronic invoice transmission and processing capabilities, which suggests that most communications with suppliers still rely on phone, fax, and face-to-face exchanges.

More IT-focused tasks such as online order status tracking or electronic payment, are practised by only 28 percent of all firms in the sample. E-business tools have not been implemented as widely as expected. Despite an intense interest in supply-chain applications, there has not been widespread progress toward e-business supply chain management.

This lag in BtoB implementation applies to both production supply chain and maintenance, repairs and operating supplies (MRO) procurement. Nearly two-thirds of all firms use online procurement for less than 20% of their MRO needs. The average online MRO procurement of all firms is about 19%, with a median of 5%. Only about 9% of the firms say that they procure more than 50% of their MRO requirements online. Similar numbers of firms utilize online procurement for production suppliers, although a slightly higher percentage say that they procure more than 50% of their requirements online.

This suggests that there is significant potential for firms to gain operational efficiency by switching to online procurement and supply chain management. The Internet is increasingly perceived as a tool to build supplier relationships, manage quality, and reduce inventories and lead time. A few of the most common BtoB practices that must be implemented include processes to:

- communicate customer feedback and field incidence reports to their suppliers in real time
- share process quality information electronically with their trading partners
- share inventory information with trading partners
- share production-related information (for example schedules, man-power availability, machine downtime) with suppliers
- provide expected demand information to suppliers online
- have online communities for suppliers to share information online
- provide supplier/vendor evaluation reports online.

Physical versus pure digital firms

Digital firms produce digital products such as online content and services, whilst physical firms sell physical products. *Pure* digital firms employ digital means, such as the Internet, for distribution and other business processes. Physical firms rely heavily on physical means and markets for such functions.

In previous sections, we have described an increasing level of investment in IT and a general drive toward transforming physical businesses into e-businesses. Key to success in this process is the appropriate investment in e-business "drivers," and the readiness of customers and suppliers to achieve operational excellence; simply increasing the share of IT investment and cap-ital stock will not transform a physical business into an e-business. This can be seen from the less vigorous implementation of BtoB drivers compared to BtoC drivers. As firms change their organization in a continuing drive toward digitization, a critical factor is whether IT investment will have the same effect wherever a firm resides on this spectrum.

For example, would IT capital stock have the same effect on firms that are "bricks and mortar" physical companies as on pure digital, virtual firms? The answer is that IT investment seems to bring about more fundamental changes if a firm is closer to the pure "dotcom" organization. As a result, IT capital produces higher levels of sales, profit, and other performance measures for dot com companies than for physical firms. This result is based on a statistical estimation of a sample of 199 US public firms (Barua, Whinston, and Yin 2000). Using 1998 figures for sales and gross margin as dependent variables against number of employees and IT and non-IT capital stock, this study tests several related hypotheses on IT investment's effectiveness in different forms of companies.

The regression results show that IT capital's effect on sales, gross margin, sales per employee, and gross margin per employee differs significantly between digital and physical firms. In digital firms, IT capital has a significantly positive effect, on all four measures, but this is not the case in physical firms.

The result indicates that the same IT equipment and software has differential effects on performance and business success depending on the type of company, that is, IT capital is more effective if a company is organized in such a way as to exploit it. Prime examples are firms that sell a purely digital product, but the organizational features of a digital firm may also be fully adopted by a physical firm. Cisco Systems, which sells physical products, conducts about 80 percent of its business online and provides customer service through the same channel. Half of its online orders are shipped directly to customers form contractors. This is digitization of processes, if not products, and results in a higher revenue per employee.

Organizational impact of IT

Just as new products have been born out of the technology of the Internet, so the nonlinear technology of the Web makes it possible to have an organizational form that represents the highest level of flexibility. In this virtual environment, it can be very difficult to define or classify firms and markets that are based on traditional organizational structures such as a hierarchy or an M-form that is based on functional divisions (such as marketing, personnel, accounting, customer service, etc.). Indeed, a very flexible organization may exist only as a network organization that defies any structural formula.

A firm in the physical market is organized into a functional hierarchy, from the top-level executive down to divisions and managers. It may structure its divisions following various product groups that rarely intersect in the market. The markets are organized under the natural order of products and producers from materials, intermediate goods, consumption goods, distributors, and retailers. On the other hand, a networked economy is a mixture of firms that are not restricted by internal hierarchies, and markets which do not favour the controlled coordination of an assembly line. Businesses operating in this virtual marketplace lack incentives to maintain long-term relationships – based on corporate ownership or contracts – with a few suppliers or partners. More and more, functions are outsourced to any number of firms and individuals in a globally dispersed market. This highly fluid form of organization confounds our task of assigning any static classification scheme to what we call network organizations.

The complex web of suppliers, distributors, and customers doing business on the World Wide Web is evolving from markets and hierarchies into a new form called a network organization. Unlike hierarchies and centralized markets, this structure allows a high degree of flexibility and responsiveness. A network organization is defined by three characteristics: co-specialized assets, joint control, and collective purpose. Co-specialization means that interconnected assets like computers and databases, as well as organization units, are complementary and interoperable. These assets may or may not be jointly owned by participants, but a critical factor is that they must provide an integrated platform for communication, joint decision-making, and transactions. Organizations and units must also have joint control over how these assets are used, and a common purpose or objective in their collaboration. Therefore, decision-making members collaborate when their decisions constrain or affect other members' decisions.

The World Wide Web – like a spider's web – is an example of a network organization with co-specialized assets, joint control, and a common purpose. Unfortunately, we often restrict our view of the network economy by focusing on BtoB or BtoC transactions, neglecting the fact that they are not only part of a whole but are also intertwined with each other. The focus on either BtoB or BtoC commerce stems from the prevailing view of a linear value chain. In a flexible and responsive economy, the increased level of interaction among economic participants results in integrated products, real-time pricing, and the need to respond to continuously changing customer preferences and demand. Decisions made by businesses, consumers, and governments affect each other continuously. Despite rosy expectations for the future of the digital economy, it is not yet clear exactly what types of values the Internet and e-commerce will create and how the value creation process will be shaped.

What is clear is that commerce on the World Wide Web enables several types of changes in the value chain. It can support existing value chains through, for instance, automation. It can also open up new ways to add value. For example, disintermediation implies reducing unnecessary middlemen, thereby decreasing costs and prices, and creating value. When products and services which were not available in physical markets become available, new value is created. Finally, commerce on the Web can collapse, reorganize, and leapfrog existing value chains through disaggregation, reorganization, and intermediation. This last, unique to the popularly referred to as a web-like value chain, entails fundamental transformations in conventional business processes and is made possible by the nonlinear nature of the value web and interactive commerce.

Production location and management under Internet technology

In the digital economy, many observers note that the trend toward outsourcing various business functions is growing rapidly because it offers a less costly alternative to in-house manufacturing, marketing, customer service, delivery, inventorying, and warehousing and other business processes. This would be consistent with the observation that firms in the physical economy also delegate production activities to external organizations if they find it less costly than to internalize them. As long as the cost of internal production (or service provision) is higher than the cost of contracting and monitoring, firms will prefer to outsource.

Outsourcing, subcontracting, and foreign direct investment have been the main tools for multinational corporations to diversify their production operations. For various reasons, newly industrializing countries (NICs) in East Asia now subcontract their manufacturing to other locations:

- reduction in costs or development time
- reallocation of resources to other functions
- access to new skills and technology
- access to new markets
- greater flexibility in production and staffing.

Multinational contract manufacturers such as Flextronics and Solectron have opened up factories in Eastern and Central Europe in addition to Asia and Latin America. While these contractors focus on minimizing costs or maximizing cost advantage in manufacturing by moving their production worldwide, original equipment manufacturing (OEM) and consumer-market players utilize these firms as suppliers. The effect is that most multinational companies which sell products to consumers are moving away from foreign direct investment to outsourcing for their entire production tasks.

It appears that the type of cost savings plays a critical role in the outsourcing decision. Lewis and Sappington (1991) argued that, when a firm's decision to buy versus internally produce inputs involved improvements in production technology, more in-house production and less outsourcing was preferred. Their result did not depend on whether the subcontractor's production technology was idiosyncratic (that is, only useful to produce the buyer's inputs) or transferable (that is, the supplier could use its production technology and facility to service other potential buyers). In the case of transferable technology, the supplier would be expected to invest more in production technology, and thus offer lower costs, which may favour more outsourcing. Nevertheless, the buyer still preferred to implement more efficient technology itself internally.

In cases where the buyer's production technology is substantially inferior and if monitoring costs are significantly lower, we would expect contract manufacturing to be favoured. Whether this is the case or not is mostly an empirical question. However, when evaluating the option of outsourcing, one must consider not only production cost savings but also cost savings and other benefits in product development, marketing, and distribution.

For example, by delegating manufacturing, a firm may better utilize its resources in non-production functions. Since production logistics are taken care of, it may be able to consider more diverse product specifications. In fact, many Internet-based firms are focusing on customer assets and the marketing value of their reputation among consumers while delegating manufacturing and distribution to third parties such as Solectron. The prevalence of outsourcing and subcontracting goes hand in hand with the use of IT that facilitates horizontal coordination and relationships with suppliers (Aoki 1986).

Manufacturers with a well-recognised brand name and their own manufacturing operations have used manufacturer-pushed logistics management. On the other hand, manufacturers which are concerned with product development, market competition, and other strategic issues rely on contract manufacturers for efficient bulk manufacturing and distributors for the ancillary tasks of moving their products to retailers. They often interact with only a few large distributors which are expected to push assigned products down to the retail channel. Their partners are more flexible manufacturers and distributors, which have developed closer ties to end customers. For example, channel marketers in the computer industry consist of OEMs that provide basic components to distributors, which build computers after orders are received. While well over two-thirds of PCs are sold in the old-fashioned way, new players are now taking advantage of IT to cut costs, and in the process they become focused more on marketing rather than producing the goods.

Dell Computers and Gateway began a new distribution model based on direct marketing. They now rely on contract manufacturers to distribute their products. In this case, orders received by Dell are forwarded to a third party, which assembles and ships the final products directly to consumers. This built-to-order manufacturing model attains distribution objectives by outsourcing manufacturing as well as distribution functions to those that can optimize their specialized functions. Distributors, in addition to delivering products, face the task of integrating purchasing, manufacturing, and supply chain management.

As the division of labor within the whole value added process continues on a worldwide scale, US firms tend to favor joint ventures, outsourcing, and other contractual arrangements over foreign direct investment. Contract manufacturers are responsible for maximizing cost advantages, developing and maintaining appropriate production technologies, and satisfying product specifications. In services, outsourcing and cooperative agreements are more pronounced. IBM, for example, entered into a ten-year US$15 billion outsourcing agreement with NTT in 2000, while it continues to expand its chip-making capacity at its non-US locations.

Significant factors in pushing US corporations toward outsourcing include reduced costs of coordination and decreasing share of labor costs. Using the Internet and IT, firms can monitor subcontractors' production activities and closely collaborate with them to meet product specification, quality standards, and delivery dates at substantially lower costs than before. This minimizes the need to control production in a more active role such as in direct investment. At the same time, the share of labor cost in the overall production or marketing costs is continuously decreasing. As a result, the advantages provided by lower labor costs in foreign locations are less salient to their overall profit calculation.

The use of the Internet and IT, for example supply chain management and logistics, is certainly improving inter-firm coordination for order generation, order taking and fulfilment, and distribution of products, services, and information. Suppliers, distributors, manufacturers, and retailers are closely linked in a supply chain as independent but integrated entities to fulfil transactional needs. As this allows US firms to segregate themselves from actual manufacturing, locational decisions for production have become more fluid.

The service sector, unlike manufacturing, tends to locate where customers are located. For this reason, many US service firms operate local businesses in a foreign country to serve customers in that country. The amount of commerce by US affiliates doing business in foreign countries is growing faster than the cross-border export of service. Nevertheless, the Internet provides them with an opportunity to shift many of their service functions back to the USA, while meeting the requirement for local service. Although it is certain that the same technological advantage enables other countries to provide any service function on behalf of US firms – for example, software engineering services by foreign contractors in foreign software parks – service production, unlike goods manufacturing, can be undertaken domestically even for foreign consumption.

Internet-based firms and shifts in industrial organisation

Although mergers and alliances among e-business firms, especially in the telecommunications service sector that includes Internet access providers, telephone companies, cable system operators, and content providers, indicate a distinct possibility that the electronic marketplace may come to be dominated by a few monopolistic firms, the basic economics of the digital market seems to point to fierce competition with little chance for extraordinary profits. This optimistic view is based on the conventional belief that the Internet allows new firms to enter a market with lower costs, creates a level playing-field for smaller firms to compete against larger corporations, and lowers transaction costs to make market processes and prices more efficient. In addition, transparent prices will foster competition among firms whose market is essentially the world, where many sellers and buyers exist.

In this competitive scenario, the industrial organization in the digital economy appears to be one of a highly competitive, efficient market. However, there exists a pessimistic view about the future of the digital market organisation. For example, the level of market capitalization of Yahoo, America Online, and other e-business firms overshadows that of many Fortune 100 firms – at least while high-tech stocks were flying high. Although there is little serious financial justification based on current revenues or profits, quasi-economic arguments are used to justify the hyperbolic stock prices of these firms. Basic investment principles would dictate that a high valuation today must be matched by enormous future profits, possibly by a near-monopoly in their markets. The expectation is that these front-runners will produce monopoly profits. This will depend critically on whether the Internet-driven markets are monopolistic or competitive.

Whether e-business firms can establish a monopolistic market position will depend on several factors that traditionally favor market power. Yahoo and Amazon.com, for example, have established their reputation by being the first successful businesses in their respective markets, and reputation and first-mover advantages, at least in the physical market, tend to produce long-term dominant market position.

As virtual firms, these and other Internet-native firms have low fixed costs and have aggressively embraced new technologies and practices in their organization and operation. Yahoo has successfully managed its advertizing and marketing strategies to become the most trafficked site on the Internet, giving credence to its strategic focus on advertizing dollars. Amazon.com has also succeeded in maximizing the benefits of the digital medium by offering a huge collection of books combined with services that are designed to enhance and integrate customer purchasing activities. Customers are offered services such as book reviews, periodic updates of new books, and a list of recommended books based on customers' past purchasing patterns.

Such innovations present a new business model for the digital economy. Without physical stores, Amazon.com in fact acts more as an intermediary or a broker than as a conventional book retailer. Despite this, neither existing reputation nor the first-mover advantage will be enough to shake off challenges by the likes of Microsoft and Barnes and Noble. Unlike television networks, for which the artificial scarcity of channels somewhat guaranteed a share of the total audience, the Internet will not impose such barriers on would-be competitors of Yahoo and Amazon.com.

Several economic factors further reduce the chance of generating or sustaining monopoly profits in the digital marketplace. With no need to build a chain of physical stores, firms can enter and exit readily at low cost. In addition, the costs of duplicating successful technologies or business practices of one's competitors are much lower than in physical markets. Locking in customers with proprietary technologies or reputation becomes challenging when patents and business practices are easily imitated, and rational consumers equipped with smart agents are less swayed by reputation. E-business products are customized, further segmenting the market and offering opportunities for niche competitors. Finally, the network effects and the economies of scale, which tend to drive traditional computer and software industries toward monopolization, are less prominent in personalized services.

With increased competition, the rosy predictions based on future dominance and profits may never be realized for Internet firms. The recent difficulties of Netscape, once the most touted Internet company that is now faced with Microsoft's competing Internet Explorer product, are an omen for others entering e-commerce. It is no coincidence that Netscape and Yahoo have been the two most visible Internet firms. For the Internet to be a market infrastructure, consumers must be provided with a means to access (browsers) and to find (search services) online shops. Accordingly, these two markets are the first to play out a competitive game. In the browser market, monopolization may occur naturally because of the network effects inherent in software products. One browser may actually do just as well as any other. In this free for all, the advantage of Netscape has nevertheless already evaporated as fast as it was built.

Business case studies on the Internet are full of small firms with an innovative technology, product, or business model, growing phenomenally without the large capital and scale of economy typical of large firms. Traditionally, innovations are considered to be the territory of large firms, which can afford to indulge in long-term R&D activities. IBM, Sony, 3M, and AT&T are perfect examples when it comes to pouring R&D dollars into untested technologies. But e-business firms defy this convention by succeeding with new technologies, products, and processes ahead of large corporations. In the physical economy, R&D activities are carried out in research centers and corporate laboratories with expensive equipment and support staff. The difficulties and costs in designing a new automobile or an aircraft, inventing chemical compounds, or developing new telecommunications standards have meant that large firms with market power carry out an essential social function through innovation and knowledge creation.

In this sense, the trend toward e-business consolidation is justified and, furthermore, the success of small start-up firms on the Internet may be temporary. Once the market matures, large corporations (such as Microsoft, NBC, Disney, AT&T, General Motors, and so on) will dominate e-business. The fact that the digital economy is a knowledge-based economy still further favors large corporations, which can afford to invest an equally large sum of money to develop products that must have heavy fixed costs.

Conclusions

The success of IT-based firms in terms of revenue, profit, and market share is paramount in considering future trends of the IT revolution. At this stage of development, there is still a cloud of uncertainty over whether IT investment over the past decades has had any significant impact on individual firms or the overall economy. But a clear indication from several studies discussed in this chapter is the rapid development in networked e-business firms that can maximize the benefits of IT and the Internet. Empirical evidences that firm-level, as well as industry-level, productivity has been exceptionally influenced by IT technologies are accumulating. Coincidentally or not, the strongest performance and success by IT industries and IT users have been shown since the introduction of the Internet and related worldwide network organizations.

The net effect of IT and the Internet on firms and the global economy cannot be estimated from this initial five-year period. Nevertheless, virtually organized firms are more fluid in their location decision for production. Supply chain and logistics applications in products and services allow firms to separate from the traditional linear value chain. The motivating factor in foreign direct investment in production facilities by US firms is diminished. This trend is even more prominent in the service sector that we discuss in detail in Chapter 13. An efficient IT-based e-business firm is represented by its flexible operation which precludes static relationships with partners or locational preferences. Digital product firms display an even greater tendency to operate on the Internet, becoming truly locationless.

References

Aoki, M. 1986, Horizontal vs. vertical information structure of the firm, *American Economic Review*, 76(5), 971–983.

Barua, A., Konana, P., Whinston, A. B., and Yin, F. 2000, E-business value assessment, CREC Working Paper, University of Texas at Austin.

Barua, A., Whinston, A. B., and Yin, F. 2000. Not all dot coms are created equal: an exploratory investigation of the productivity of Internet based companies, CREC Working Paper, University of Texas at Austin, http://crec.bus.utexas.edu/works/articles/digital.pdf.

Jorgenson, D. W. and Stiroh, K. J. 2000, Raising the speed limit: US economic growth in the information age, *Brookings Papers on Economic Activity 2000*, http://www.economics.harvard.edu/faculty/jorgenson/papers/dj_ks5.pdf.

Lewis, T. R. and Sappington, D. E. 1991, Technological change and the boundaries of the firm, *American Economic Review*, 81(4), 887–900.

Triplett, J. E. and Bosworth, B. P. 2001, Productivity in the services sector, in R. M. Stern (ed.) *Services in the International Economy*, Ann Arbor, MI: University of Michigan Press.

US Bureau of Labor Statistics 2000, *Multifactor Productivity Trends*, Washington DC, http://stats.bls.gov/news.release/prod3.nr0.htm.

US Department of Commerce 2000, *Digital Economy 2000*, Washington DC, http://www.esa.doc.gov/de2000.pdf.

13 Internet-based globalization and international division of labor

Soon-Yong Choi and Andrew B. Whinston

Introduction

The purpose of this chapter is to investigate whether or how the Internet and related technologies affect the way firms are organized and operated in the world economy. Depending on how firms operate, regional differences across nations – in the various factors of production such as materials, labor, and capital – will become critical factors which determine economic performance and growth levels as well as the long-term economic welfare in each country.

During the twentieth century after the full development of manufacturing-driven international division of labor, multinational firms focused on direct foreign investment in order to take advantage of varying factor prices in different regions. Due to computers and the Internet, the international division of labor in the twenty-first century will revolve around different sectors of the economy, namely the service sector, and the Internet technology's effect on communications mode, coordination costs between firms, and comparative factor prices. The expectation is that both movements by production sites and migrations by workers will be overshadowed by regionalized production and trade over the Internet. We review basic characteristics of this Internet-driven new division of labor and their impact on the world economy, and conclude by summarizing some policy implications.

The Internet as a general purpose technology

Technologies affect many aspects of production of goods and services and consumption of such goods and services. In addition to material or process-specific technologies, transport technologies ranging from simple wheels to canals, steam ships, and automobiles have changed aspects in utilization of material inputs, factory locations, the manner by which productive inputs are organized, and the way manufactured products are distributed and consumed. Similarly, communications technologies such as the telephone and the Internet have had wide-ranging effects. The Internet in particular, coupled with computers and other networking tools, has the potential to change international economic equilibrium through reconfiguring transport costs (Krugman 1992) or through realigning factor prices (Harris 1995).

The peculiar characteristics of the Internet and its related innovations in communication are similar to electricity and its effects on productive economic activities. Electricity as a technology is pervasive in almost all aspects of production and non-production activities of an economy. Such a technology is termed a "general purpose technology."

In terms of international division of labor and changing industrial structure, innovations in transportation had a much greater impact than electricity. For instance, many innovations in transport technologies have played a critical role in expanding world trade in agricultural and mining products as well as manufactured goods. In particular, the decreasing transport costs in the shipping industry were primary incentives in worldwide specialization in production of goods and in the relocations of multinational corporations in search of cheaper raw materials, lower labor costs, greater economies of scale, and other factors of comparative advantages.

The Internet, along with computers and associated digital technologies, will certainly bring about changes of a similar magnitude to transport technology. While physical goods and services may not be actually transported over the Internet, sellers and buyers meet on the electronic network. Thus, trades can occur in a virtual marketplace without regard to geographic limits as long as there is the conventional double coincidence of needs. Economic players on the Internet are said to have a form of "virtual mobility" (Harris 1998).

More significantly, the Internet as a general purpose technology reaches wider aspects of economic life than transport technology. While innovations in transportation relate to a specific process (for example, distribution) in a vertical value chain, computers and networks, like electricity, are clearly more pervasive in all segments of a value chain, thus enabling further innovations in the way a firm organizes itself in internal processes and external relationships with suppliers, partners, employees, and customers. It is this pervasive nature of the Internet that warrants a precise evaluation of the technology in terms of industrial structure and the new developments in the international division of labor. The use of IT and the Internet, for example, begins with product development process and continues through manufacturing, all the way to sales and customer service functions. An Internet-based firm, therefore, may locate and relocate its offices and functions for any of its functions beyond manufacturing and assembly.

Throughout this chapter, our focus will be on the service sector. There are a few arguments for this focus. Firstly, the service sector continues to grow and dominate national economies of developed and near-developed countries in terms of both gross domestic products and the overall employment vis-à-vis goods production industries. For example, 80 percent of the US workforce is now employed in service production. Shares of service sector employment in OECD countries range between 50 percent and 80 percent of the total employment. Secondly, trades in services, although they are less than trades in manufactured goods in absolute value, are growing more rapidly than goods trade. Thirdly, digital goods and services are heavily dependent on computers and the Internet for production, distribution, and consumption. As a result, Internet technology is expected to have greater impact on the service sector in the long run.

Finally, the new division of labor induced by the Internet seems to affect firms and economies more through communication, coordination, and service functions than manufacturing innovations. In this context, human resources and workforce training become more critical issues for policy-makers than opening up industrial projects that center on maximizing comparative advantages in labor costs or in particular divisions within the manufacturing process. Simple assembly plants could be relocated to wherever ample, disciplined workers are located. However, non-manufacturing jobs require a better trained workforce, workers with the ability to communicate, coordinate and collaborate with client firms. Since many advantages of the Internet economy revolve around diverse service functions, the international division of labor under the Internet will be more complex.

Technologies affecting international division of labor

Like the Industrial Revolution of the past, the Internet or Digital Revolution introduces new forces that determine possible growth paths of an economy. Current international division of labor that is focused on manufacturing stems from industrial innovations. Among these, the most salient factor is "Fordism," best illustrated by parts standardization, extreme division of manufacturing process, and mass production geared to maximize economies of scale. With reduced transportation costs, Fordism allowed firms to segregate production processes and move operations across regions to where such economic objectives could be achieved at least costs.

The Digital Revolution in the short run continues the process of improving production efficiency as long as technologies are applied to re-engineer existing manufacturing processes. Nevertheless, the Internet will have more fundamental effects on the economy, which go beyond manufacturing goods. This aspect of "post-Fordism" will be discussed in the next section. Here we summarize basic factors of economic processes that are impacted by new technologies.

An industry or a firm in an economic sense relies on several factors of inputs: raw materials, labor, and capital. In addition, non-traditional factors include management and technology inputs, which are often called indirect inputs. Raw materials have been a major component of a manufactured goods, determining price and availability. Although in most industries raw materials now account for a small proportion of a product's total cost, if they are significant firms will locate their production facilities as close to materials' sites as possible.

Technologies and labor inputs

A factor that is clearly dominant in location and international division of labor is the cost related to labor input. Some technological innovations reduce required skills so that relatively unskilled labor can be employed in the production process. Fordism and other technologies in the Industrial Revolution are skill reducing. For example, industrial machines and procedural engineering allow unskilled workers to produce highly sophisticated products. In some cases, the fine division in the production process enables firms to transport materials and intermediate goods across regions to take advantage of minute differences in labor costs.

Computers and the Internet, to the extent that they are productivity enhancing and process simplifying tools, also contribute to deskilling of the workforce. Highly automated or computer-assisted production facilities may be located wherever labor costs are lower.

In most instances, however, the Internet revolution brings forth skill-increasing technologies. Workers who operate computers and networking may requires higher levels of training and skills. As a result, production processes under the Digital Revolution may be finely segmented but choices of location may be limited by the skills available in a region.

To some extent, labor inputs are substituted by machinery and other capital inputs. Industrial technologies are capital intensive in the sense that much of the skilled labor is replaced by advanced machinery and production process innovations such that products can be manufactured by less skilled workers. Some incentives for US companies to move their operations to Asia and Latin America come from the lowered skill requirement, and therefore the current international division of labor is a direct result of industrial technologies.

Computers and the Internet may possibly reverse this trend, at least in the short run. Unlike production facilities under the industrial division of labor for which capital intensive operations often allow relatively unskilled workers to find employment, digital production of goods and services depend on skilled labor. Using computers requires highly advanced skills. Production of goods and services that rely on computers and digital technologies may be limited to advanced economies where skilled workers are readily found. Developing countries face the increasingly difficult task of training their workers in high-tech industries. Until they are successful, production of digital goods and services will be concentrated within developed economies and a few areas in the developing countries where a pool of highly skilled workers can be found.

Capital goods and investment

The accumulation of capital goods during the industrial mode of production tends to be intensive. Capital goods are machines and tools that are used to produce other intermediate and final goods. Due to increasing economies of scale, the minimum level of production facilities has grown rapidly, and developed economies spend as much as 10 percent of their gross national product (GNP) to replace existing capital stock. During the growth period in the 1960s and the 1970s, Japan invested about 33 percent of its GNP in capital stock and the USA 17 percent.

As massive investment is needed for facilities, overseas operations of industrial manufacturers revolve around direct investment of capital in countries where cheaper material or labor costs justify such investment. Materials and intermediate goods are frequently imported to such production sites and re-exported to other production sites or to final consumption destinations. The Internet technology is poised to alter such requirements. For example, direct investments are no longer needed since production can be outsourced to manufacturing firms. Most firms are focused on marketing and brand competition in various consumption markets instead of manufacturing. Coordination and service functions done on computers and over the Internet imply less dependence on direct investment and more on taking advantage of virtual organization. Contracting and outsourcing increase and, as a result, service trade, rather than goods trade, will dominate world trade.

Technological inputs

Technological inputs are any type of knowledge that is applied to production and service. Although technological inputs are clearly evident in improved materials (for example, substitute material technology) and capital goods that embody knowledge, they are even more critical in other areas of production such as product design, marketing, and management. Technology plays an important role in increasing productivity. And it is in the service and management functions that computer technology will have the greatest impact.

Nevertheless, as we discussed in previous chapters, it remains to be seen whether computers and the Internet contribute substantially to increasing productivity. Regardless of such evidence, the Internet technology allows firms to operate better in different countries and markets through reduced coordination costs, less hindrance from language barriers, easier compliance with local trade and legal conventions, etc.

Technologies affecting management

Management inputs are perhaps most conducive to natural division of labor. Finance, marketing, production, and technology, for example, are carried out by specialized managers within an organization. The Internet and digital technology, to the extent that they make processes clearer and coordination and collaboration more effective, will have substantial impact on how a firm organizes and locates its management functions.

In a traditional corporate structure called M-form organization, a firm consists of multiple functional units, each of which carries out a specific task. Such a multidivisional firm applies management models that are based on behavioral and managerial practices within an organization. As seen in such examples as General Motors and Sears, variations and refined forms of multidivisional firms have dominated the theory of organization and management during the second half of the twentieth century (Williamson 1975).

The advent of the Internet and networked organizations is now creating a new organizational model that is akin to distributed enterprises. Unlike traditional corporations that tend to agglomerate at certain locations, IT-intensive firms utilize technologies that enhance coordination and collaboration among their operational units, managers, and employees, who may be widely distributed and located throughout the world. Unlike multidivisional firms with strict hierarchical control, distributed firms encourage flexible decision-making in order to support on-demand production, demand-sensitive product development and pricing, and customization of products and services.

Production locations as well as managerial functions become locationless in the virtual markets as the Internet and IT continue to reshape corporations in the twenty-first century. The rapidly decreasing cost in coordination allows a higher degree of disaggregation and further division of labor which enables vertical as well as horizontal division of labor, which we will elaborate on in later sections.

Technology, operation and structure of virtual firms

An industrial firm that strives to achieve a maximum economy of scale follows the example of Henry Ford's technique of mass production. Firms under Fordism are characterized by an extreme division of labor. Any or all parts of its value chain can be moved to different locations, for example where labor costs are lowest. Some theorists have put forward a term "post-Fordism" to denote organizational changes in post-industrial firms. A firm characterized by post-Fordism include following features (Hall and Jacques 1991):

- a shift to the new information technologies
- more flexible, decentralized forms of labor process and work organization
- decline of the old manufacturing base and the growth of the sunrise, computer-based industries
- the hiving off or contracting out of functions and services
- a greater emphasis on choice and product differentiation, on marketing, packaging, and design, and on the targeting of consumers by lifestyle, taste, and culture rather than by categories of social class
- a decline in the proportion of the skilled, male, manual working class, and the rise of the service and white-collar classes and the feminization of the workforce
- an economy dominated by the multinationals, with their new international division of labor and their greater autonomy from nation-state control; and the globalization of the new financial markets, linked by the communications revolution.

These characteristics are close to what is defined as a virtual firm. To distil these elements, we argue that the key aspects of a virtual firm are its decentralized organization that enables flexible operation. Flexibility opens up new options for businesses in all spheres but it at the same time compels them to rethink their basic business processes and assumptions.

Flexibility in production

Flexibility in production is often equated with customization. This in turn redefines the meaning of efficiency in the new economy. The most efficient manufacturing plant will no longer be a cost-minimizing assembly plant – the overarching principle of mass-production industrial economics – but one that can respond rapidly to changing demands. For instance, operating in the old industrial economy, an automobile plant is optimized for producing 300,000 units a year. Below or above that level, the average cost of an automobile increases – due to lowered plant capacity utilization, overtime pay, idle workforce, etc. Its optimal plan also calls for a standard model that can benefit from mass production. In contrast, a flexible manufacturing process or arrangement is concerned with meeting customer preferences rather than lowering average costs. Instead of offering a one-size-fits-all product of an average quality, firms will offer their customers choices.

At its extreme, customization implies individualization of a product or service. While it will be unnecessary to literally individualize each unit, even physical goods such as automobiles can be personalized by offering an almost infinite number of options and combinations of features or by individualized configuration of special computer-driven features.

Injecting flexibility into product design will require companies to change other business processes and relationships as well. In order to manage flexible manufacturing, for example, a firm will need to run a flexible organization, opening up to need-based or order-based contract manufacturing. Today, many computer sellers like Dell Computer and others focus on marketing and providing customized solutions to their customers. The computer systems themselves are built by contractors that are specialized to handle complex orders. Flexible manufacturing also changes inter-firm relationships, as managing supply chains on the versatile World Wide Web often involves a virtual firm in a virtual chain of suppliers. Thus, online retailers like Amazoniom and CDnow are a collection of firms specializing in marketing, warehousing, distribution, and fulfilment, not actual product manufacturing.

Flexibility in manufacturing companies in the smart economy will necessarily mean close integration with the non-manufacturing activities of a firm as well. Flexible manufacturing and customized products and services also imply the need to understand customer preferences. A flexible market allows product customization based on tastes and time-sensitive needs. Even the advertisements are tailored for individual profiles, targeted and delivered on demand.

Product configuration is also affected by the degree of flexibility. The economics of mass production – and the reliance on advertiser support – has prevailed in newspapers and magazines. In the Internet economy, information products, when created in digital format, will be easily configured, unbundled, and rebundled. Similarly, a package tour is based on the principle of the scale economy, sold at lower prices because of standardization. The Internet economy's flexible product configuration opens up new possibilities in this industry, too. For example, a travel agent can offer smart services by individualizing a vacation package that includes airline tickets, hotel accommodation, entertainment, and meals, according to each customer's schedule, tastes, and budget.

Customization requires inputs from end users who seek out responses from the sellers. Interacting with end users is an integrated process that involves not only finding out the preferences of individual customers but also dealing with them throughout the pre-production research, marketing, negotiation and purchasing, and after-sale customer service phases. The objectives of a flexible business therefore go far beyond custom manufacturing into targeted marketing, interactions with potential customers for market research, on-demand services, and support.

Flexibility in the workforce

In a decentralized, flexible virtual organization, employees are no longer lifetime workers doing the same work with minimal changes in skills and training. Instead, employees tend to be part-time; otherwise they are often self-employed

Table 13.1 *Labor characteristics in the USA, 1997 (percent)*

	Full-time	Regular part-time	Others[a]
All	71.3	13.6	15.1
Women	66.3	21.3	12.4
Men	75.7	6.9	17.4

Note:
[a] Includes employment through temporary help agency, on call/day labor, self-employment and independent contractors.
Source: Hudson 1999.

or independent contractors. The increasing degree of flexibility in the workforce means more mobility for firms that are no longer tied to specific locations where a ready pool of potential employees is available. On the Internet, virtual firms can be truly locationless as they disperse not only their offices and factories but also their employees.

Some characteristics of the labor composition should be noted. In many developed countries, part-time workers account for over one-third of the total employment. This is largely explained by female workers who are disproportionately part-time. While non-standard male workers are largely self-employed or independent contractors, one in three women are employed only part-time (see Table 13.1).

In the USA, waged and salaried workers in 1997 numbered 119.5 million (92% of total employment), self-employed workers 10.4 million (8%), and unpaid family workers 0.2 million (less than 1%). Part-time workers numbered 22.0 million (18% of all wage and salaried workers). In February 1997, 6.7% of workers (8.5 million) were classified as being independent contractors, 1.6% (2.0 million) as on-call workers who are called to work only when needed, 1.0% (1.3 million) worked for temporary help agencies, and 0.6% (800,000) worked for contract firms. Workers with temporary help agencies are paid by the agencies, whether or not their job is in reality temporary. Workers provided by contract firms are employed by companies that provide them or their services to others under contract. They are usually assigned to only one customer and usually work at the customer's work site.

The use of part-time and fixed-term workers indicate a more flexible, albeit unstable, labor market, which is consistent with the development of IT-intensive e-business firms which pursue flexible operations. When favouring networked, virtual organization, e-business firms rely increasingly on contractual partners and outsourcing arrangements, which minimizes stable and centralized labor relations.

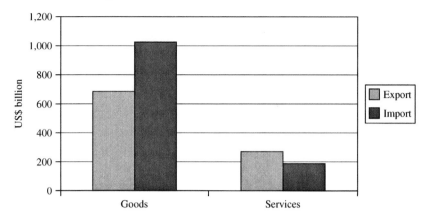

Figure 13.1 Total cross-border trades for the USA, 1998 (Source: US Bureau of Economic Analysis 2000)

Global trade in knowledge-based and service goods

Trade occurs when production processes can be broken up and carried out in different locations. The act of trade is a movement of commodities from a production location to where they are consumed. While this adequately describes cross-border trade in manufactured goods and some digital goods that can be traded over the Internet, trends in service trades indicate quite a different picture.

In absolute terms, the US trade – imports and exports – in services is only one-third of that of goods trade (see Figure 13.1). However, much of goods trade is explained by selling and buying by multinational corporations (MNCs), who export and import between foreign affiliates and local firms (see Figure 13.2). Such trades include shipments of parts, intermediate goods for overseas assembly, and final products shipped to foreign affiliates for local sales. The role of MNCs is more prominent in export than import. The reduced level of imports can be explained by the fact that foreign corporations have increased their local US operations during the past decades. With direct investment in the USA by foreign corporations, US affiliates of foreign parents accounted for US$418 billion (7 percent of GDP) in terms of output.

Service trade is relatively smaller than goods trade in terms of conventional cross-border trade. The service trade represents a wide variety of non-manufacturing activities. Major components include travel-related services, business services, and royalty payments (see Table 13.2).

However, cross-border trade in services does not give a total picture of the growing importance in that sector. For example, unlike movable manufactured goods, services are often provided at the point of consumption. That is, many US

Table 13.2 *US service trade, 1999 (US$ billion)*

	Export	Import
Travel	75	59
Passenger fares	20	21
Other transportation	27	34
Royalties and license fees	37	13
Other private services	97	47
Others[a]	17	17
Total	272	191

Note:
[a] Includes transfers under US military sales contract and government miscellaneous services.
Source: US Census Bureau 2000.

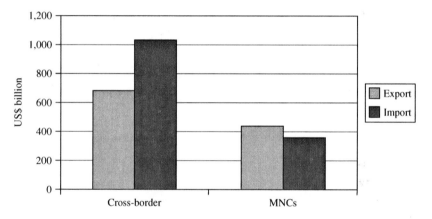

Figure 13.2 Trade of goods by MNCs for the USA, 1998 (Source: US Bureau of Economic Analysis 2000)

firms sell services through their affiliates operating in countries of consumption. A better picture is gained from comparing cross-border and intra-firm trades.

Cross-border trade in services measures the amount of billing by US-located firms for services rendered in other countries, while intra-firm trade refers to business done by local affiliates. Intra-firm trade, which is not included in the cross-border figures, is larger than the latter and continuously increasing for the USA (see Figure 13.3). In the intra-firm trade, exports are sales to foreign persons by foreign affiliates of US parents. For example, IBM Japan's sales in the Japanese market will be considered an export as intra-firm trade. Imports

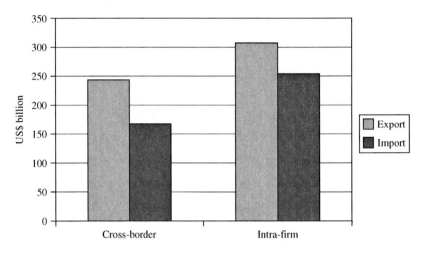

Figure 13.3 Cross-border and intra-firm trade of services for the USA, 1998 (Source: US Bureau of Economic Analysis 2000)

are sales to US persons by US affiliates of foreign companies (for example, Japan's DoCoMo's sales in the USA).

Service trade is growing in the USA and other countries more rapidly than trade in manufactured goods. Although the service trade represented about 20 percent of world trade in goods and services, at US$1.3 trillion in 1999, it has been the fastest growing component of world trade during the last decade. This figure will be an underestimate, considering service trade that is not accounted by cross-border trade as discussed above. This growth is being driven by powerful forces, including the relentless shift to knowledge-based services from goods production, the impact of e-commerce on trade in services, the deregulation and privatization of service industries, and the reliance of global MNCs on services. Services account for close to 70% of GDP in industrialized nations, and close to 50% in developing countries. Employment in services in G7 countries accounts roughly for 70% of total employment. Worldwide, trade in services now exceeds US$2 trillion annually. It has grown faster than trade in goods and accounts for 20% of world trade. Services account for close to 60% of the world's foreign direct investment through an increasing number of affiliates. Figures 13.4 and 13.5 show geographical and sectoral distribution of foreign direct investment positions by US firms.

Emerging trends in international division of labor

During the industrial production mode, differing factor costs in material and labor inputs across regions have played an important role in locating and

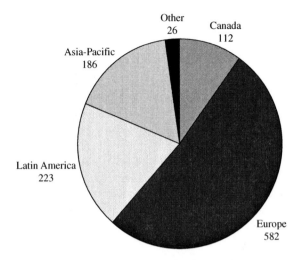

Figure 13.4 US direct investment abroad (US$ billion), 1999 (Source: US Bureau of Economic Analysis 2000)

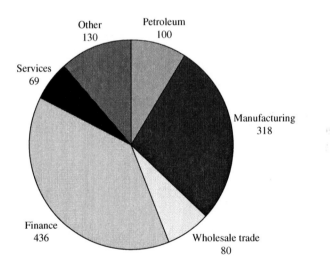

Figure 13.5 US direct investment abroad by industry (US$ billion), 1999 (Source: US Bureau of Economic Analysis 2000)

relocating manufacturing facilities. Most such determined locations are often far from the locations where end consumers reside. Consequently, intermediate and final products have to be moved. A characteristic feature of such an economy is a vertical division of labor.

Vertical division of labor

The Fordist mode of production organization and subsequent international division of labor has its root in Adam Smith's original postulation of the division of labor. According to Smith, the manufacture of any product can be broken down into steps and each worker is specialized in one of these steps, becoming better over a period of time. This type of division of labor leads to substantial productivity gains and was perfected in Ford's assembly line technique and other industrial production schemes.

Such a division of a production process can be characterized as a vertical division of labor. This refers to segmenting of a manufacturing process in a linear value chain from raw materials to intermediate goods and to final products. With lower transportation costs, firms could now separate any vertical segment of a process and move its operation to wherever comparative advantage exists.

As a consequence, location became one overriding factor in the production process. For example, easy access to raw materials or markets dictated that a firm could only be located near a river or a railroad line. But as transport technologies advanced, firms were afforded greater flexibility in location. Not only could a production process be broken up and located in different places – for example, factories near raw materials and distribution centers near a river – choices of location also expanded into foreign countries. Ricardo's formulation of comparative advantage shows that international division of labor and trade among nations are always advantageous to all trading partners even when one country has absolute advantage in all products. Coupled with such trade postulations, a vertical division of labor among countries produced extraordinary economic growth in countries that provided workers with comparative advantages during the late twentieth century.

Horizontal division of labor

The division of labor afforded by the Internet and related communications technologies is more horizontal than vertical, although efficiency gains and decreasing transaction costs will certainly have positive effects on further deepening the international division of labor we witnessed in manufacturing industries. However, advantages of the Internet technology squarely reside in the flexibility it brings to firms' organization. Lowered coordination costs allow virtual firms to operate in a web of partners that specialize not in a vertical value chain but in specific functions, which are more horizontal.

For example, a virtual firm may outsource its financial, programming, marketing, manufacturing, and service functions. Operating partners in this model require close cooperation and coordination rather than absolute gains from streamlined, linear production process. The need to respond rapidly to consumer preferences and changing market conditions also dictate rapid assembly and servicing of customers rather than a carefully mapped out production chain that is not flexible once it is put into practice.

Such a horizontal division of labor is a dominant feature in service trades. Service trades differ from goods trades because of the nature of services. Often those who provide services must be relocated to where services are to be provided. Instead of materials and goods, workers are moved. Associated problems include immigration issues, such as currently ongoing debates on H1-B temporary work visas in the USA. Another example is the case of migratory agricultural workers from Mexico who must be moved to where crops are to be harvested.

In the new horizontal division of labor seen with Internet-induced reorganization, training the workforce is a critical success factor, especially in circumstances where technological changes necessitate retraining. Developing countries can no longer rely on occupying a lower end of the production process where only cheap, unskilled labor may be sufficient incentive to attract foreign investment.

As the economy progresses toward the Internet-driven service economy, increasing gains in service sector productivity will translate into higher wages and employment for those countries that can provide ample workers in this high-tech service sector. In the USA, the level of employment in the IT sector shows an extraordinary growth while maintaining high wages. High wages and growth come from great productivity gains in the IT sector, which is reflected in increasing multifactor productivity. Labor and multifactor productivity measures show a higher growth rate in the 1990s than the previous two decades, with a rapid acceleration since 1995 when the Internet began to be used widely.

Location in the new horizontal division of labor

In the service-dominated economies, comparative advantages are found in human resources – in knowledge and training, not just in relative wages – which tend to move to where services are to be rendered. The dilemma is to reconcile the issues between migration and educating a local workforce. Highly educated workers who migrate to developed countries result in brain drain. When workers instead of goods are transported, as in the service sector, that might be unavoidable. However, the Internet also provides a viable solution for such a problem.

The efficiency achieved by the Internet and digital communications networks indicates that many service functions can be provided independent of location. For example, high-tech workers in programming and computer-related services may be located in one country while providing essential work for clients and customers in another country. Consequently, services may be moved via the

Internet, in the same way that goods are transported, preventing the need to migrate. Like export-oriented development projects during the past decades, similar efforts and policies may be pushed forward in the case of the service sector. Only, in this case, relatively low wage levels are not so much important as the quality of a region's workforce. Digital products and services that can be exported through the Internet tend to be centered on highly skilled, high-paid jobs.

New policies aimed at initiating or maintaining economic growth in the twenty-first century must now deal with the new horizontal division of labor brought on by the Internet technology. A great number of developing countries are now experimenting with software parks and other network centers which are designed to retain highly educated and trained workers within their countries (see Figure 13.6). For example, in India software technology park projects can be created anywhere in the country and receive numerous benefits promised by the government, such as project cost support, lax foreign equity holding requirement, exemption from duties, reduced corporate income tax, and so on.

The quality and reliability of the Indian software workforce presents a somewhat unique opportunity in developing software parks. Its close connection to Indian-born entrepreneurs in Silicon Valley works as a further incentive. As a consequence, during 1999–2000, the IT software and services industry in India reached an annual revenue of US$5.7 billion. This represents almost 53% of growth from the previous year. Out of the total, 70% (US$4 billion) was exported, accounting for 10.5% of India's total exports. With the Silicon Valley connection, it is not surprising that 62% of its software exports went to the USA and Canada.

Most of the companies depend heavily on MNCs that outsource their work to these Indian companies. More than 185 of Fortune 500 companies sent outsourcing contracts to these firms. In turn, India's own off-shore software development is increasing rapidly. During 1999–2000, off-shore operations accounted for 42% of total exports, a growth from 5% in 1991–1992.

More interestingly, Indian firms are focusing on IT-enabled services for continued growth of its service industry. IT-enabled services, or "remote processing" services, include call centers, medical transcription, data digitization, legal databases, accounting, data processing, back-office operations, Web content development, and so on. These services are provided by Indian firms in India via the Internet and IT for clients in other regions and countries. India expects to create 1 million jobs in this sector by 2008.

Primary incentives for US firms to outsource their software and service needs are found in lower costs, faster product cycle time, and other benefits such as better documentation, 24-hour operation, and so on. Other countries such as Ireland, China, and Pakistan have begun promoting software parks as the next stage of high-tech-driven growth.

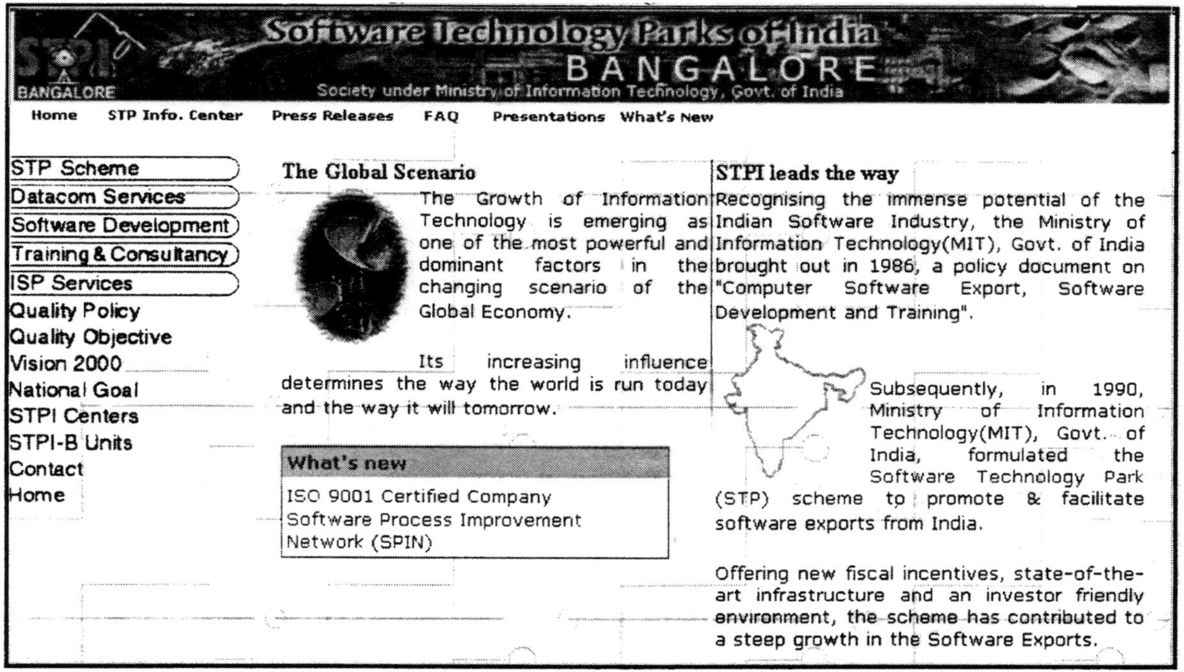

Figure 13.6 Software technology parks of India, Bangalore

However, there may be important costs involved in outsourcing software and services which may counter such developments. Kogut and Turcanu (1999) have argued that there are significant costs involved in Internet-based software and service industries, namely coordination costs, lack of face-to-face communication, and disadvantages associated with "not being close to where innovations occur." They argue that off-shore services may impose high costs so that on-site software and services may be preferred, or alternatively there should be a mixture of on-site firms and off-shore ones which would participate via communities on the Internet.

Policy implications of Internet-based globalization

India and China have implemented various initiatives for software parks and other network centers designed to promote local employment opportunities in the highly skilled service industries such as computer programming and telecommunications services. However, China's main exports are still low value added labor-intensive products, over half of which are simply processed products with 10 to 20 percent value added. But its long-term goal is to play a greater role in the new international division of labor, especially in technology trade:

> In technology trade, we shall abide by international norms and practices and protect intellectual property rights according to law so as to safeguard the legitimate rights and interests of the cooperative parties. We shall introduce and learn the advanced technology and experience of other countries so as to promote domestic economic development. We shall encourage the active exploration of technology export market and extensively participate in international division of labor in an effort to gradually make China's technology-intensive industries one of the important links of the international industrial technology chain.   Ministry of Foreign Trade and Economic Co-operation (MOFTEC) Basic Policies

To achieve such goals, a focused effort toward worker education and training as well as an adequate provision of local employment opportunities in skilled, service sector must be paramount. Unlike unskilled, disciplined, hard-working laborers that industrial division of labor required, Internet-driven service economy demands well-educated, highly skilled workers. They may be highly mobile. Without local jobs, service sector workers are easily migrated to where service consumers are located. In the US, fully 40 percent of the engineering graduate students in universities are from foreign countries, typically from countries with little or no advanced technological infrastructure. A large majority of these graduate students stay in the USA when they complete their studies. US immigration laws also favour immigrants with advanced scientific or technical education. This intensifies the disparity between the advanced countries and those with widespread poverty. To offer local employment, developing countries must prepare for better technological infrastructure to support software parks and other areas of network connection. At the same time, unlike manufacturing operations, services must be highly customizable to meet the requirements of their consumers. For example, one of the reasons behind India's success in exporting computer-related services from Bangalore and other software parks has been the ease in using the English language. Besides language barriers, however, services and many digital products present cultural, legal, and organizational problems when countries attempt to offer services to those who reside in foreign countries. For example, financial services require understanding in the financial systems of the client's country. Many commercial services must adhere to the latter's legal and commercial norms. Digital products such as music and games must be tailored to the tastes and preferences of the clients. Exporting such goods and services may necessitate broader understanding or integration within the global world economy.

Conclusions

The so-called new international division of labor that promoted a selected few countries to industrial development and economic wealth is closely related to the industrial mode of production which favours mass production and finer division of labor. Countries with low wages and a pool of disciplined workforce reaped the economic benefit from pervasive movement of capital in search of lower costs. Technological advancements in transportation provided further incentives to relocate manufacturing facilities almost anywhere in the world. Now, we are in the digital mode of production which centres around customization rather than mass production and the service sector rather than the manufacturing of physical goods. The Internet and IT provide technological innovations comparable to those in transport technologies of the past. As a result of the combination of these digital age technologies, we can expect significant and comparable changes in the way firms are organized and regional economies are affected by Internet-driven globalization.

Again, the IT revolution is reshaping the international division of labor, affecting the decisions of US firms in their location, organization, and concurrent movements of workers. In this chapter, we have focused on the increasing importance of the service sector and some implications of the use of IT and the Internet in this sector. Foremost, the type of service sector labor being affected by IT is highly skilled, highly paid jobs. Traditionally, workers of this type moved to where services are to be provided, unlike unskilled workers who are employed in duty-free export zones in developing countries. The Internet and IT offer an alternative to migratory employment in the service sector. Through software park projects, highly skilled Indian workers can enjoy highly-paid jobs while staying close to their families. High value added generated by this sector has also boosted the country's economic outlook.

Unlike the vertical division of labor we witnessed in the manufacturing sector, the Internet and IT enable a horizontal division of labor, which addresses the need to be flexible in the newly emerging value web. Firms dependent on IT are virtual firms, often producing digital products and services which can be transported via the Internet. In this sense, the service sector is highly conducive to horizontal division of labor, relying on efficiencies in communication and coordination afforded by the Internet and IT. Despite the locationlessness of the Internet, a notable trend among US firms is to expand operations through foreign affiliates, often minimizing cross-border trades, which have been the hallmark of goods trade based on international division of labor.

For developing economies, the shift toward the service sector and the reliance on IT and the Internet pose a serious threat in development policies. On the one hand, highly skilled workers can be retained, lowering the risk of brain drain, by promoting IT infrastructure and software and other digital product and service projects. On the other hand, the required level of education and training is far higher than manufacturing jobs. Software and digital products will certainly demand more skills to produce than shoes, clothes, and other manufactured items. The gap between developing countries and the underdeveloped world seems to be growing and will get worse, not better, as we move into a full-fledged service economy of the digital age.

Those who are in front see an increasing trend toward outsourcing instead of foreign direct investment by firms in developed countries, although with deregulated capital markets, funds and capital may migrate as well. For developed economies, service sector coordination requires a different set of relationships between parent and affiliates. To operate locally, firms must be able to collaborate with local firms and address the needs of local customers. Although off-shore service operations are still possible, the need to employ domestic workers more productively means that on-site facilities will present a better alternative. The lagging wage level in the broader service sector in the USA is one reason why IT-driven service sector re-engineering must occur, especially when 80 percent of the workforce is employed outside manufacturing industries. There seems to be ample room to first expand domestic employment. Whether service sector jobs will migrate to foreign countries remains to be seen.

References

Hall, S. and Jacques, M. 1991, *New Times: the Changing Face of Politics in the 1990s*, London: Lawrence and Wishart.
Harris, R. G. 1995, Trade and communication costs, *Canadian Journal of Economics*, 28, S46–75.

1998, The Internet as a GPT: factor market implications, in E. Helpman (ed.), *General Purpose Technologies and Economic Growth*, Cambridge, MA: MIT Press, 145–166.

Hudson, K. 1999, *No Shortage of "Nonstandard" Jobs*, http://www.epinet.org/briefingpapers/hudson/hudson.html.

Kogut, B. and Turcanu, A., 1999, *Global Software Development and the Emergence of E-Innovation*, http://cbi.gsia.cmu.edu/newweb/1999SFconference/Kogut/Kogut.html.

Krugman, P. 1992, *Geography and International Trade*, Cambridge, MA: MIT Press.

National Association of Software and Service Companies (NASSCOM) 2000, *Indian IT Software and Services Industry*, http://www.nasscom.org/template/itinindia.htm.

People's Republic of China, Ministry of Foreign Trade and Economic Cooperation(MOFTEC), http://www.moftec.gov.cn/moftec.

People's Republic of China, Ministry of Foreign Trade and Economic Cooperation(MOFTEC), *Basic Policies Governing China's Foreign Trade and Economic Cooperation*.

Software Technology Parks of India, http://www.soft.net.

US Bureau of Economic Analysis 2000, *US International Services: Cross-Border Trade in 1999 and Sales Through Affiliates in 1998*, *Survey of Current Business*, October 2000, Washington DC.

US Census Bureau 2000, *US International Trades in Goods and Services*, Washington DC, http://www.census.gov/foreign-trade/Press-Release/2000pr/10.

Williamson, O. E. 1975, *Markets and Hierarchies: Analysis and Antitrust Implications*, New York: The Free Press.

Conclusion

Emanuele Giovannetti, Mitsuhiro Kagami and Masatsugu Tsuji

The IT revolution of the 1990s brought mankind many benefits, but also created a number of problems. Its extraordinary nature, especially its transcendence of time, place, and social status, dramatically changed people's lives and their ways of thinking.

In the eighteenth century, the first industrial revolution followed the introduction of the steam engine and mechanization then, at the end of the nineteenth century, the invention of electricity led to a second revolution with the development of mass-production techniques. IT has created a third industrial revolution, starting with the application of artificial intelligence pioneered during the "space race" in the 1960s, followed by cheap, reliable computers in the 1980s and, finally, the creation of the Internet or the information revolution through IT-related technologies.

Cyberspace creates a way of reaching beyond national boundaries and this casts a new light on the concept of national sovereignty. The Internet transcends time zones so 24-hour working becomes possible by setting assignments in different locations around the globe. This enormously increases the efficiency of business activities, particularly in software industries. Faced with the reality of electronic data interchange (EDI), traditional business hierarchies are disappearing, and intermediaries and vertically integrated parts procurements are vanishing. Moreover, changes ranging from cost minimization to customer choice are occurring over the entire supply chain.

The Internet has improved industrial efficiency through its ability to transmit large volumes of data instantaneously. The World Wide Web has provided consumers with access to entertainment, fashion, education, cultural information, etc., changing their lifestyles as well as their ways of thinking. This will be further augmented when broadband facilities become more widely available.

The process of deregulation and privatization is closely linked to the development of IT. In many developing countries, infrastructure such as telecommunications and electricity supply tends to be run by state-owned enterprises, so progress toward deregulation and privatization is a prerequisite for further development of the IT revolution. IT can speed up industrialization by allowing a country to leapfrog intermediate stages. India and Israel, for example, have enjoyed a leapfrogging pattern of industrialization by moving into the supply of software services and skilled technicians. The IT revolution, therefore, has had a number of serious impacts on society, both positive and negative.

To summarise the benefits:

1 E-mail facilities save time and money by making worldwide, one-to-one communication possible.

2 The Internet connects us into instant information exchange and gives us access to such domains as education, academia, medical treatments, industry, culture, mass media, and entertainment.

3 Economic productivity (multifactor productivity) has increased through the use of IT, especially since the latter half of the 1990s. The IT industry itself has created many jobs and functions as an engine of growth for the world economy. Applications such as EDI and electronic fund transfer (EFT) have made business easier, quicker, cheaper, and more efficient.

4 New types of business and new IT utilizations have emerged, such as e-commerce (BtoB and BtoC), e-government, e-education, and e-medicare.

5 Leapfrogging patterns of industrialization based on technological development can help developing countries grasp the momentum for growth and enable them to bypass traditional developmental stages ("digital jump").

6 Individual participation has made people happier and has resulted in more decentralization at every institutional level, thus enhancing democracy.

On the other hand, there are real problems to be overcome:

1 **Digital divide**: those with access to the Internet can enjoy the benefits of the IT revolution but those without are left behind. This gap occurs both within and between countries.

2 **Unemployment**: new models such as BtoB and B2C cut out existing intermediary processes, resulting in redundancies, albeit IT industry job-creation counters this to some degree.

3 **Supporting industries**: because of EDI, MNCs can purchase their parts and components worldwide, so domestic supporting industries (small and medium-sized enterprises) do not grow in developing countries.

4 **Monopoly**: ideas-based industries are apt to dominate their market due to knowledge intensity and network externalities. Microsoft is a

good example. Large incumbent firms with huge sunk costs tend to retain their monopolistic position and impose high access charges.

5 **Online crimes**: in cyberspace it is easy to violate laws relating to copyright, taxation, fraud, money laundering, hazardous information, and cyber terrorism.

6 **Privacy**: infringement of privacy, especially by public authorities, is also easy, through wire and wireless tapping, hacker activities, etc.

7 **Human resource bottleneck**: computer literacy becomes very important and the IT industry faces a lack of trained people worldwide. Given this, advanced countries further become 'brain magnets' whilst developing countries such as India and China face 'brain drains.'

We definitely need international measures and cooperation to overcome these negative aspects, especially the digital divide and computer-related crimes. Further IT progress is expected and its influence will bring about an unprecedented but irresistible transformation of our society in this new century. However, the recent US economic slowdown at the beginning of 2001, and the supply shortage in California's electricity supply industry, highlight the fact that the IT revolution is not always going to be a bed of roses and does not guarantee a recession-free future. Furthermore, we have to be mindful that deregulation and excessive reliance on competition may lead us to ignore the long-term stable supply of deregulated products. Therefore, we have to examine carefully the effects of the IT revolution and globalization for each economy and learn from the past in order to chart our own way forward to make best use of latecomer's advantage.

Index

9 780521 823722